Kilwaughter

The Unknown Castle

Jacqueline Agnew

Copyright © Jacqueline Agnew, 2025

Published: 2025 by Latharna Press, Leschenault, Western Australia

ISBN: 978-1-923454-25-5 – Paperback
ISBN: 978-1-923454-26-2 – E-Book

The right of Jacqueline Agnew to be identified as author of this work has been asserted by her in accordance with sections 77 and 78 of the copyright, designs and patents act 1988.

The author asserts that no Artificial Intelligence methods, techniques or tools have been used within the researching or production of this novel. Without in any way limiting the author's [and publisher's] exclusive rights under copyright, any use of this publication to "train" generative artificial intelligence (AI) technologies to generate text is expressly prohibited. The author reserves all rights to license uses of this work for generative AI training and development of machine learning language models.

All rights reserved. No part of this publication may be reproduced or transmitted in any form or by any means, electronic or mechanical, including photography, recording, or any information storage or retrieval system, without permission in writing from the publisher.

The book is sold subject to the condition that it shall not, by way of trade or otherwise, be lent, resold or otherwise circulated without the publisher's prior consent in any form of binding or cover other than that in which it is published and without a similar condition, including this condition, being imposed on the subsequent purchaser.

Cover Design by Brittany Wilson | Brittwilsonart.com

Table of Contents

Table of Contents 3
Preface i
Acknowledgements v
    List of Proprietorial Characters vii
A Scottish Agnew Prayer ix
Introduction xi
Chapter 1
    The Early Years 1
    The Kilwaughter Plantation House 4
    Captain John Agnew, agent to Sir Patrick Agnew 7
    Captain John Agnew's part in the 1641 Rebellion 8
    Death of Sir Patrick Agnew, 8th Sheriff of Galloway 10
    Sir Andrew Agnew, 9th Sheriff of Galloway and heir to Sir Patrick Agnew 11
Chapter 2
    Patrick Agnew, 1st of Kilwaughter (son of Captain John Agnew) 12
    Patrick Agnew, 2nd of Kilwaughter and visit by Sir Andrew Agnew of Lochnaw 13
    Visit by Sir James Agnew of Lochnaw. Relinquishes ownership of the Estate 14
    Children of Sir James Agnew 15
    The Kilwaughter Estate ends its relationship with the Agnews of Lochnaw 19
    Patrick Agnew, 2nd of Kilwaughter 19
    Patrick Agnew, 2nd of Kilwaughter dies 21

Chapter 3

William Agnew, son of Patrick Agnew, 2nd of Kilwaughter, inherits the Estate 23
William Agnew and his role as Landlord 24
William's Family Life 25
William Agnew dies and his grandson Edward Jones Agnew becomes Heir 27

Chapter 4

The Jones Dynasty 29
Valentine Jones (the Elder) 30
Valentine Jones (Barbados 1) and the Slave Trade 31
Disgrace brought upon the Jones and Agnew Families 34
Valentine Jones (Barbados 3) 34
Valentine Jones (the Elder), his Business and Political Life 36
Valentine Jones (the Elder), Death and Family 39

Chapter 5

Edward Jones Agnew inherits the Kilwaughter Estate 43
Nomination to become a Member of the Irish Parliament 44
Edward is Elected into the Irish Parliament 45
Edward loses his Parliamentary seat, but finds a new Political Cause 49
James Agnew Farrell, second cousin to Edward Jones Agnew 55
His Role in the 1798 Rebellion 55
Family Life of James Agnew Farrell 59
The Sale of the Family Home, the Magheramorne Estate 59
James Agnew Farrell seeks to prove connections with the Lochnaw Family 60
The Magheramorne Estate is sold again 61
The Kilwaughter Estate continues to Survive 62
Edward Jones Agnew begins to Renovate Kilwaughter House 63
The Tenants on the Estate 65
Edward Jones Agnew attempts Marriage 66
Scandalous Behaviour 67

 Edward Jones Agnew becomes a Father to two Children *68*
 Edward Jones Agnew Dies *71*

Chapter 6
 Margaret Jones, sister to Edward takes over the Estate *74*
 Margaret changes conditions for the Tenant Farmers *76*
 The Great Famine *78*
 Margaret Jones Dies *80*
 The Illegitimate nephew of Margaret Jones becomes Heir *82*
 William Agnew moves to France with John Hay Lambert *83*
 Maria Agnew, Sister to William. Marriage, birth of Daughter and Death *84*
 William Agnew Dies *87*

Chapter 7
 A New Era – The Balzani Family *99*
 The Galt Smiths add an American Dimension *101*
 Elizabeth Bringhurst Smith *103*
 The Galt Smiths return to Ireland *105*
 Family Connections *107*
 Kilwaughter Castle undergoes another Refurbishment *108*
 Auction *110*
 Court Case *114*
 The Refurbishment is complete and the Galt Smiths begin socialising *114*
 The Balzanis visit Kilwaughter *120*
 The Countess Balzani Dies *123*
 Count Balzani and his Daughters *125*
 Guendalina and Guido begin Married Life *126*
 Nora becomes sole Heiress *127*

Chapter 8

- The Galt Smiths Entertain *130*
- The Servants *131*
- Life continues at Kilwaughter for the Galt Smiths *133*
- Public Duty and more Travels *135*
- Summer Return to Kilwaughter *136*
- Bessie's Brother Edward Visits *138*
- John Galt Smith Dies *140*
- Bessie's Relationship with her Step-Children *141*
- Bessie's Father and Edward visit Kilwaughter *142*
- Bessie meets King Edward VII and Queen Alexandra *144*
- Bessie's Father Dies *146*
- Bessie returns from America *146*
- Bessie hears about the 1914 Gun-Running *148*

Chapter 9

- Outbreak of World War 1 .... *151*
- More Servants Exploits *153*
- Local Politics *156*
- Entertaining Continues *156*
- Bessie Meets Edward Carson *159*
- Kennedy joins the UVF *159*
- Bessie's War Effort *160*
- Suspicious Signalling on Agnew's Hill *162*
- Disharmony in the Kitchen *164*
- Life Continues with Entertaining *166*
- Christmas Alone *168*
- Bessie spends another Christmas at Kilwaughter *169*
- Yet More Trouble in the Kitchen *170*

    Kennedy Marries *173*

    The Final Year of the War *174*

    Kilwaughter becomes a Convalescent Hospital *175*

    War Finally Ends *176*

Chapter 10

    Things begin to Change *177*

    The Balzani Family can finally visit Kilwaughter Castle *177*

    Bessie leaves for America to visit her Family *179*

    Kilwaughter Castle's Protector Relinquishes her Responsibility Permanently *181*

    The Guest Book *183*

Chapter 11

    What next for the Castle and Estate? *184*

    World War Two looms which causes problems for the Balzani Family *185*

    Kilwaughter Castle seized as Enemy Property *186*

    Troops Arrive at Kilwaughter Castle *186*

    Kilwaughter's Final Demise *189*

    Kilwaughter in Ruins *191*

Afterword 192

Appendix 1
   The Extended Jones Family *193*
Appendix 2
   Sir James Willson (sic) Agnew (1815-1901) *198*
Appendix 3
   The Agnew Slave Plantation *201*
Appendix 4
   Thomas Agnew (1794-1871) *203*
Appendix 5
   Thomas Frederick Andrew Agnew (1834-1924) *205*
Appendix 6
   Kilwaughter Castle Ghost Stories *206*
Postscript 207
References
   Books *209*
   Primary Sources *213*
   Secondary Sources *216*
   Theses *220*
   Web References *220*
Index 225

Preface

A chance remark by a relative, some years ago, began my intrigue about the characters of Kilwaughter Castle in Northern Ireland. Amongst other tales, she relayed the story to me of how this Irish Castle was once owned by a noble, aristocratic family from Italy and so began my journey into the Castle's history. I did not know then, just how many stories lay hidden behind its thick stone walls, or just how far I would get in unearthing the histories of the characters who once lived there, after all it was a very long time ago.

I discovered that whilst Kilwaughter Castle was named in some printed works because of its architecture, nothing could be found on the intimate history of the people (called Agnew), who had resided there or their connections to others. There was information on the earlier Agnew bards the Ó Gnímhs, though this story will not expand on their lives. Another more recent book dealt with the connections between the Kilwaughter and Lochnaw Agnews. In fact, outside the Larne area, it seemed that the Castle was unknown to most people, which was surprising considering that it was designed by one of the foremost architects of the day, John Nash (1752-1835).

I began my search with a visit to the Castle and saw a disappointing ruination that had long been forgotten, but that only encouraged me to try and unearth some of the mysteries of the people who had once lived there. To begin with and to give me a little background, some use was made of the two volumes written by Sir Andrew Agnew of Lochnaw Castle, (1818-1892), entitled, "The Agnews of Lochnaw: a history of the hereditary Sheriffs of Galloway", which covered the period when the Kilwaughter area was leased by the Scottish Agnews of Lochnaw in the seventeenth century. Whilst the volumes are considered fanciful, I did glean enough information to help me with names.

The discovery of the three volumes of the Drennan-McTier letters, edited by Jean Agnew (general editor Maria Luddy), was a fantastic source of reference and I made good use of them. I learned much about the habits and stories of the Valentine Jones era.

Then the letters I received from some members of the 644th American Tank Destroyer Battalion who were stationed at Kilwaughter Castle from January to May 1944, were also very enlightening and kind and I was grateful for the time they took to reply to me.

One excellent source I found was the unpublished thesis of Katino Manko which introduced me to Elizabeth Bringhurst Smith. Bessie as she was known, kept a remarkable record of life in Ulster and the day to day running of the Kilwaughter estate during the thirty year period from 1891 that she and her husband Galt leased the Castle. The information I obtained from her many hundreds of letters was unsurpassed.

Once I had something to work on and the names of some of the occupants, the records at the Public Record Office of Northern Ireland (PRONI) provided much new authentic information and confirmed or corrected various assumptions that I had made. Many hours were spent there perusing some ancient documents and the staff were very helpful in finding them.

Discovering the relevant books, documents and odd bits of information that serendipity sent my way, was all very necessary. Finding people though, who could add to the colour of the story was an invaluable source of knowledge. Amongst those who provided not only pictures of some of the characters, but much detail, was the Italian Balzani family who had owned the Castle and estate from 1891 until the Second World War. Locating this family was important and meant much detective work as I didn't know in which part of Italy the family resided. It took around two years before I found them through the help of Francesca Balzani (no relation), an Italian politician. She very kindly helped me to pinpoint the family to Bologna and I received my first email from Alessandra Gatti who was intrigued by the idea and was keen to help. She thoughtfully provided the first photographs from portraits, of some of the people of Kilwaughter and gave me family information. In particular, I owe a great deal of thanks to Lorenza Gatti Balzani[1] who has been a wonderful help in providing yet more information about the family and was also kind enough to arrange for me to visit the Balzani ancestral home in Bologna. This was a delightful experience, to see the 500 year old residence and private chapel and to meet other family members. I am very grateful to her late aunt, Stefania Balzani, for allowing this to happen.

Like all research it wasn't without its problems and one of those was the frequent name use of some of the characters. For example, the name Patrick Agnew was used at least twelve times within the Kilwaughter family tree. The name Valentine Jones was found six times and the name John Galt Smith was found eight times. Not all of these people have been mentioned, but finding a way to disconnect their personal histories from each other and to use only those important to the story, as well as making them accessible to the reader, was a discerning task.

The story is interspersed with historic events that hopefully helps provide a context and setting in which to place the characters during the times they lived. In the end it is a story that gave me great pleasure in both researching and writing and any mistakes that are found within it must be my responsibility. I hope though, that the reader will come to the same conclusion that I have reached, that this Castle contained so much fascinating information that it deserved to be told.

Jacqueline Agnew
Kilwaughter
2025

---

[1] Articles written by Lorenza Gatti Balzani on the Countess Augusta Balzani (No. 52) and her daughter Nora Balzani (No. 69), published in the Newsletter of the Friends of the Non-Catholic Cemetery, Rome. https://cemeteryrome.it/press/newsletter.html

Acknowledgements

This story could not have been told without the generous help of many people and I would like to acknowledge them and give thanks to them.

The late Albert Agnew, California. Sir Crispin Agnew, Scotland. Jean Agnew, Northern Ireland. Balzani family – Lorenza Gatti Balzani, Alessandra Gatti and their late uncle Andrea Balzani, also his wife the late Stefania Balzani, Italy. Francesca Balzani, Italy. Centre for Migration Studies, Ulster-American Folk Park, Omagh. The late Nelson Bell, Northern Ireland. Connie Cooper of the Delaware Historical Society, Wilmington, USA. Director, National Library Service, Barbados. Corinne Durand, Paris. Anne Ferguson, Australia, owner of Kilwaughter Castle and her late father Frank Ferguson. The late Nancy Agnew Ferns, Nova Scotia. Ryan Greer, Northern Ireland. John Hopkins Medical Institution, Baltimore, USA. Linda Hooke, Northern Ireland. Angeline King, Northern Ireland. Linen Hall Library, Belfast. Larne Museum. Linde Lunney, Royal Irish Academy, Dublin. John Marsden, County Kildare. John Mead, England. Members of the 644th Tank Destroyer Battalion, USA. Rosalind Moad, King's College Library, Cambridge. The Public Record Office of Northern Ireland, Belfast. Raymond Refaussé, The Representative Church Body Library, Dublin. Colum O'Riordan, The Irish Architectural Archive, Dublin. Jimmie Robbins, USA. Paul Robinson, Japan. Juliet Scaife, Tasmanian Parliamentary Library, Tasmania. Ulster Folk & Transport Museum, Belfast. Penny and Leslie Underwood, Canada. Robert and Elaine Wade, Australia. I am also grateful to Maimi Agnew Hanna, her late sister Nance Agnew Wallace, Jacob Hanna and the late Muriel Agnew, Northern Ireland, who have all spent many hours in discussion about the Kilwaughter Agnews.

List of Proprietorial Characters

Sir Patrick Agnew (1578-1661), 8th Sheriff of Galloway.

Captain John Agnew (1586-1656)

Patrick Agnew (ca. 1639-1686)

Patrick Agnew (-1724)

William Agnew (1706-1776)

Edward Jones Agnew (1767-1834)

Margaret Jones (1764-1848) – held in Trust for

William Agnew (1824-1891)

Countess Augusta Balzani (1847-1895)

Count Ugo Balzani (1847-1916) – held in Trust for

Guendalina Valensin (1882-1957) and

Nora Balzani (1883-1975)

John Galt Smith (1839-1899) and

Elizabeth Bringhurst Smith (1863-1934). Rented property for 30 years.

Countess Bianca Molteni Balzani (1908-2008). Second cousin to Nora Balzani.

A Scottish Agnew Prayer

(Circa 1803)[2]
"Bless a' the Agnews and a' the Agnew childer:
Their sons and childer and their dochiter's for a
Thousand years to come.
Be ye gracious an' send doon mountains o' snuff
An' rivers of whisky.
An' oh Lord, send doon swords an' pistols an'
Daggers, as monie as the sands on the seashore.
To kill the Clan MacDonalds, the Clan Ranalds,
And the Campbells.
An' oh Lord, bless the wee coo,
An' make it a big coo.
An' oh Lord, bless the sucklin' and make it a grand board.
An' oh Lord, bless the wee bairns,
Yon Angus, Alex an' Bessie,
an' Maggie an' Florrie.
An' oh Lord, build a great wall between
us an' the Irish,
an' put broken bottles on the top,
so they cannae come over.
An' oh Lord, if ye hae anything to gie,
Dunna gie it to the Irish,
But gie it to your chosen people, the Scots,
Especially to the Clan Agnew an' a' their friends.
Glorious ye are for ever more".

---

[2] Agnew Newsletter 1999.

Introduction

Kilwaughter Castle stands secluded on the outskirts of Larne in Northern Ireland. Today it is a wreck of a John Nash building awaiting its final fate, but even a brief look at its past starts unravelling a much longer story of intrigue, politics, the slave trade and international connections. It introduces complex characters who each had their own stories to tell and who involved themselves in the lives of their tenants and the politics of the day. They did not forget to enjoy themselves either, whether in gambling, in entertaining the local aristocracy or in scandalous behaviour. They frequented the theatre in Belfast and were said to have come by private coach from Kilwaughter to attend performances by Mrs. Sarah Siddons, a Welsh actress from the 18th century who was the best known leading lady of her day.

The Agnew family of Kilwaughter House as it was originally known, was the prominent family of the Larne area from the 1600's until WW2. By then, having been redesigned into the Castle it is today, their descendants the Balzani family, owned it. It has been a somewhat difficult family to research as its name originally was Ó Gnímh in Irish and that name in itself was corrupted to many different forms which also added to the confusion. The Ó Gnímhs were bards to the wealthy MacDonnells and O'Neills in the mid seventeenth century. It is thought that the Kilwaughter Agnews 'grew' out of the bardic family which is plausible as the name simply anglicised, but there is another stumbling block. Across the North Channel in Galloway lies Lochnaw Castle, just outside Stranraer, where yet another Agnew family resided for centuries, traversing back and forth to the Kilwaughter area to visit the land they had leased. It would make sense if all these families were related, having the same name and leasing the same land, but so far documentation remains absent to confirm this one way or other, so we must resort to circumstantial evidence instead. That part of the story though, is left for another researcher to unravel, this story will involve only the characters of the Castle and their connections.

The narrative has many layers beginning with problems for their Agnew Scottish landlords, ranging from the reneguing of rent, to the intrigues of two family members supporting the United Irishmen, one of whom fathered at least three illegitimate children (one died). This of course was considered an outrage in the strict religious Irish society of that time. Then the Great Irish Famine of 1845 brought about more problems for the collecting of the estate rents. Another incumbent decided that life in Paris was much more exciting and so he and his male friend left the Kilwaughter estate for approximately forty years, to enjoy life abroad. They settled eventually in Bossy-St-Léger in a charming Château. The Kilwaughter estate was left in the hands of an agent.

Bit by bit the research unravelled some fascinating connections which were a rich source of information and brought in such people as the aristocratic Italian Balzanis, who in themselves introduced their niece Lady Hailey, a descendant of Prince Lucien, a younger brother of Napoleon I. Then there was Elizabeth Bringhurst Smith who introduced an American influence from Delaware. She and her Irish husband who was a distant relative to the Agnews, contributed greatly to the story's enhancement. Bessie, as she was known, took it upon herself to refurbish the Castle and bring a more up-to-date approach to making it a comfortable home for entertaining her rich friends. Meanwhile her husband took charge of the estate to make it more profitable. The Castle was also turned into a recuperation home for WW1 soldiers.

An unaware and truly shocking side of the story (and indeed a major part of it), stemmed from the discovery of the Castle's connection to the slave trade in Barbados. This slave link lasted over thirty years with the family and it would be remiss not to mention that the update of Kilwaughter House to the present day Castle, was more than likely paid with money from this odious trade. Their accumulation of vast wealth did not always go smoothly as it resulted in a serious case of fraud for one of the family who was imprisoned for his behaviour. It is unfortunate that the Will belonging to the main catalyst of the Kilwaughter Castle slave trade (Valentine Jones the Elder), has been impossible to locate and it is more than likely that it was lost during the Irish Civil War in 1922. It would have given a very strong indication of just how much money had been accumulated through his various business interests and of course the slave trade.

The Castle was used again during WW2 when both British and American troops were billeted there for several months. During this war the decline of the Castle and its estate began in earnest. The Italian owners resided in Italy and as that country was then a belligerent state, the whole demesne was sequestrated by the Custodian of Enemy Property for Northern Ireland. The Balzani family had cared deeply for their Irish home as it was a very strong link to their Irish mother and wished to keep it, but the authorities did not allow that under the Act. Various land acts earlier, had removed almost all the land.

It is ironic that during the Irish Civil War when other stately homes were being burned to the ground, Kilwaughter Castle stood aloof from it all. Through reasons unknown to the public, the Castle was not handed back to its original owners after the end of the WW2 when normal relations had already been established between Italy and the United Kingdom. The Northern Ireland administration appear to have retained control of Kilwaughter and allowed it to be stripped of anything of value. Auctions had been held and the lead and copper sold. In fact, the lead was only removed from the roof in 1951 and this desecration was photographed and published in a newspaper. It was only then that the vandalised building was returned to its Italian owners, who in 1983 sold on the wrecked Castle and the gate lodge.

With the roofless building long since open to the elements, it had no chance of remaining secure and intact, and so the obliteration of this proud building began its path of destruction. The future of the ruined building is unpredictable and the Castle faces a bleak future.

This story is setting out to give a glimmer of the lives of some of the occupants of Kilwaughter Castle, those of their family and their associates.

Chapter 1

The Early Years

The area of Kilwaughter is situated in the Barony of Glenarm and in parts is mountainous and boggy and it incorporates Agnew's Hill, taking the name of the main family of this story. The Agnew family was never ennobled (possibly due to the fact that they supported the United Irishmen), but were landed gentry and were certainly wealthy enough to maintain lives of high satisfaction for themselves. They were considered to be reasonable and at times kind, landlords. Its family history with the Kilwaughter area covered at least 400 years, but the family name then however, was not the modern anglicised version Agnew of today, but they used the native Irish name, Ó Gnímh[1] and were important bards to the MacDonnells and the O'Neills.

In 12th century Ireland new invaders arrived to conquer the island. These Anglo-Normans were powerful people and proceeded to wrestle large portions of land from the indigenous population. Amongst them were the Bissetts, the Fitz Warins, the de Mandevilles and the Savages - and the Kilwaughter area did not escape their clutches. Adam Bissett who aligned with Hugh de Lacy,[2] appeared in the early 13th century and built a fort at Kilwaughter,[3] but in 1281 a fracas with the de Mandeville family resulted in his fort being razed to the ground.[4] The Fitz Warins had lost their estate in Shropshire, but a timely marriage connected to the Ormond family in Ireland, gave them the chance to change their allegiance from England to Ireland. Part of their territory was Twescard which was one of the counties of the old

---

[1] There are several spelling variants of the name.
[2] McDonnell, 2013, p.6.
[3] Remnants of the motte still survive today.
[4] Brown, 2023, p.54.

Earldom of Ulster and centred around Glenarm.[5] The Savage family from Derbyshire, had also been granted land by Hugh de Lacy before 1243 and they continued to gain vast tracts of territory in Counties Antrim and Down, but lost their Antrim lands to the native Irish over the next three decades, though managed to hang on to their lands in County Down. Patrick Savage was granted 25 townlands from Queen Elizabeth 1 in 1571 and amongst them was Tullagharnan, known today as Tullycarnan in the Barony of Upper Ards in County Down. It was once known as Listyagnew,[6] and also known as the *House of the Ó Gnímh,* and we find mention of one, Andrew Agnewe *(sic)* of Carnie living there. Not only was the Gaelic and English surname interchangeable, but it also indicated a close connection to the Savages.[7] [8]

When and how the bardic Ó Gnímh's possessed the Kilwaughter land before it was taken from them by these Anglo-Norman families, is obscure, as indeed is the earlier history of the Ó Gnímh family itself. We know that they had already been established in the area before the 1600's and that they eventually had their old lands returned to them by another patron Sir Randal MacDonnell. This might suggest that indeed, they did possess these Kilwaughter lands in earlier times and quite possibly from the powerful MacDonnell family whose ancestry they shared through Somerled, a Norse-Scot warrior. Sir Randal appears to have been a generous landlord and was keen to reinstate the lands that had been usurped by the Anglo-Norman incomers much earlier.[9] He was also on good terms with the Agnew family of Lochnaw Castle at Leswalt, just outside Stranraer in Scotland, who were said to be connected to the Agnews of Kilwaughter, though documentation to confirm this is scarce.

By 1620 Sir Randal had been granted the Earldom of Antrim and it seemed that after he achieved this accolade he persuaded his friend Sir Patrick Agnew of Lochnaw in Galloway, to hold several estates within the vicinity of Larne,

---

[5] Ibid, p.49.
[6] Hughes, 1998-2000, p.244.
[7] Placenamesni.org
[8] Hughes speculated that it was possible the Savages were also patrons to the Ó Gnímhs, but as Dr. Angeline King points out in her thesis, this may or may not be correct. She notes that the name Andrew is a Lochnaw name and therefore he could have been an incomer from Scotland. King, 2023, p.312.
[9] McDonnell, 1993, p.14.

Glenarm and Kilwaughter.[10] Sir Patrick Agnew was no stranger to Sir Randal since both had been friends from childhood. They had met through their fathers (Sorley Boy MacDonnell and Sir Andrew Agnew, the 7th Sheriff of Galloway), who were contemporaries. Both Sir Andrew and Sir Patrick had made frequent visits across the Irish Sea to visit the MacDonnell stronghold.[11] It would not be surprising and an obvious natural extension of the two sons' friendship, if they were to cement this relationship by holding lands in a similar vicinity, being close to the coast and the journey to Galloway.

It should also not be forgotten that the early 17th century was an explosive time in Irish politics and was the beginning of what came to be known as the *Plantation of Ulster*. (An earlier plantation had begun in Elizabeth's reign, but had been abandoned). The mighty O'Neill family of Tyrone was very much involved in this social revolution by waging war against Elizabeth's proposal. Hugh O'Neill enlisted the help of the Spanish, but he was defeated at the Battle of Kinsale in 1601 and again at Omagh, by Lord Mountjoy where O'Neill capitulated and signed the Treaty of Mellifont in 1603. After this in 1607, Hugh and other Gaelic lords fled Ireland in what came to be called *The Flight of the Earls*, thus forfeiting their estates to the Crown. This was taken as evidence to the English once and for all that they were traitors.[12] Hugh finally died blind, in Rome on 20th July, 1616 and was buried alongside his son in the church of San Pietro.[13]

The vast majority of planters were settlers from Scotland who very soon realised that their arrival in the new country, far from being welcomed, actually resulted in tension with the native Irish. The Scottish settlers who arrived in Ulster then were mostly Presbyterians, many of whom spoke Lowlands Scots (Lallons), or Scots Gaelic.

This then was the state of affairs that prevailed in Ireland at the time when Sir Patrick decided to hold an estate in County Antrim. The ambitious Patrick saw a chance to enlarge his empire and join the rest of the Scottish speculators who arrived at that time to purchase or lease the vast tracts of land that existed. Land along the north east coast of that part of Ireland, would have been

---

[10] Agnew, 1893, p.43.
[11] Ibid, p.43.
[12] Stewart, 1977, p.22.
[13] O'Faolain, 1992, p.281.

particularly attractive as it was a convenient place to live for those who wished to continue to traverse the short distance across the North Channel.

By now Sir Patrick who was born in 1578 (the same era as Brian Ó Gnímh father of Fear Flatha Ó Gnímh, the most famous of the Ó Gnímh poets), had become the 8th Sheriff of Galloway and Baronet of Nova Scotia,[14] as he had inherited his father's title in 1617.[15] The Baronetage of Nova Scotia had been devised in 1624 by King James VI, in order to settle the Province. The King wished to create one hundred baronets and each baronet had to support six colonists for two years or pay a sum which was 2,000 marks in lieu. Sir Patrick was chosen as one of the baronets. His grandfather (another Patrick), lived during the time of the great reformer John Knox and was the first of his family to be buried a Protestant when he died in 1590.[16] Having acquired the lands from Sir Randal, Sir Patrick established a base at Kilwaughter and appointed a relative, Captain John Agnew as his County Antrim agent.

The Kilwaughter Plantation House

Sir Patrick was not the first settler to build at Kilwaughter for beside the plantation house[17] was the ruin of an ancient Danish or druidical fort from yet another much earlier invasion.[18] Added to that the Ordnance Survey Memoirs of the mid 19th Century described an old oak door having the date of 1566 marked on it, but which was within part of the house.

A detailed description of this early plantation house has been documented by Professor E.M. Jope and he described it as a castellated dwelling of the early 17th century similar to Scottish types. It was built of rubble chalk blocks with very little basalt included and was said to have been slate-roofed.[19] Some of these original slates were used again in 1807 when a descendant (Edward Jones Agnew), converted the tower house into the castle building that remains today in decimated form.

---

[14] Agnew, 1926, p.377.
[15] Agnew, 1864, p.247.
[16] Ibid, p.218.
[17] Kilwaughter Castle as a building, was not yet in existence.
[18] Ordnance Survey Memoirs of Ireland, Vol.10. p.107.
[19] Jope, undated.

Kilwaughter – The Unknown Castle

From what can be deduced it appears that the plantation house at Kilwaughter was built to be a stout defence which was needed considering the continuous conflict in the country at the time and was a sagacious move.

The building had four floors and built in a T-plan manner, but one special feature was the spacious staircase of straight steps and landings known as a scale and platt staircase which occupied a separate projecting tower and which was considered to be a somewhat English feature of the late 16th/early 17th centuries, though it was also found in Scotland. Professor Jope also made a comment that Dunluce Castle on the north Antrim coast contained the remains of a similar scale and platt staircase in the early 17th century mansion of English style which had been built within the Castle walls. Another characteristic indicated that slits were often used as windows, which seemed to give the structure a somewhat austere appearance from outside and would certainly have meant that natural light flooding inside the building would have been restricted. These slits can still be seen today in those sections of the Castle that still remain. Fireplaces were built at the end walls of each floor.

The external building to the North, was a bawn (a word derived from Gaelic, meaning *cattle-fort*), which would have offered some extra defence for the occupants if required, as the entrance and staircase of this bawn were within the property's boundary.[20] (The bawn also had a much more practical use some years later and one which the builder could never possibly have envisaged , for it became the birthplace of at least two illegitimate Agnew children about whom we will read later).

Outside the tower house, in the surrounding lands, the agricultural pursuits which took place on the estate were mixed, both arable and livestock. The individual leases were inclined to be small, five to thirty acres and could have been because the estate was so close to Larne, one of the main ports of entry where the planters arrived and the desire to live there would have made the journey back to Scotland easy. The farms were by necessity then, forced to be compact. The livestock numbers on the Kilwaughter estate were also small as cattle were very scarce, only an average of 0.2 cows per acre on the estate, is recorded. Cattle became a highly valued commodity then because of this scarcity. Sorley Boy MacDonnell for example, had a huge herd of 50,000 cattle, but of that only 1,500 gave milk, but because they were regarded with

---

[20] Jope, undated.

such high esteem, they were kept even though they were of little practical use. In fact the new migrants were advised at the time to bring over their own livestock which helped in due course to increase the numbers locally. The Kilwaughter land did lend itself very well to one particular aspect of farming though, the rearing of sheep which produced large quantities of wool and meat. The arable nature of farming on the Kilwaughter land was very weak. Labour supply was limited and the soil was not fertile because of the shortage of cattle waste to fertilise it, so only crops that were virtually maintenance free could be grown.[21]

Due to the difficulty in farming the estate, it is questionable just how much revenue Sir Patrick obtained from his tenancies and it is tempting to ask if the estate was financially successful and if not, just why he maintained it?

Sir Patrick married Margaret the daughter of the Hon. Sir Thomas Kennedy of Culzean. Her mother Elizabeth was the daughter of David McGill of Cranstoun Riddell. (The Kennedy's had been the original possessors of Leswalt, in 1482 when John, Lord Kennedy and son of Gilbert, obtained the Barony of Leswalt). Some property had been granted to the Agnews in 1426 though small, however, it came with the appointment of the Sheriffdom which gave the Agnews some power.[22] The Agnews first patrons were the Douglas family, William Douglas putting his seal to charters in the same year of 1426, thus transferring the Constabulary of Lochnaw and the privileges of the Barony to Andrew Agnew.[23]

Sir Patrick and Margaret had nine children - Andrew the heir, who later became the 9th Sheriff of Galloway; Alexander of Whitehills, a Lieutenant Colonel in the Earl of Galloway's Regiment and who travelled back and forth with Andrew to the estate in Ireland; James of Auchrocher, an army Colonel who married Marion Kennedy, daughter of the Laird of Ardmullan. James died in 1648.[24] Patrick of Sheuchan[25] who married Elizabeth Gordon the daughter of William Gordon of Craichlaw. Their five daughters were – Agnes

---

[21] Gillespie, 1985, pps.71,73,74.
[22] McKerlie, p.427.
[23] Ibid, p.456.
[24] Agnew, 1864, pps.251, 300
[25] Thomas Agnew of Culhorn, Inch Wigtonshire, founder of Agnew's Art Gallery in London, which celebrated 197 years as art dealers in 2013, claimed descent from Patrick of Sheuchan. (See Appendix 4).

Agnew who married Uchtrad McDowall of Freugh in 1622; Jane Agnew who married Alexander McDowall of Logan in 1621; Elizabeth Agnew who married J. Baillie of Dunragit; Marie Agnew who married Hew McDowall of Knockglass and Rosina Agnew who married John Cathcart of Genoch in 1632.[26]

It is not clear just how much time Sir Patrick spent at Kilwaughter, as his main home continued to be in Galloway where he was elected to serve in Parliament in 1628 for a five year term.[27] This was during the first parliament of Charles I.[28] During his absence from Kilwaughter he left the estate in the hands of his agent Captain John Agnew. Little is known about his relationship with Sir Patrick, except that he was referred to as *Kinsman*. He was born around 1586, some eight years after Sir Patrick's own birth and is thought to have lived on the corner of Shaw's Hill.[29] We know that Sir Patrick, sublet the land of Ballykeel to his namesake, Patrick Agnew in 1622 who is possibly the father of John.

Captain John Agnew, agent to Sir Patrick Agnew

John married his cousin Eleanor Shaw of Ballygally. The Shaw family was another enterprising Scottish family who had arrived in the North of Ireland in 1606 during the Plantation, from Greenock. Captain James Shaw was the younger son and had ventured forth to seek his future in Ireland where his sister had already settled. She had married Sir Hugh Montgomery of County Down and James stayed with them for a few years before moving north to County Antrim where he received grants of land in the parish of Cairncastle, from the Earl of Antrim. Here he built Ballygally Castle in 1625.[30] He married Isabella Brisbane. In later years when the Shaw family fell on hard times, this Castle would be purchased by another Agnew, a colourful character about whom we will learn much more later.

John and Eleanor had two sons that we can identify – Patrick and Francis. In Tennison Groves Genealogical Notes and Abstracts of the Agnews, a Will of Captain Francis Agnew of Kilwaughter dated 1681 is noted as having been

---

[26] McKerlie, 1994, p.106.
[27] Ibid, p.106.
[28] Agnew, 1926, p.383.
[29] The Corran, 1997, No.4.
[30] Porter, 1901.

proved.[31] This is more than likely John's son as the date and address fit and in the list of Scots-Irish links, we find Patrick Agnew of Kilwaughter, 1665, who is presumably John's other son.[32]

Ulster was still, at this time, in its usual unsettled agitation. From the beginning of the plantation the Protestant settlers had lived in an anxious state for they were very aware that the land on which they lived, had been appropriated under duress from the native Catholic Irish. Far from having an exciting new life in an exciting new country, it had turned out to be disastrous. The settlers found themselves living a life full of fear with rumour of retribution from the Catholic Irish. Gossip was rife that one day they would seek revenge. The settlers knew that whilst they lived in relative prosperity, the dispossessed Irish whom they referred to as *Woodkerne*, roamed the hills and forests or were homeless.[33] This was an intolerable and unsustainable situation.

Captain John Agnew's part in the 1641 Rebellion

The 23rd October 1641 was the day of reckoning. Whilst the leaders of the old Gaelic families in Ulster amongst whom were the O'Neills, MacDonnells and Magennises, did not attack, their followers did and in a matter of hours the place was overrun by the insurgents.[34] Captain John Agnew was said to have been in charge of the Larne Refugee camp. He had taken control of Larne and both that and the bordering lands were fortified under his command.[35] The tenants of the Kilwaughter estate fled to Larne as their nearest shelter and did not return again for four years.[36] Captain John Agnew and his troops appeared ruthless. In a Deposition of 30th April 1653, he and his men were accused of killing Mary Savadge *(sic)*, wife of Bryane *(sic)* Oge Magee, together with four more women and three children, for no apparent reason.[37] Another Deposition dated 7th May 1653, described how he and his Company chased John McLaugherty, a servant, accused of, "*Running to the*

---

[31] PRONI, T808, p.47.
[32] Scots-Irish Links, p.3, 2010.
[33] Haddick-Flynn, 1999, p.33.
[34] Elliott, 2000, p.98.
[35] Agnew, 1864, p.318.
[36] Dickson, 1901, p.170.
[37] Depositions, 1641 (Katherine Magee).

enemy" to his Mistress's house in Magheramorne where he was caught and violently killed.[38]

Ballygally Castle too, at that time was under siege, but was successfully defended[39] and as John Shaw had secured his property against attack, he was able to take in many of his servants and tenants to the Castle for their protection.[40] At the same time, some miles to the south of Ballygally Castle in Inver, Larne, a much more immediate struggle was taking place. Inside St. Cedma's parish Church which had become a refuge for some of the residents of Larne, a heavily pregnant woman was about to give birth to a daughter. This baby girl was named Helen Agnew and is said to have lived well into old age. It is not known how she is connected to Kilwaughter, but she went on to marry Mr. Getty of Larne and together they had several children, one of whom married John McCullough of Cairncastle. Helen was obviously much revered because the McCullough family kept an old armchair belonging to her and on it were carved the initials, *"H.A. who was born in Larne Church in 1641".* It is likely that this chair had been presented to her as a reminder of her unusual place of birth.[41]

The rebellion lasted for the rest of the decade before Cromwell managed to crush the insurgents. What happened to Kilwaughter and the estate during this time is open to conjecture.

In the book, *"Irish Landed Gentry – when Cromwell came to Ireland",* we find three Agnews mentioned – Alexander, James and John. They are referred to as, *"Of the 49 Lots"*, meaning that they served either Charles I or Charles II as commissioned officers in Ireland before 5 June 1649, during the Irish land settlements.[42] These three Agnews were most likely relatives of the Lochnaw family supporting the cause.

Before leaving John however, there is some more information to consider. The Scottish Presbyterians came under fire because of their political attitudes against the Government and in 1653 Parliament decided to rid themselves of the troubling Scots once and for all and to transplant them to Connaught, Munster and Tipperary. Amongst the proscribed were – Captain John Agnew,

---

[38] Ibid, 1641 (Owen Magee).
[39] Porter, 1901.
[40] McKillop, 1987, p.21.
[41] Ibid, 2005, p.39.
[42] PRONI, DA/106/57-10

Patrick Agnew, Francis Agnew (presumably his two sons) and another, William Agnew.[43] The scheme was never enforced and one of the reasons for this must have been due to some shrewd negotiating skills during this uncertain period in their lives.

Death of Sir Patrick Agnew, 8th Sheriff of Galloway

Sir Randal MacDonnell who died in December 1636 at Dunluce Castle, did not live to witness the rebellion. Since the family was on the opposing side to the Agnews, one is inclined to wonder what impact the rebellion would have had on the lifelong friendship between him and Sir Patrick if he had lived? From information we have, based on letters, Sir Patrick appears to have been a loyal friend to Sir Randal and to have treated him with great courtesy, so his family taking the opposing side, may have caused him some anxiety. He also seems to have been a loving father to his son Andrew who by that time, had come over from Galloway to look after the Kilwaughter estate and in one letter to his son, Sir Patrick implores him to write soon and signs it, *"Your luffing father"*. (John had died in 1656, two years before he and James Shaw of Ballygally penned Depositions concerning the lease on the land granted by the Earl of Antrim to Patrick[44]). In the same letter, as an after-thought, Sir Patrick also requested that on Andrew's return to the Scottish estate, he should bring with him a new saddle and described the type he wanted.[45] Sir Patrick appeared to have been methodical in detail, as even into old age he was still particular about the management of his estates and was continuing to proffer advice by letter to Andrew on how to handle various situations concerning them.[46] He died in 1661, aged 83 years, at his estate at Lochnaw. He was remembered not only as the, *"Best of fathers"*, but as a man of great wisdom during his service in public life.[47] He is buried with his wife in the Agnew family vault at the old church in Leswalt.

---

[43] Agnew, 1893, p.52.
[44] National Archives of Scotland, GD154-517, 30th November, 1654.
[45] Agnew, 1864, p.323.
[46] Ibid, p.322.
[47] Ibid, p.347.

Sir Andrew Agnew, 9th Sheriff of Galloway and heir to Sir Patrick Agnew

Sir Patrick's son and heir Andrew married Lady Agnes Stewart in 1625, the only daughter of the Earl of Galloway whose finances at the time of her marriage, appeared somewhat stretched.[48] A story survives describing how the Earl was finding it difficult to come up with the £450 cash which was part of her dowry and which still remained unpaid some eleven years later. The Earl couldn't even manage the instalments. Sir Patrick sued for the money and the Earl was charged to pay up within six days.[49]

The following year Andrew, who by now, was again living in Scotland, returned to his estate at Kilwaughter, not with any serious intent it seems this time, but to make merriment with his tenants as was shown in the accounts which were sent to him at Lochnaw, highlighting the cost for the amount of *drink* that had been partaken during the festivities.[50] In 1653 the estate comprised 452 acres for farming and the rental was worth £92 2s. 1d. though on the rental roll this read £87 2s. 1d. instead. Was the discrepancy deliberate or a mistake? The land was divided amongst 19 tenants and the largest farm numbered 66 acres and was combined and farmed jointly by two tenants, whilst the smallest farm of 5 acres, was farmed by one tenant only.[51] Several Agnews appear amongst the tenants (Thomas, Gilbert and Patrick). By 1693 a further 12 acres of land had been added and in 1695 the total had reached 471 acres. From the rent rolls it is easy to see how the Lochnaw Agnews continued to have problems recouping rental money. Some tenants paid just a little, presumably what they could afford and in the second quarter of 1699, more than £200 debt was written off which corresponded with the amount owing. Three years later a further debt of £159 18s. 4d. was also written off.[52]

Andrew died in 1671 only ten years after his father. The names of his children were not included in his Will though they were provided for, but his eldest son, also Andrew is mentioned as his heir, thus becoming the 10th Sheriff of Galloway.[53]

---

[48] Ibid, p.251.
[49] Ibid, p.252.
[50] Dickson, 1901, p.171.
[51] National Archives of Scotland, GD154-515, 1653.
[52] Ibid, GD154-532, 1693-2702.
[53] Agnew, 1864, pps.372,374.

Chapter 2

Patrick Agnew, 1ˢᵗ of Kilwaughter (son of Captain John Agnew)[1]

Earlier in 1659, Andrew the 9th Sheriff sublet his Kilwaughter estate to Captain John's son Patrick.[2] Information on this Patrick is scant though from his son's Will we know that he had at least two children – Patrick and Jean or Jane.[3] Another daughter Helen is mentioned in the Stewart genealogy.[4] John's son Patrick was called *cousin* by Sir James Agnew of Lochnaw who was the son and heir of Andrew, the 10th Sheriff of Galloway, but this would probably have been a distant cousin. We know that Patrick married into the Stewart family of Killymoon Castle in County Tyrone.[5] The Stewart family had also been settlers in the North of Ireland and had arrived from Scotland during the plantation. Their home at Killymoon, had been built originally in 1671 by James Stewart who bought the land lease in 1666 from Alan Cooke, the progenitor of Cookstown. This Castle later became the first Irish project for John Nash, one of England's finest architects when he was called upon to refurbish it in 1802. Some twenty years later on a visit to Killymoon by one of their Tyrone neighbours, John Ynyr Burges, he described it as both romantic and beautiful and, *"Its equal is not to be found in any country for the most perfect combination of wood, water, mountain and undulation of ground".* [6] Nash would also go on to refurbish Kilwaughter House sometime later.

---

[1] Named 1ˢᵗ of Kilwaughter as he was permanently based there.
[2] Agnew, 1893, p.59.
[3] PRONI, D300/1/5/1, p.17.
[4] PRONI, T559/36.
[5] Agnews of Kilwaughter.
[6] PRONI, T1282/1, pps.10-13.

Patrick's daughter Helen also married into the Stewart family of Killymoon. She married James in 1709 who was born in 1665 and was considered to have been somewhat headstrong in his youth, but went on to have an audacious career both at home and abroad. He became a friend of Emperor Joseph I of Austria and received a commission in the Austrian artillery in 1703 when he was 38 years old. James and Helen had three children – William, Patrick and Margaret.[7]

Patrick Agnew, 2nd of Kilwaughter and visit by Sir Andrew Agnew of Lochnaw

Patrick (1st of Kilwaughter), is believed to have died in 1686 by which time he was succeeded by his son, also named Patrick (2nd of Kilwaughter), who became an agent for the Agnews of Lochnaw.[8]

Two years later in 1688, Andrew, the 10th Sheriff, decided to visit his Irish estate purely as a tour of inspection because it was becoming so difficult to obtain the rent from his leases and he wished to find the reasons for this. Before his arrival he sent a letter to Patrick, his agent, saying that he hoped his journey would not be in vain and spelt out in no uncertain terms that he was becoming impatient about the debts owing him. His financial situation unfortunately, was compounded by the fact that at the same time, his Scottish tenants were also finding it difficult to pay up.[9] A situation that was both frustrating and untenable. (It was only much later on 20 November, 1693 that Patrick was officially appointed Sir Andrew's rent collector in Kilwaughter through a bond dated 1 August, 1695).[10]

It seems unlikely that Andrew succeeded in achieving his goal of improving the situation because when he died in 1701, his Irish estate was still causing financial problems for his heir Sir James. In a letter to him, his agent Patrick declared that he, *"Can make no money of the (tenants) goods"* and pointed out that Sir James ought to be able to, *"Tell the state of our country"* from the frugality of his profits.[11] The letter also mentioned that what money was owing to Sir

---

[7] PRONI, T559/36.
[8] Agnews of Kilwaughter.
[9] Agnew, 1864, p.435.
[10] Scots-Irish Links, p.3, 2010.
[11] Agnew, 1864, p.489.

James depended upon the price of the butter produced on the estate which had to be taken to Belfast for weighing. Butter was the prime export thanks to the industrious merchants in Belfast who had begun exporting it in the mid 17th century to countries as far away as Norway. In the year 1694 though, the revenue netted only £3 13s. 4d.[12], but we can still see just how much the Kilwaughter estate had improved from the 1640's when cattle were so scarce, to having big enough herds to benefit from the butter export which brought in more revenue.

By then of course, Ulster was again in the throes of coping with another wave of immigrants caused by a population explosion in Scotland which had begun during the last decade of the 17th century.[13] This invasion of Scottish Presbyterians was to cause the most disruption so far with regard to land leasing. There was also a grave shortage of tenants who were capable of paying their rent, presumably why it was so difficult to recover debts. The majority of those tenants who did move over, probably came from small crofts in Scotland with less arable land and therefore had little experience if any, of farming and no financial back-up.

Visit by Sir James Agnew of Lochnaw. Relinquishes ownership of the Kilwaughter Estate

In 1708 Sir James chose to visit the estate to see for himself and after an uncomfortable journey and receiving very little of his estate income, it seemed that he had had enough with all the difficulties in holding an estate in Ulster which was still very politically turbulent. The rent rolls in that year show that a further debt of almost £460 had to be written off.[14] He came to the conclusion that he would have to get rid of it as it was more trouble than it was worth. Added to that the Earl of Antrim had imposed a surcharge for renewing the lease at the end of the 77-year period in 1713 which didn't help and so Sir James decided that he had to sell the estate to Patrick which he did.[15] He sold the estate so cheaply that it was, *"Most detrimental to the family*

---

[12] National Archives of Scotland, GD154-532, 1693-1708.
[13] Elliott, 2000. p.121.
[14] National Archives of Scotland, GD154-532, 1693-1708.
[15] Deed by Randle McDonnell Earl of Antrim to Patrick Agnew of Kilwaughter, 1713.

interests".[16] Another interesting reason might also have provoked the sale for it seemed that Sir James and his wife Lady Mary who was the daughter of Alexander Montgomerie, the 8th Earl of Eglington, were becoming used to a considerably higher standard of living than their income allowed. Added to that, the couple had, by then, 19 children, (they eventually went on to have two more), so they were very glad of the money from the Kilwaughter sale, even though it was not as much as it ought to have been.[17] He is said to have sold it for £11,000.[18]

We can see from one purchase account sent to Sir James on 18th August, 1704, by a merchant in Belfast, Samuel Smith, that Sir James lived well. He purchased large quantities of goods – 61 yards of material, linen, ratine; 18 dossn *(dozen)* buttons, nails, salt and not only that but enormous quantities of milk and cheese and astonishingly, 312 pounds of butter.[19]

Sir James could also have been a somewhat impulsive character and just wanted to move on to some other pursuit. He certainly 'was whimsical in nature and gave no thought to the historical value of his own home at Lochnaw. Within its history he is infamous for having drained the loch beside the Castle which was one of its enhancing features, just to get at the small fort. Having destroyed this he used the material to extend the Castle by adding an extra wing as well as some stables and offices. He then had the initials of himself and his wife carved on to the building (dated 1704). It never occurred to him that whilst Lochnaw Castle looked much grander, there remained a boggy eyesore in the loch for all to see.[20] He died in Edinburgh in 1735 and was buried there at Holyrood Abbey.

Children of Sir James Agnew

We know a little about some of his children. Their eldest son and heir Andrew was born on 21st December, 1687. He joined Marlborough's army after the Battle of Blenheim and continued to serve in various other regiments long after his father had passed on to him the mantle of responsibility that came

---

[16] Agnew, 1864, p.490.
[17] Ibid, p.491.
[18] Kindly recounted by Ryan Greer. The amount equates to approximately £2,000,000 at today's value. (Bank of England Inflation Calculator).
[19] Ramsey. Undated. (Courtesy of the late Mr. Nelson Bell).
[20] McKerlie, 1994, p.109.

with his inheritance. He brought some shame to his family when he married Eleanor, a relative, who was only 15 years old and a daughter of Captain Thomas Agnew of Creoch. Both families objected to the union, but Andrew persuaded Eleanor to elope to London where they married in May, 1714.[21] The couple were eventually reconciled with their families. Like his parents before him, Andrew had a large family of 18 children and when he died at Lochnaw in 1771, he was succeeded by Sir Stair Agnew, his fifth son.[22]

Another of Sir James' son George, was a Captain in the First Royal Scotch Regiment based in King's County (County Offaly) in Ireland. His first marriage to Elizabeth Dunbar, the daughter of Sir James Dunbar of Mochrum produced no children, but a subsequent marriage did and his daughter Susanna, married William Ware[23] who was the first organist in St. Anne's Parish Church in Belfast, which was later to become St. Anne's Cathedral. William held his position for 49 years from 1776 to 1825. In 1784 he was called away to London and needed a temporary replacement so invited a young musician of eleven years old to replace him during his temporary absence. This was Edward Bunting who is best known for his arrangements of ancient Irish music which eventually led to the more modern renditions.[24] Edward proved to be an outstanding organist, better that William. He became William's assistant at this young age and at times his youth was not that popular because he would scold some of William's pupils who were much older than himself.[25] Susanna occupied herself by opening a boarding school for young ladies in 40 Bank Lane, just off Castle Street in Belfast. The school taught the usual academic subjects such as English, geography, arithmetic, together with music, dancing, art and French embroidery.[26]

A more serious scandalous story is told about Sir James and Lady Mary's daughter Margaret, who married her namesake John Agnew. He was a Supervisor of Excise at Arbroath. In time, something went seriously wrong with their marriage and as a result Margaret left John and moved to the Orkneys to live with her sister Anne Nisbet. Anne's husband James was a

---

[21] Ibid, p.110.
[22] Oxford Dictionary of National Biography, 2004, p.463.
[23] Information courtesy of the late Albert Agnew, California, USA.
[24] St. Anne's Cathedral, Belfast.
[25] O'Regan, 2010, p.99.
[26] The Belfast Newsletter Index.

clergyman there and the *Second charge* of St. Magnus Cathedral in Kirkwall, which put him in a somewhat difficult position, having a sister-in-law who had shunned her husband, come to live with him and his wife in the Manse. James' brother William was also a clergyman and came to the rescue and offered Margaret accommodation at his home. It is difficult to see how this arrangement made it any better considering that William was due to marry soon, but for some reason this change was deemed more acceptable. In fact Margaret's mother Lady Mary Agnew was so pleased that she wrote James the following letter of gratitude, *"Sir I wrote you last Decr., and returned you my most sincere thanks for your kind and tender concern for my unhappy Daughter. Allow me to make my most grateful acknowledgements for all your favours and friendly care of yt. most unfortunate woman, but particularly for getting her so well settled, for I am much better pleased she is Lodged in your house than anywhere Else; so if you are so kind to allow her to continue there, it will give me great pleasure to have her under your roof and instruction of one who is so capable to advise and direct her. (Locknaw, Nover. ye 12th, 1763)".*

Lady Mary Agnew could not have known just how settled Margaret was at her new abode because it wasn't long before rumours started circulating of the somewhat unusual arrangement of a married woman who was no longer with her husband, living alone with the unmarried Minister of the Manse who was about to be married. The rumours of the affair were justified, but William's marriage took place nonetheless on 12th January 1764, though did not last long and his new wife soon returned to live with her father. William was found guilty of adultery by the Presbytery and, *"Liable to a public prosecution"* as it was a capital offence. His punishment was harsh for his misdemeanour and he was given two months' prison sentence with nothing but, *"Bread and water"* followed by permanent banishment to a plantation in America. He was not allowed to return to Scotland for the rest of his life and if he did so would be, *"Whipped periodically"* before being returned to the plantation. The General Assembly thought a little of his ex-wife who must have felt totally humiliated and arranged for a collection to be taken up to help support her. William accepted his punishment and remained in Jamaica, eventually purchasing some property there. Shortly after his transportation other members of the Nisbet family in Kirkwall emigrated to be with him.[27]

---

[27] Hossack, 1986, pps.290,291,292,293.

A story of some interest too, exists about Sir James' grandson, also James, who fought for the British in America. He was born in 1724 the same year that Patrick died and was the son of Major James Agnew of Howlish Hall[28] in Bishop Auckland, County Durham and his wife Elizabeth Wilkinson. Their son James married Elizabeth Saunderson in September 1747 in St. Andrew's Church, Bishop Auckland. He was a Brigadier General of the 4th Brigade and the 37th Regiment of Foot and ADC to King George III in 1775.[29] James commanded the 4th Brigade at the Battle of Brandywine, during the Philadelphia campaign in 1777. He was killed at the Battle of Germantown on 4th October of that year by a civilian sniper and was buried in the DeBenneville family cemetery in Philadelphia. His death was mentioned by George Washington in his writings from camp at Pawlins Mill on 7 October 1777.[30]

His granddaughter Margaret, daughter of his son Captain Robert Agnew, Lieutenant-Governor of the Isle of Man, created scandal when she married her uncle, Harman Blennerhassett around 1796. Harman was a younger son of Conway Blennerhassett, a wealthy Irish landowner whose estate was in County Kerry. Before marrying Margaret, Harman completed his education at Trinity College, Dublin in 1790 and was called to the Bar at King's Inn when he was twenty-five years old. Having succeeded to his father's estate and with a ready supply of money, he gave up his career and went to Paris which was then in the aftermath of the Revolution. This suited Harman well since he was a secret sympathiser with the revolutionaries in Ireland, a political view which was in direct opposition to his family. Tiring of the constant arguments, Harman sold his estate to a relative Thomas Mullins of Burnham (who later became Lord Ventry) and moved with Margaret to America where he purchased an island of 170 acres in the Ohio River, hoping to make his fortune. Sadly for him, once more he aligned himself with the revolutionaries which cost him any future he had hoped to have in his new land. He made some dubious contacts which ended all ambition of remaining wealthy. Margaret, a poet, who was considered an intelligent and beautiful woman, died in New York in 1842. By then her husband was gone and she had been left in poverty.[31]

---

[28] Howlish Hall still survives and is now a residential care home.
[29] The Newsletter of the Agnew Family, 2004, p.3.
[30] The George Washington Papers, 1741-1799.
[31] Agnew, 1926, pps. 426-428.

Her brother James who was heir to Howlish Hall, disgraced himself and cost his descendants their inheritance when he squandered the estate and had to sell up.[32]

The Kilwaughter Estate ends its relationship with the Agnews of Lochnaw

Patrick Agnew, 2nd of Kilwaughter

A significant turning point in the history of Kilwaughter had now been reached with Patrick's purchase because from then onwards, it became a truly Irish family home with no further interference from the Agnews of Lochnaw, though Scottish connections were still maintained, since Patrick had been admitted as a Burgess and Guilds-Brother of Ayr on 11 March 1675.[33] Patrick married Martha Houston the daughter of William Houston of Craigs and she had given birth to eight children - William the oldest son, inherited the Kilwaughter estate and had six children: Francis who had two sons: John, 1st of Craigs who had at least one child and who, when his Will was proved in 1798, was living in Ahoghill parish.

Another son James, 1st of Larne, married Margaret the daughter of James Wilson and had six children, one of whom was Margaret who married James Farrell from County Fermanagh and was a midshipman in the Royal Navy. He was assigned to *The Hynd*, a Sloop of War which was commanded at the time by Captain William McCleverty from Glynn near Larne. James' brother-in-law William was an officer on the ship at the same time.[34] [35] Margaret and James later became the parents of James Agnew Farrell who was instrumental in the 1798 Uprising and was a Commander in the United Irishmen. When James died, according to his Will, his estate was to be sold apart from a few legacies.[36]

Patrick and Martha's son Patrick, married Margaret Haywood and had one child. There was yet another son Patrick born about whom nothing is known,

---

[32] Burke's Peerage, 2003.
[33] Scots-Irish Links, 2010, p.3.
[34] William's address at the time was Highbury Grove London.
[35] Porter, The Agnews of Ireland. Undated.
[36] PRONI, T206/1

indicating that this child most likely died young and his name was used again in his honour. Hugh who had two sons and Henry who married Grace, the daughter of Edward Harries.

Many of Patrick and Martha's grandchildren and great grandchildren went on to serve in the army in India. One, Major General William Agnew, became the Judicial Commissioner for Assam in 1861. Their great grandson Charles (grandson of James, 1st of Larne and a Captain in the 16th Queen's Lancers), was murdered in March, 1873 in Suez whilst on his way home on sick leave.[37] He had stopped off at a café and having accused the Italian croupier of cheating at the roulette table, was stabbed in the stomach which brought about his untimely death. He was buried at Ismailia in Egypt. A tablet in his memory was erected in Canterbury Cathedral in Kent.

After Patrick (2nd of Kilwaughter) acquired Kilwaughter he added to his holding by building a farm house which became known as Kilwaughter House. His Will dated 1st July, 1724 ran to twenty pages in length including several codicils.[38] Patrick was thorough in its execution and made provision for any financial arrears owing to him to be distributed to named people, the Earl of Antrim having first rights. He followed on in the Irish tradition of primogeniture, by leaving the estate to his eldest son William. His wife Martha was well provided for, in that she was allowed to remain in the family home and enjoy the financial rewards of the land leases and the farming returns. Whilst William inherited, Patrick also took care of his remaining six sons and they were left a legacy. His daughter Margaret who had married James Crawford of Ballysavage, was bequeathed £10 sterling, as she had already received a dowry at the time of her marriage.

Patrick's sister Jean (or Jane) had married the Rev. William Ogilvie who was the grandson of Lord Airlie and before marriage her family had helped with the financing and reconstruction of the Manse called Ballyloran House, which the newly married couple would occupy.[39] William became the third Presbyterian minister of Larne and Kilwaughter from 1699 to his death in 1712. The couple had a son called William and he married Elizabeth the daughter of Major James Blair who had earlier taken part in the Siege of Derry.

---

[37] Porter, Agnews of Kilwaughter. Undated.
[38] PRONI, D300/1/5/2.
[39] Agnew Association Newsletter, January 1985, No.3.

In time this couple also had a son called James Blair Ogilvie who went on to marry Margaret the daughter of Willliam Shaw of Doagh.[40]

Two years before Patrick (2nd of Kilwaughter), yet another Patrick (relationship unknown) and his wife Jenny Shaw who was the daughter of Thomas Shaw of Ballygally Castle, set in motion the construction of the boundary wall of the Kilwaughter deer park. The first section of this was built by a stonemason named William Agnew who resided on Andrew Greenlees' farm and Patrick Gingles of Hightown.[41] The work however, was halted for a lengthy period, due to illness and then the deaths of both Patrick and Jenny, but was later finished around 1749, by members of the Gingles family, William, Andrew and John, of the *Red Rock*. Some of the people who lived alongside the old walls were the Boyds who had been planters and the Rocks who originated in Ahoghill, but another family, the Galbraith's also took up residence there. This family was to become much closer to the Agnews in later years when one of them Eleanor, known as Nellie, became the Mistress of Edward Jones Agnew and mother of his two surviving children.

Patrick Agnew, 2nd of Kilwaughter dies

In December 1724 Patrick died leaving Martha a widow. He was buried in the graveyard of the old Corporation Church, in High Street, Belfast.[42] His heir William, was still a young man of eighteen years of age, when he became the proprietor of Kilwaughter. So far the building and its occupants had survived the continuous political turmoil that was ongoing in Ulster. The Siege of Derry had taken place in 1689 and the harsh Penal Law system had been introduced against Catholics in order that a Protestant ascendancy could be secured in the province. Anti-Catholicism was rife. Catholics were not allowed to purchase land; there was a restriction time levied on their land leases (not more than 31 years); they could not carry arms or keep a horse which was worth more than five pounds. Those Catholics who had an estate were under an obligation to split this between the male heirs, unless the first-born converted to Protestantism, in which case he would be the sole owner. Other restrictions

---

[40] Rutherford, 2004, pps.100-101.
[41] Another Agnew stonemason built the towers of Kilwaughter Castle beside the front gates.
[42] This church was pulled down in 1774 and was replaced by St. George's Church which was built over both the old church and the graveyard. No record was kept of the graveyard inscriptions. (Agnew, 1995, p.4).

were placed on them by Parliament, including being prohibited to join the legal profession. They could not work in local government and were banned from the only university in Ireland.[43]

Catholics however, were not the only people in Ulster society to suffer such a draconian regime. Presbyterians were also disadvantaged as they too, were not considered to be part of the Established Church. Huge numbers of Presbyterians had arrived during the Plantation process and as the 18th century dawned, they became more and more uneasy about their position in Ulster. As tenant farmers they had seen their rents rise and agricultural prices fall and it was at this time that many of them decided to emigrate to America where religious bias was not an issue and where there were greater opportunities for a higher standard of living for their families.[44]

---

[43] Elliott, 2000, p.167.
[44] Holmes, 1992, p.12.

Chapter 3

William Agnew, son of Patrick Agnew, 2nd of Kilwaughter, inherits the Estate

It was during this period that the next proprietor William, lived, but notwithstanding the current problems of unrest and prejudice, compared to the decades before, life was relatively calm during the beginning of the 18th century. There was however, still polarisation abounding in society and it must have been quite a depressing and frightening place in which to live. The Protestant nobility was still very concerned about losing land and William would have been no different from any of the other gentry, but his problems would have been minor in comparison with those of the tenants. He did though, have one issue with land near Ballymoney that had been sold to him by Alexander, the 5th Earl of Antrim, to pay off a gambling debt.[1] The Earl sold William not only part of Kilraughts, but the townlands of Drumaquern, Islandmore, Upper and Lower Magherboy, Crosstagherty and Artiferral.[2] He could not take possession of it because another, Brian O'Hale, claimed ownership on the grounds of an alleged lease which had also been granted by the Earl of Antrim. Although O'Hale produced the sealed document, it was proven to be a forgery. He still didn't give up his claim and in the end the Earl of Antrim sent his Glenarm militia to Kilraughts so that William could take possession of his land.[3]

---

[1] Porter, The Agnews of Ireland. Undated.
[2] Blair, Undated.
[3] The Corran, 1986.

William Agnew and his role as Landlord

There is some suggestion that William was not a compassionate landlord and evidence certainly exists to show that he was a somewhat authoritarian one. In 1765 it was the custom for householders to give six days' labour every year for the maintenance and repair of the county's roads. Added to that, everyone who owned a horse was also compelled to lend the use of this animal for the six days. Afterwards when the maintenance had been carried out it was against the law for vehicles with narrow wheels to be used on these same roads. The tenants who did this work were sometimes taken advantage of because the members of the County Grand Jury who were responsible for the scheme, were known to use the men's labour to carry out repairs on their own private roads or build bridges for their convenience. (It was known that William had made sure that there were plenty of byroads leading into his Kilwaughter estate). The landlords did not always pay the men either which must have created plenty of disharmony amongst them.

William Agnew was one of the Grand Jurors and his reputation was such that he seemed to be particularly strict in making sure that this six days' law was carried out. In fact he seemed to have upset the local people so much with his stern approach, that on lst August 1765 at the Summer Assizes at Carrickfergus, an anonymous petition was presented in the Crown Court from the combined parishes of Kilwaughter, Cairncastle and Larne, against William for his, *"Harsh enforcing compliance of the statutable six days labour"*. The first petition was ignored, but the people of the same parishes presented another one against him. The second one was more threatening. Yet again the petitioners' requests were ignored however, this time the Grand Jury only succeeded in provoking them by confirming the, *"Irrepproachable character of William Agnew"* and by demanding obedience to the laws and in particular to that related to the six days' labour. They also offered 20 guineas for the conviction of the writer of the petition. One of the signatories to this declaration was none other than William Agnew himself.[4] This resulted in some riots, the rioters wearing the small twigs of oak in their hats which identified them with the *Oakboys*, a militant group. Very soon afterwards the riots were quelled. There was another side to William though because the

---

[4] PRONI, D2095/18.

weather for successive weeks in autumn, had been so bad that the farmers could not collect the harvest from their fields. One Sunday it improved substantially and as they gathered in church and the Minister Mr. Sinclair, about to begin preaching, William stood up and addressed him and said that it would be better if he had no sermon that day, but let the people go and collect their grain. This the Minister duly did.[5] [6]

Many landlords were unscrupulous in the dealings with their tenants. There was much gazumping over the land leases of tenant farms and the poor cottiers or farm labourers, who were lower in status than the tenants, had the worst time of all. They had no security of tenure and at times lived in abject poverty with preciously few belongings. This contrasted greatly with the Marquess of Downshire at Hillsborough in County Down, who was said to have built a mansion in part, with imported Bath stone. He had also used white marble from Italy, together with mahogany and walnut timber and had had Robert Adams' fireplaces installed in the rooms.[7] Such grandeur between the various divisions in society must have been greatly resented by the lower social strata.

William's Family Life

William too, will inevitably, have lived a comfortable lifestyle by virtue of his position within society and he engaged the services of a jester called Jock the Fool, just to keep himself amused and of course he employed a brewer who kept the house supplied with homemade ale to entertain the guests. Life wasn't all devoted to pleasure though and it had its moments of risk, because once after a visit to England to sell his cattle, on returning home and reaching Newry, Willam was robbed of a large quantity of golden guineas resulting from the sale of the cattle. These were taken from his portmanteau. He was able to recover the money which says something about the tenacious determination of his character.[8]

At the age of 18, he took on the task of running the Kilwaughter estate though he would have had help and advice from the Trustees appointed in his

---

[5] Congregational Memoirs of the Old Presbyterian Church of Larne and Kilwaughter, 1864, p.78.
[6] The Agnews of Kilwaughter Castle were Presbyterians and had been patrons of the Larne and Kilwaughter Church for generations.
[7] Haddick-Flynn, 1999, p.109.
[8] Porter, Agnews of Kilwaughter. Undated.

father's Will. He married Margaret, his cousin who was born in 1714 and the daughter of James Stewart of Killymoon Castle in Co. Tyrone, strengthening yet further the family alliance between Kilwaughter and Killymoon. The marriage produced six children, two boys and four girls. Sadly though, we know little about most of the children, apart from his daughter Ellen who had her own history and her story is told later.

In writing his Will, it must have been rather more of a sad affair for William than usual because no mention is made of his wife or indeed, his one remaining daughter Ellen, so we can probably assume that all his children had died before the Will was written. It was dated 27th January 1775, had one codicil and was proved on 24th February 1776.[9] In this he chose to name his grandson Edward Jones as the main benefactor. He was to inherit the Kilwaughter estate at 21 years of age, with one proviso, that he would take the name Agnew. Edward and his sister Margaret were the two children born to his daughter Ellen and her husband Valentine Jones. Various bequests of lands were given to members of his family including his grand-daughter Margaret Jones and Edward's sister. She was to be given £2,000 on the day of her marriage provided that her marriage had been "*Approved*", but was not to be paid to her if she remained unmarried. Margaret never married, so forfeited her legacy. William Crawford, a nephew, was given the responsibility for the collection of all rents until Edward reached the age of 21 years and this included liaising with the agent in County Tyrone, where William had recently acquired some land.

William appointed three executors – William Stewart of Killymoon, his brother James Agnew of Larne and his nephew William Crawford of Dublin. He also appointed guardians for his two grandchildren Edward and Margaret – his brother James Agnew of Larne, his two nephews William Crawford of Dublin and James Stewart of Killymoon and the children's father Valentine Jones (the elder) [10]then of Belfast. The Will would appear to have been the source of some gossip because news of his less than generous endowment to his grand-daughter Margaret reached Lisburn and in particular Martha McTier who was her friend. Martha wrote to her brother William Drennan who was studying medicine at Edinburgh University *(in)*, "*Old Agnew's Will, he had not*

---

[9] PRONI, T808/46.
[10] Hereafter known as Valentine Jones (the elder)

been very generous to the females of the family and in particular Margaret, who was left only £3,000 to add to the £4,000 she already had". The estate was not to pass to her either should anything happen to her brother Edward.[11] There is however, no mention of this money in her grandfather's Will so this may have been a rumour.

William Agnew dies and his grandson Edward Jones Agnew becomes Heir

William Agnew who by then was referred to as the *Old Squire*, died in 1776, the same year as the signing of the Declaration of Independence in Philadelphia. Whilst in William's final year, American affairs may have been of little significance to him, the Agnew family of Kilwaughter would be loosely connected to this historic event and in particular to one of the descendants of the North Carolina *Signer*, William Hooper. Hooper's grandson (also called William Hooper), would go on to marry Frances Pollock Jones who was the daughter of Edward Jones Agnew's half-cousin.[12] Hooper, an erudite scholar had studied theology and taught for many years before combining his career with that of the Baptist ministry.

After his grandfather's death, Edward Jones who then became Edward Jones Agnew, inherited Kilwaughter and its estate at the tender age of nine, having been born in 1767. His mother Ellen had been married before to James Ross from Portavo in County Down. He was a merchant and business partner of Valentine's (the elder) and the couple had had several children all of whom seemed to have died young. (A death notice of one of their children appeared in the Belfast News Letter on 15th September 1769) announcing the death of William Ross aged 11 years, son of James Ross).[13] Ellen's husband James was a relative (through his grandmother Jane Ross Waddell), of Waddell Cunningham, a merchant and slave trader. He also acted as agent to Lord Antrim. James traded between Belfast and the West Indies and was part-owner, together with Valentine (the elder) and a consortium of others, of several trading vessels,[14] but by August 1762 he was dead. When James died

---

[11] Agnew, 1998, p.3.
[12] Dictionary Of North Carolina Biography, Vol.3. See more in Appendix 1.
[13] The Belfast Newsletter Index, 15th September 1769, DOC, ID 129965.
[14] Truxes, 2001, p.216.

Ellen's father William who was a shrewd man, had hoped that the Ross estate could be brought into the Kilwaughter family, but this wasn't to be. Instead he was one of the executors of his Will.[15] A year later on 4th October 1763 Ellen, married Valentine (the elder) in Belfast becoming step-father to her remaining son William.[16]

---

[15] The Belfast Newsletter Index,, 31st August 1762, DOC, ID 38488.
[16] Ibid, 4th October 1763, DOC, ID 89437.

Chapter 4

The Jones Dynasty

Valentine's (the elder) ancestors are said to have arrived in Ireland at the time of the Plantation from Wales. In William Petty's census taken around 1659, we find two names in the townland of Portadown – Thomas Jones and Valentine Jones.[1] Probate of a Will for a Valentine Jones of Kilmoriarity, near Portadown, in which his wife Elizabeth was the beneficiary, was sought on 1st September 1693.[2] This person was more than likely, Valentine's grandfather who had acquired the sobriquet *Bumper* mentioned in an interesting article in the Belfast News Letter in March 1940 referring to *Squire Jones* of Portadown. Bumper Squire Jones died on 9th January,1694 and is buried in the parish of Drumcree. His seems to have been a somewhat jovial character and was popular. At the end of the article there is a poem which states, *"For pray, what would you more than mirth, with good claret, and bumper Squire Jones."*[3]

Valentine's own father (also called Valentine) married his first wife Margaret Peers on 7th December, 1699 at Lisburn Cathedral. The Peers family was connected to the Rev. Thomas Peers who had been vicar of Derriaghy Parish Church in 1622 and to the Waring family of Waringstown as John Waring had married Mary Peers, the vicar's daughter.[4][5] The couple had one surviving child – Valentine (the elder). In the Blaris (Lisburn) parish register, another marriage is recorded as having taken place on 6th November, 1715,

---

[1] The Belfast News Letter, 7th March, 1940.
[2] PRONI, T281/1/8.
[3] The Belfast News Letter, 7th March, 1940.
[4] Information kindly recounted by Linde Lunney.
[5] PRONI, T2625/1

between Valentine Jones and Miss Mary Close.[6] At that time Valentine (the elder) was only four years old. This was presumably the second marriage of Valentine's (the elder) father.

His father chose the Lisburn or Lagan Valley district to reside. The area was occupied by Lord Conway, another Welsh man. The region was agriculturally important. Added to that, the linen industry was about to gather momentum with the arrival of Louis Crommelin and the Huguenots at the close of the seventeenth century. Crommelin (1652-1727), had been invited by William III to expand the linen industry as he had been an astute banker and also had previous experience working with linen in his home region of Picardy.[7]

Valentine Jones (the Elder)

Valentine (the elder) was born in 1711 and became the third generation to be named Valentine Jones (the next three generations at least, also embraced the same name).[8] When he was merely sixteen years old, he entered into his first marriage. Amongst the Huguenots who had arrived with Crommelin was a family from Picardy named Rochet. Louis Rochet had two daughters, Alice and Mary. Both sisters were married young, Alice to Edward Maslin in 1725 and Mary to Valentine Jones (the elder) in 1727 when she was only fourteen years old.[9] [10] The girls' father died the following year in 1728.[11] Louis's brother, curiously named Lewis Poiriez in his Will, also came with him and he too settled in Lisburn. In the Will he leaves his brother Louis, niece Mary and members of the Truffet family, certain legacies. The father of Louis and Lewis

---

[6] Information kindly recounted by Jean Agnew.
[7] Collins, 1994, p.12.
[8] The continual use of the name Valentine has been a source of great confusion. The following example highlights this. At the same time that Valentine Jones, our present subject, was in the middle of his thriving business interests and making his fortune, another Valentine Jones appeared in Ireland and spent much of the 1760 decade there. He was also a native of Wales, from Llanidloes in Montgomeryshire, born around 1723. This Valentine however, was a military officer fighting in Europe and beyond, before distinguishing himself in America where he was promoted to Major General in 1776. He died in Wales on 16 November 1779. (The Belfast Newsletter Index, 2-5 April 1776. DOC. ID 162805). www.62ndregiment.org/Valentine_Jones.htm)
[9] Best, 1977, chpt. 3.
[10] Benn. 1879, p.4.
[11] Information kindly recounted by the (Galt) Smith family descendants in Brisbane, Australia.

was Jean Moses Poirie Rochette.[12] Valentine (the elder) and Mary were still only children at the time of their marriage and it is stated in Benn's History of Belfast that as a married couple they were most, *"Amusing"* since some of their behaviour was considered to be very immature and childlike. Nevertheless, the couple went on to have at least five children – Valentine, Edward, Louis; Jane who married John Galt Smith on 2nd July, 1765, and another daughter Mary Anne, who became the wife of Robert Harrison. Family life would have been quite entertaining for the couple with overtones of French, Welsh and Irish cultures influencing their lives.

Whilst Mary's time was fully occupied with her family, Valentine (the elder) began in his youth, trading with the West Indies, a trading route that had been established with Ireland for some time, but when Valentine (the elder) became involved, Irish trade with these islands was not as easy as it had been in the latter half of the previous century due to increasing competition with the mainland of America. Valentine (the elder) though, was an astute business man and made it work for himself. Tobacco, sugar, rice, cotton and rum, would have been well received in Belfast. Eighteenth century Belfast was a small, but vibrant and thriving town. It was dominated by a group of intelligent merchants who were intent on making their fortunes. People such as Valentine Jones (the elder), Thomas Gregg and his partner Waddell Cunningham amongst others, were enthusiastic entrepreneurs. Not only were they all friends and in some cases relatives, but they were interlinked with the sole purpose of procuring a sound financial future for themselves and their descendants and in so doing gaining the power that came with great wealth.

Valentine Jones (Barbados 1) and the Slave Trade

The benefits of great wealth sometimes come at a cost and the cost here came in the form of the slave trade. This ancient form of people dominance really began to take shape in 1619 when the first African slaves were transported to North America. In the mid 17th Century the Royal Africa Company was formed in Britain leading to the forced removal of some 90,000 slaves during the decades of the 1670's and 1680's. Ireland though, could not directly trade in slaves as it was not a member of this Company and in fact, for the most

---

[12] The French surname of this family has been spelt variously, Rochet, Rochette, Rouchet, Roche.

part of the next century, it was banned from slave trading altogether,[13] but this didn't stop the merchants of Belfast from finding a way around the ban in order to build upon their wealth. One of the ways of doing that was either to own a ship or have part–shares in one or several, using the vessels for the transportation of goods that the slaves had exhausted themselves in producing. For example, Valentine's (the elder) friend Waddell Cunningham at the time, had shares in at least seven vessels. Another method of trading was to expand the family empire abroad, exactly what Valentine (the elder) chose to do by sending out his son Valentine (Barbados 1)[14] to Barbados. He was at the real heart of the Jones slave trade at the Jones plantation in Providence in Christ Church parish, which comprised 167 acres[15] and not far from the capital Bridgetown.

The thriving West Indies trading would not have been possible at this time without the slaves. They had a grim and miserable existence and their working conditions were atrocious. Working within the sugar houses in particular, was a dangerous job with the boiling liquid and fetid smells.[16] We know something of this Valentine (Barbados 1), during his 33 years in Barbados. Initially he worked in the Bridgetown trading firm of Law, Satterthwaite and Jones. The partnership traded in sugar and their products and also salted provisions. The firm was also involved with the trading of enslaved people. Most of the slaves were taken to be sold in South Carolina. The partnership was dissolved in 1756, but Valentine (Barbados 1) stayed on working as a merchant. He was also made a judge in the Court of Common Pleas.[17]

He was a member of the House of Assembly in Barbados and is first noted as having been elected in 1774 representing St. Michael's Lodge. He continued to sit on the Assembly until 1781[18] and was summonsed to sit on the panel that was dealing with the sale of property and of slaves.

His last session (1780-81) proved to be a difficult one for the Assembly as they reduced the Governor's salary (Major-General James Cunninghame), to £2,000 because of the, *"Present impoverished state of the colony"* and in so doing

---

[13] Rodgers, 2009, p.95.
[14] Hereafter known as Valentine (Barbados 1).
[15] Barbados Plantation History.
[16] Rodgers, 2009, p.36.
[17] Truxes, 2001, p.70.
[18] The Journal of the BMHS. Vol.XIV, pps.185-187.

caused him to be so angry that it affected the rest of his administration which was considered to be, *"One of the most unfortunate and tyrannical in the annals of colonial administration"*. In the midst of all of this came a devastating hurricane on 10th October 1780 which would probably have reinforced the members' view regarding the reduction of the Governor's salary because now even more money would be needed to help pay for the damage on the island. Cunninghame's anger was not to be quelled and the fracas continued until he dissolved the Assembly on 9th December.

When the new session opened on 14th February the following year there were more immediate problems for Valentine (Barbados 1) and his fellow members to deal with. The damage to the island was substantial, though the hurricane failed to reconcile the Governor and the Assembly because he was still seething with anger. The French were expected to invade and there was potential for war with Holland. Reparations were quickly carried out, as were the preparations for war. The Governor still seeking revenge got his own retribution and dissolved the Assembly because he felt that the money being used had not been approved by the people and he now had grounds to call for a new election. Valentine (Barbados 1) was not re-elected, but the Governor did not survive much longer either as he was removed two years later. An address was sent to the King by the Assembly, thanking him for the Governor's recall.[19]

Life on the island, in between the Assembly business, was rather pleasant for those in high office. The Irish would get together to celebrate the Festival of St. Patrick and there were balls in honour of various dignitaries, including the celebration of the Queen's birthday, but normal island activities continued including cock-fighting and the selling and bartering of slaves.

In 1787 Valentine (Barbados 1) was elected one of the Vestrymen for the parish of St. Michael on 15th January. On 20th January 1789 he entertained Prince William Henry, the son of George III and the future King William IV, at his home in Pinford Street.[20] The Prince had come to Barbados to attend the celebrations of the birthday of his mother the Queen by reviewing the troops.[21] By then Valentine (Barbados 1) was Secretary of the Island (he had been elected deputy Secretary on 8th November 1783 followed by the

---

[19] The Journal of the BMHS, Vol.XV, pps.163,164,165.
[20] Ibid, Vol.XVII ,pps.23,106,107.
[21] Ibid, Vol. XXV, p.162.

appointment of Registrar of the Court of Vice Admiralty and Deputy Remembrancer of the Court of Exchequer).[22]

Valentine's (Barbados 1) son (Barbados 2)[23] continued to fill the family coffers and carried on trading in Barbados. He married Elizabeth Graeme and the couple had two children – yet another Valentine (Barbados 3)[24] and Elizabeth. This Valentine (Barbados 3) was to dishonour the family and become a criminal, ending up in prison for his misdemeanours.

Disgrace brought upon the Jones and Agnew Families

Valentine Jones (Barbados 3)

The continual trading in the West Indies through the generations of the Jones' family must have given the family a very comfortable lifestyle, but this was to change in a most embarrassing way. One of Valentine's (the elder) descendants, his great grandson, also called Valentine (Barbados 3), brought shame and disgrace to the family at the beginning of the 1800's. This time not only was it to do with the slave trade, but another frailty of human nature – that of greed which was also thrown into the mix. The younger Valentine Jones (Barbados 3), who was related to Edward Jones Agnew by his half-brother Valentine (Barbados 1), had embezzled very substantial funds in the West Indies. This scandal followed him back to Ireland because Martha McTier in a letter to her brother William, described a dinner party she attended with the Jones' family. It appeared that the young man was, *"Under some cloud"* and indeed was in the house that evening incognito, so that his grandfather (Valentine Barbados 1) didn't even know he was there.[25]

The younger Valentine's (Barbados 3) crimes were extremely serious. He had been appointed Commissary General in 1795 and through this and his earlier experience in the West Indies, had become very well acquainted with the routines of army expenditure, which from the period 1792-1800, had been £2,064,894 6s. 10d., an enormous sum of money. Valentine (Barbados 3) had spotted some loopholes in the procedures and even though he had a salary of

---

[22] Ibid, Vol.XVI, p.144.
[23] Hereafter known as Valentine (Barbados 2).
[24] Hereafter known as Valentine (Barbados 3)
[25] Agnew, Luddy, 1999, Vol. 3, p.386.

£1,800 p.a., a huge sum in those days, this outlet gave him the opportunity to enter a life of dishonesty because he began misappropriating funds. One of the charges brought against him was that of colouring new rum to give it the appearance of old rum which had already been aged. New rum was cheaper, but it was sold as old and Valentine (Barbados 3) pocketed the price difference. As if this wasn't bad enough, unfortunately the colouring used had severe consequences because it was considered to be a deleterious mixture that resulted in loss of life. Another charge also involved alcohol, this time wine that Valentine (Barbados 3) sold at vastly inflated prices as indeed he also did with flour. His behaviour was infectious amongst his assistants and other resident commissioners on the neighbouring islands because he turned a blind eye when they too, participated in making personal gain from the army stores. False documents and dubious vouchers were sanctioned by him to cover up the practices of both himself and his peers.

This deception continued, but by 1797, two years after his senior appointment had been granted, the Treasury was beginning to waken up to the fact that money was being continually requested to be sent to the West Indies without full written justification. The deceit and greed of Valentine (Barbados 3) was obvious and the following excerpt taken from one of the Commissioners' reports summed up his conduct.

"It appears therefore to us, that Valentine Jones very early framed and established, by means of combinations and intricacies almost impervious, an over-ruling and highly injurious influence over the whole transactions of the public, connected with the pay and enormous extraordinaries of the army in this part of the world. This influence was disseminated in various directions, through every branch of the department, and embraced persons of even the lowest description employed therein; and this influence, matured into a regular and far-extended system, produced an immediate loss and injury almost incalculable; and its remote consequences have been little less prejudicial by furnishing examples and precedents, that are to be clearly traced since that period, in nearly all transactions of a similar description."[26]

Valentine (Barbados 3) tried to redeem himself, but it was too late. His conundrum led to him selling his house and personal effects. Although he refunded £100,000, it was not enough and in court on 19 June 1809 as the late Commissary General in the West Indies, he was found guilty of fraud and peculation and given a three year custodial sentence at Newgate prison. He

---

[26] The Times Newspaper, 19th May 1809, p.3.

was also banned from serving the King ever again.[27] His greed had cost him dearly. The sum involved for him alone was colossal at that time - £87,179, but this was but a moiety when taking into account the amounts embezzled by those who colluded with him - £41,300 (Mr. Graeme), £62,000 (Mr. Gordon) and £61,000 (Mr. Sayers).[28] The Graeme family was already associated with Valentine (Barbados3), since his mother was called Elizabeth Graeme and in fact Valentine (Barbados 3) later changed his name from Valentine Jones to Valentine Jones Graeme. Thomas Graeme was also a West Indian sugar baron who had plantations in both Barbados and Grenada, inherited from his father Alexander. He died in 1820 followed by his heir Valentine thirteen years later. Perhaps a reason as to why Valentine (Barbados 3) changed his name to include Graeme due to his inheritance?[29]

Valentine Jones (the Elder), his Business and Political Life

By that time Valentine Jones (the elder) had died in 1805, so did not live to know the consequences of his great grandson's appalling behaviour. Considering the family's social standing, this unfortunate incident must have been of great embarrassment to them and to the Agnews of Kilwaughter. It was widely reported in many columns in The Times newspaper over several days and one can only guess at the level of gossip which permeated high society in the North of Ireland amongst the family and their friends.

Long before this however, and back in Belfast, Valentine (the elder) was continuing his accumulation of wealth. His thriving wine business occupied substantial premises off High Street (White's Tavern today), in Winecellar Entry, which Valentine (the elder) had rebuilt as a spirit warehouse in 1790.[30] It seemed though, that he did not concentrate solely on his business ventures, but he also found time to help build the town of Belfast, so many of his schemes had the sole aim of benefitting the city and in fact he is acknowledged as one of the Founders of Belfast. He was active in raising funds to set up the Belfast Dispensary; he contributed together with his son Valentine (Barbados 1), to the establishment of the town's water supply as well as to the old Poor

---

[27] Newgate Calendar, Vol.3, p.208.
[28] The Times newspaper, March, May and June, 1809.
[29] It is calculated that within the Ross, Jones and Smith connections there were seven families (including Graeme) who either owned slave plantations or traded in slavery.
[30] Wilsdon, 1998, p.43.

House building which was erected in 1774. He also recognized the need for a library and became a committee member of the Belfast Library (now the Linen Hall Library). He was listed as one of the financial contributors (£100), for the building of the White Linen Hall in 1785 as it was decided that a market hall was needed to both sell and promote the awareness of linen which was a major industry then in the North of Ireland. Amongst the other contributors were his son-in-law John Galt Smith (£100) and a friend, Dr. Alexander Halliday (£100) Another friend, Waddell Cunningham was elected to the Committee to oversee the construction of the building.[31] Valentine (the elder) also purchased leases in the Malone area of Belfast, together with others such as Robert Legg and Henry Joy.[32] When he died his son Valentine (Barbados 1) put the lease of a farm in Malone up for sale.[33]

Politically Valentine (the elder) was a liberal. He was a friend of Dr. William Drennan (who later became a famous member of the United Irishmen) and his sister Martha McTier. The middle class salons of people like the McTiers and Drennans, would have exchanged much political discussion around their dinner tables. By this time the Protestants were feeling less insecure about their status in the North of Ireland as the Catholics for the time being, had given up all thoughts of seriously confronting the Protestant Ascendancy, so this hiatus gave them something less to worry about. Many hundreds of miles away however, in America, the colonies were revolting. Their quarrel with England about legislation had degenerated to such an extent that Parliament declared war on the country in 1775. A side-effect of this was that Ireland was left bare of protection since her troops were sent as reinforcements to America. The Protestant middle classes were not slow in filling this vacuum and the Irish Volunteer movement was formed. Valentine Jones (the elder) became a member of this fashionable political movement which was meant to defend the coasts of Ireland and to prevent minor political skirmishes. Although led by the middle class, members gained prestige and above all else, power. Whilst no invasion took place, another equally disheartening event began to unfold in Ulster. At that time an economic depression was descending in Ireland and this was compounded by the Irish trade embargo with the colonies which had been imposed by the English Parliament. A

---

[31] Belfast News Letter Database, 1891.
[32] Ulster Journal of Archaeology, 1978, p.94.
[33] Belfast Commercial Chronicle, 1805.

distorted reason to substantiate this was used: the freedom fighters of America were surviving because of imported Irish provisions.[34]

The American colonists hit back by prohibiting the import of Irish linen which in turn meant that many thousands of Irish textile workers were now unemployed. Valentine Jones (the elder) who came from Lisburn, the heart of the linen industry, must have reacted to this as he understood the hardship that his own community would now endure. At a meeting in 1775, to discuss the ensuing problems which had resulted with the American colonies, Valentine (the elder), representing the merchants and traders, was second to sign a petition to the King (George III), complaining about this state of affairs.[35]

Back home, the Volunteer movement continued to try and cut Ireland's apron strings from England. Initially and to some extent, this was successful; commercial restrictions were done away with in 1779; the English Parliament repealed its right to legislate in Ireland in 1782 and the Volunteers felt they had achieved much.[36] Nonetheless, a schism occurred in the Movement between the aristocracy and middle classes when new objectives such as further Catholic emancipation and parliamentary reform were sought. This proved too much for the organisation to accommodate and the Volunteers eventually disbanded.

By that time Valentine Jones (the elder) was within the closing years of his life. Without doubt he was a man of many strengths and some would say he even had a charmed life to have survived so long. He was a merchant of some distinction who made his fortune in trading; a contributor to society, not only by giving money, but was a man of some vision as was displayed in his wish to improve the town's water supply, which in turn improved the health of its people. He had also addressed the Earl of Donegall on the Lagan Navigation system, explaining his enthusiasm for the use of this, suggesting the river as an alternative to the use of carts.[37] He moved amongst the upper levels of society, participated in the life of the town and kept involved in politics to the end for in his seventieth year he was granted the honour of becoming the

---

[34] Haddick-Flynn, 1999, p.117.
[35] Benn, 1879, Vol.II, p.4.
[36] Stewart, 1977, p.105.
[37] Benn, 1879, Vol.II, p.6.

High Sheriff of the County of Antrim. We can't though, overlook the huge involvement he had within the slave trade which will have made him a fortune.

There was another side to him however, as not only was he a man with serious intentions, but he also knew how to have fun. At ninety years old, he was considered to have kept all the, *"Freshness and vigour"* of youth and indeed, records show that in what were the Exchange Rooms in Belfast, he, his son, grandson and great grandson – four Valentine Jones' in direct succession – all took part in the same dance and that, *"The old man displayed on the occasion unusual vigour and hilarity".*[38]

By 1805 it appeared that his life was moving to its end, because in a letter from William Drennan to Martha his sister, he noted that Valentine Jones (the elder) was dying. This though, was not to be the end of Valentine (the elder), because his robust good health enabled him to recover, but the recovery was short-lived because in a further letter, this time from Martha to her brother, she mentioned that although well again, Valentine (the elder) had fractured his leg.[39]

Valentine Jones (the Elder), Death and Family

On 22nd March 1805, Valentine (the elder) died at the age of 94, almost blind. The latter part of his life had been spent in his home in Donegall Place in Belfast where earlier he been responsible for the building of five houses.[40] He was buried with his son-in-law John Galt Smith (1)[41] and other members of his family at the New Burying Ground in Clifton Street, Belfast. Unfortunately his Will is not to be found, but a snippet from the Belfast Commercial Chronicle dated 8th April, 1805, stated that the Belfast Charitable Society received £100 from him and the Belfast Dispensary, £22 15s.[42]

The children from his first marriage have already been named. His son Valentine (Barbados 1) who was born in 1729 has already been mentioned. As we know he lived most of his working life in Barbados (33 years) carrying out his father's wishes and making sure that the family funds were full. Afterwards he came home to live with him in 1783. His character seemed best summed

---

[38] Merrick, 1991, pps.151-2.
[39] Agnew, Luddy, 1999, Vol.III, pps.322,335.
[40] Merrick, 1991, p.151
[41] Hereafter known as John Galt Smith (1)
[42] Belfast Commercial Chronicle, 1805.

up in the following public testimonial which was presented to him on leaving the island:-

"In testimony of an affectionate and honourable regard, from the merchants and other principal inhabitants of Bridge Town, Barbadoss (sic) to Valentine Jones, Esq., whose public and private virtues, during a residence of 33 years in that island, have claimed the applause and esteem of a grateful community. His fellow citizens having experienced his steady and disinterested principles as a member of the General Assembly, his assiduity and impartiality as eldest Assistant-Judge of the Common Pleas, the benevolence, candour and readiness with which he acted as an Arbitrator, and the rectitude wherewith he always supported the eminent character of a merchant, present this to Mrs. Jones, his amiable partner, having parted from him and her with sincere regret, on the first day of July, 1788".[43]

He too, was involved with the Belfast Dispensary in 1792 and was a member of the Belfast Charitable Society. He married Katherine Moore, daughter to John and Marbella Moore of Moorgrove, County Antrim, by whom he had three children – a son Valentine (Barbados 2) who married Miss Graeme and had two children, Valentine and Elizabeth. (Their son Valentine (Barbados 3) was the fraudster previously mentioned). The couple also had two daughters – Maria who remained unmarried and Kitty who married Roger Moore, but had no children. Kitty's marriage settlement was £2,500 and her father also gave her husband, the use of the various lands that he owned.[44] Valentine (Barbados 1) died at Portpatrick on 26th October 1808, only three years after his father and was buried in the New Burying Ground in Belfast together with his wife who had pre-deceased him on 28th October 1806.[45]

One of Valentine's (the elder) daughters Mary Anne married Robert Harrison. She too was very close to her half-siblings, Margaret and Edward Jones and was very involved in their lives, especially with Margaret since she accompanied her on many social occasions. By 1804 she was a widow and died herself in 1810. Amongst her legacies were the poor pensioners, who were left £2,000 to help them.[46]

---

[43] Benn, 1879, Vol.II, p.6.
[44] PRONI, T956/54.
[45] Merrick, 1991, p.153.
[46] Agnew, Luddy 1999, Vol.III, p.662.

Of the three known remaining children to Valentine's (the elder) first marriage, we know what happened to two of them. His son Louis was a legal practitioner in Belfast and became a Freeman in 1754.[47] Valentine's (the elder) daughter Jane married John Galt Smith (1) on 2nd July 1765[48], a West India slave merchant of Belfast. Both Jane and John were born in the same year, 1731. John's parents were Samuel Smith (a friend of Valentine's (the elder)) and Ann Galt, Samuel's second wife. Samuel's first wife was called Sarah Boyd and he had three daughters to her and appears to have been married for about ten years before his second marriage to Ann took place around 1730. The Smith's ancestor William was a merchant of some standing. He arrived in Ireland in the mid 1660's but by 1663, in a list of ships owned by Belfast merchants, he is noted as already possessing six of them. He died in 1684 after having become extremely wealthy and is said to have left the princely sum of £3,600. Samuel descended from one of William's sons called John (Jack) who died in 1760.[49]

Jane Jones and John Galt Smith (1) were both great grandchildren of Irish settlers, so had something in common. They both came from families who had become exceedingly rich in their adopted land and who had contributed and participated greatly in its growth and development. John was active in rope and pottery manufacture and he was also a West India merchant. The couple had at least nine children, four daughters and five sons. One son William, became a slave owner of Barbados and Surinam, like his father.[50] [51] Those that survived childhood married well and had good careers. Jane like her other siblings seemed to have kept close company with the family and socialised within the same group of friends. When, at 56 years of age, she became ill, her condition was frequently mentioned in correspondence between Martha McTier and her brother William Drennan. It seemed that everyone was showing great concern for her health and well-being. William who was a doctor thought that she may have had a liver complaint.[52] Jane died

---

[47] Information kindly recounted by Jean Agnew, 2003.
[48] Belfast Newsletter Database, DOC ID 89437.
[49] Information kindly recounted by the (Galt) Smith descendants in Brisbane, Australia.
[50] Centre for the Study of the Legacies of British Slavery.
[51] William was the great uncle of another John Galt Smith who married Bessie Bringhurst, but more about him later.
[52] Agnew, Luddy, 1999, Vol. I, pps.262, 263.

on 8th August 1787 in Bath where she went for a cure. She too, was buried in the family plot at the New Burying Ground in the Clifton Street graveyard in Belfast.

One of their grand-daughters, another Jane, married her second cousin the wealthy banker, James Bristow. This couple later purchased a very substantial residence called, *Wilmont* in Dunmurry around 1858.[53]

John Galt Smith (1) like his father-in-law Valentine Jones (the elder), demonstrated an active interest in local affairs and became a member of the Irish Volunteer movement. He too, signed the petition to King George III in 1775 as Valentine (the elder) had done and was a member of the Volunteer movement. He was also a member of the Northern Whig Club. The two men therefore, had much in common. In 1802 John had a second stroke, which left him paralysed and on 14th December that year he died, three years before his father-in-law. He is said to have died a beggar as he had spent his last years in decline, drinking and paying scant attention to his business interests.[54] By then his wife had been dead 15 years. His grandfather William would probably have been disappointed in him for allowing the business to deteriorate since he had spent his life building up a wealthy establishment to pass on to his family. John Galt Smith (1) was buried in the New Burying Ground in Clifton Street, Belfast.

---

[53] More information can be found about the Wilmont residence in Rankin, The Linen Houses of the Lagan Valley,
2003, pps.126-129.
[54] Agnew, Luddy, 1999, Vol. III., p.90.

Chapter 5

Edward Jones Agnew inherits the Kilwaughter Estate

Edward Jones Agnew like his grandfather before him, inherited Kilwaughter and the estate at a young age. He was not meant to inherit since some of William's brothers were still alive, but his grandfather made him heir nonetheless. Guardians had already been put in place for both Edward and his sister Margaret – their uncle James Agnew of Larne; two cousins William Crawford of Dublin and James Stewart of Killymoon Castle and finally their father Valentine Jones (the elder). William had already taken control of the Castle's future and of the family name by appointing Trustees within the family whom he could rely on and by adding a proviso in his Will, that Edward, on claiming his inheritance at 21 years of age, would become Edward Jones Agnew.

It is probably likely that Edward and Margaret were born in Belfast where their father lived and carried out his wine business in Winecellar Entry. In the intervening period between Edward becoming heir at 9 years and taking on the responsibility of his inheritance at 21, his estate was put in the hands of the Trustees. At 13 years old he was sent to Harrow, the prestigious public school in England. The school register noted that he attended there from 1780 until 1785. Curiously his father's name is shown as Valentine Agnew and Edward as Edward James Agnew. When Edward returned to Ireland he pursued his further education at Trinity College in Dublin. He matriculated on 17 January 1785 when he was 18 years old and qualified in 1788 with a Bachelor of Arts degree.[1] During his time at University (in 1787), he suffered

---

[1] Gun, 1934, p.31.

from scurvy, a vitamin deficiency disease and is said to have gone to Ballynahinch (probably to the Spa) with his sister Margaret.[2]

In 1788 he was 21 years of age and able to claim his inheritance. With Edward's arrival, Kilwaughter probably gained the most colourful character of its history. He was young, educated, had experienced life outside Ulster and his Jones background was that of a well-to-do family that was prominent both in Ireland and abroad. Edward must have relished the idea of becoming the latest Squire and he would go on to refurbish his home in some style, by enlisting the help of John Nash the distinguished English architect. His personal life too, would become somewhat less conventional as he would father at least three children out of wedlock.

It would have been natural for Edward to set about the task of becoming acquainted with the routine of running the estate and assuming responsibility for the tenant farmers. He employed an agent to help him with this. He kept it in the family and appointed his half-brother Valentine (Barbados 1) on a salary of £300 per year, though wanted to increase this by a further £100, however, this was opposed by his father. Even though Edward had claimed his inheritance, his father as one of his Trustees and as someone more experienced in these matters, continued to advise him.[3] Depending of course on the financial circumstances of the estate at the time (and there had been a vacuum of 12 years since his grandfather's death), the management of the whole estate must have needed re-assessing and this became obvious when he and Margaret went to view the house as there was virtually nothing there - even the books, pictures, papers and cutlery were all gone[4] which does not say much for the Trustees including his father, who were supposed to protect the home for Edward and Margaret. Edward employed Philip Breen as his first servant at Kilwaughter to make the house habitable before he and his sister moved in.[5]

Nomination to become a Member of the Irish Parliament

Edward would have been reared in a home where politics were much spoken and argued over. His father was very much not only into business and

---

[2] Agnew, Luddy, 1998, Vol.1, p.279.
[3] Agnew, Luddy, 1998, Vol.1, p.306.
[4] Porter, Agnews of Kilwaughter. Undated.
[5] Ibid.

philanthropy, but also public affairs and no doubt encouraged by this, Edward wasted no time in becoming politically active as it would have been intuitive. He put his nomination in to be MP for County Antrim in 1792 and in the meantime, he and Margaret embarked on a journey that could have ended their lives, because they decided to visit France which was, at that time, still in the throes of the Revolution. They had a very narrow escape from death, helped by a French valet called Peo. (Edward offered the valet to return to Kilwaughter and stay as long as he wished and he did for a time, but didn't like Ireland and returned to his native France). Edward had to cut his trip short because his friends wrote to tell him that he needed to get back to Ireland to prepare for the forthcoming election. It is intriguing to know why both Edward and Margaret would have decided to visit France at such a menacing time as they must have known what was happening there. The year before in Ireland, the United Irishmen had been formed by Theobald Wolfe Tone, Edward would later become associated with that, so it may be that he wished to avail himself of what was happening in France, that might just help bring about a new Ireland of political reform under the auspices of this newly created Irish organisation.

Edward is Elected into the Irish Parliament

On 22 March 1792, Edward was elected a Member of the Irish Parliament for County Antrim.[6] The election was celebrated in Kilwaughter by drinking vast amounts of alcohol and by the burning of bonfires.[7] Edward also donated £50 to the Old Poor House in Belfast and £100 to the County Antrim Infirmary. For a young man who had spent considerably little of his life in the county he represented, he must have been keen to promote himself and his father must also have been supportive of his plans. He was certainly wealthy enough to provide the money needed in order to achieve this. He was also well known by people of significance who would have supported his son to victory in the election. At that time too, the buying and selling of parliamentary seats was the norm of the day because the Irish Parliament was still very much the preserve of the Protestant landed gentry. Valentine (the elder) would have been an enormous influence on Edward's political thinking since he also had

---

[6] Johnston-Liik, 2002, Vol.4, p.510, No.1124.
[7] Larne Times, 14th June 1951.

been politically active throughout his career. Both were Liberals (Edward being one of the Founder members of the Whig Club)[8] and both would have exchanged views in the many political discussions of the middle classes. In earlier days Edward's older half-brother Valentine (Barbados 1) had been involved in the community as indeed had his brother-in-law John Galt Smith (1) (husband of his half-sister Jane) and all had worked closely with Edward's father.

Edward was elected after some stiff competition and replaced John O'Neill, who had been raised to the peerage. O'Neill[9] of Shane's Castle had been a member of the Volunteer movement and had been active in trying to make powerless such Protestant dissenter militant groups as the *Hearts of Steel* and the *Hearts of Oak*.[10] The *Hearts of Steel* (so named because they carried steel bars for use as weapons) claimed a John Agnew as one of its members. He turned Government informer and unfortunately for him was found out by his associates. Lots were drawn to see who would *dispatch* him and one of the leaders, Sam Blair of Ballyvallagh was given the task of killing him. This he did by slitting his throat and he then threw the body down a quarryhole at Toby's Brae.[11]

Edward supported Catholic emancipation.[12] Surprisingly however, when it came to voting for the Convention Bill in 1793, to give Irish Catholics the same rights as their English counterparts, he voted against it. His liberal politics would no doubt, have been firmly based on the value of democracy. The work on Catholic emancipation surrounding the campaign for the Convention in 1792, was perceived a threat to Irish democracy and would have gone against Edward's fundamental principle to sustain this. This may well have been the over-riding priority for him in his wish to help modernise Ireland and therefore he would have felt compelled to vote against the Bill. In the Division Lists it is also noted that in 1795 he voted for a Short Money Bill.[13]

---

[8] PRONI, D2095/18.

[9] O'Neill died from a stomach wound on 18th June 1798, having been wounded in the Battle of Antrim, 11 days earlier. (Agnew, Luddy, 1999, Vol.II, p.410).

[10] O'Laverty, 1881, Vol.111, p.308.

[11] PRONI, D2095/18.

[12] He and another relative, Patrick Agnew, took part in the consecration service of a new Catholic chapel in Larne in November, 1831. (The Belfast Newsletter Database, 1831).

[13] Johnston-Liik, 2002, Vol.4, p.510, No.1124.

His parliamentary career was short-lived because in 1797 after just one term, he was not returned at the General Election. One of the opponents he had been up against was similarly unlucky. He was Arthur O'Connor, the youngest son of the enormously rich and historic family from Cork. Arthur was President of the United Irishman and issued a challenging and damning address to the electorate of County Antrim as part of his campaign, which pledged to get rid of the British.[14] The address was considered almost an act of treason and *mad,* by O'Connor's friend, General John Knox. It resulted in his arrest on a charge of seditious libel and he was imprisoned in February 1797. Arthur's ebullience cost him the Antrim seat as he languished in prison until July of that year by which time all the elections were over. The authorities made sure that he was not released from prison until the day after the Antrim election.[15]

It is difficult to know just why Edward lost his election, but there are one or two clues. He appeared to have been a popular man and Dr. Alexander Haliday, another Whig, on writing to Lord Charlemont the Commander-in-Chief of the Volunteer movement and an Irish statesman, referred to him as such, *"Agnew is a man of independent fortune and principles and an excellent character"*.[16] Edward may simply have totally and naively mis-judged the mood of his constituents by his stand on the Convention Bill and thus lost his seat, but another reason emerged though from Martha McTier's gossip. It seemed that when Edward was defeated, this was to the, *"Great satisfaction of his best friends"*.[17] His down-fall strangely, seemed to have been of little concern to them. One reason for this could have been due to the fact that Edward was on very friendly terms with the Establishment and was said to have voted with the opposition. He was constantly seen with members of the ruling administration and a sarcastic comment was made by William Drennan, *"I suppose Agnew will become more democratical (sic) now than he was, for I met him always with the Chancellor's cronies, such as Stewart the Surgeon General".* (He was the Surgeon General of the English Army in Ireland).[18] This possibly accounted for Edward's bizarre voting record of not voting with his own party and it would have been easy to

---

[14] Hames, 2001, p.131.
[15] Ibid, p.153.
[16] Johnston-Liik, 2002, Vol.4., p.510, No. 1124.
[17] Agnew, Luddy, 1999, Vol. II., pps.333,334.
[18] Agnew, Luddy, 1999, Vol. II., p.335.

understand his friends, if they were not at all upset when he lost his seat and they may even have been smugly satisfied that Edward had got his comeuppance. Martha McTier went on to say that Edward seemed to have been a lazy thinker and relied on others for ideas. She made the point that the Whigs were missing opportunities and perhaps unknowingly had but a short time left. Her perception was indeed accurate because the Irish Parliament was abolished in 1800.

There is one item that allows us some insight into Edward's mode of transport from Kilwaughter to parliament in Dublin, his coach, which is said to originate from 1791. In 1891 Cassie McCay composed the following poem about it:-

"A hundred years have passed away
And left but little trace
Of Valiant deeds by heroes done
In this historic place.
But firm and fast, through sun and shade
Defying Time's approach
There stands a link with other days –
The Old Kilwaughter Coach.

What stirring scenes of old times
It brings beneath its view,
When in the Irish Parliament
Sat jovial Squire Agnew.
He nobly stirred the Antrim men
And never won reproach;
Their case was often argued
In the Old Kilwaughter Coach.

What many tales were gaily told
Within its friendly shade;
What vows of love were sweetly pledged
And plots for marriage laid;
What jars of purest old poteen
The gaugers feared to broach,
Were drained beneath the cover

Of the Old Kilwaughter Coach.

How often has it bowled away
Along the rocky road
To Dublin gay and city grand
With merry-hearted load;
Its going always gave "the boys"
A night or two to poach,
Because the Squire had travelled
In the Old Kilwaughter Coach.

Then come what may, 'twill nobly stand
Whate'er the future brings
And all will prise its yellow coat
And good old leather springs;
Although the years will come and go
Decay will not encroach
For care will be the guardian
Of the Old Kilwaughter Coach."[19]

Edward loses his Parliamentary seat, but finds a new Political Cause

Edward's period in parliament coincided with one of the most difficult, but interesting times in Ulster's history, but the years following his grandfather's death until he became an MP, had been, to a large extent, a period of some calm and reform in that part of Ireland, headed by members of the Volunteer movement. In the latter part of the 18th Century, the North of Ireland became embroiled once more, in sectarian disturbances. In 1791 both Catholics and Protestants and in particular the Presbyterians who were also discriminated against by the Establishment, decided that they would join forces to promote both religious freedom and political independence from Britain. They had taken their cues from a country hundreds of miles away – France. The French Revolution of 1789 ignited the intelligentsia in Ulster to action. They too

---

[19] The Corran, Summer 1980.

began to think that the Irish problem could be solved by following the example and approach of the French and so the United Irishmen came into being, but establishing this organisation was far from smooth as was described by Wolfe Tone in his diary. *"A furious battle"* over dinner in Belfast with some Presbyterians (reformed Whigs), who were still against Catholic emancipation, was how he described one evening.[20]

The newly formed organisation followed developments in France avidly and began reporting them in their own newspaper, the Northern Star, in 1791.[21] The newspaper became a popular medium to reach the masses manipulating them to rebellion in the process. Poetry and catchy tunes printed in the newspaper were not only good marketing ruses, but were clever subliminal ways of arousing the people to insurrection.[22] By 1797 the country was in such a state of anarchy that martial law in the North of Ireland was declared by General Lake who was the British Military Commander there. An oath of allegiance to the English Crown was required and all unauthorised weapons called in. Beatings were common place and many people were killed in the process of bringing order. This was not an approach that would guarantee peace. Life then in Ireland and particularly in that part of Ireland, the epicentre for the United Irishmen, must have been almost unbearable. Rumours and counter-rumours of massacres by militant Protestants were common too and many people escaped to the hills to save themselves from certain death.

On 8th May a public notice was issued calling for a meeting of the landowners in County Antrim. The meeting took place in the Linen Hall in Ballymena and at the meeting Chichester Skeffington (the 4th Earl of Massareene) and Edward Jones Agnew proposed to send a petition to the King (George III). They protested against the, *"Wicked and unprincipled ministers"* whom they held responsible for the very serious situation that the country was in and the King was also reminded that the people were tense and apprehensive because of the arrests and imprisonments – many without proper judicial proceedings.[23] [24] The petition was seconded by James Agnew

---

[20] Elliott, 2000, p.228.
[21] Clifford, 1989, p.5.
[22] Elliott, 2000, pps.231,232.
[23] PRONI, D2095/18.
[24] Dickson, 1997, pps.110,111.

Farrell, Edward's second cousin. The restrictive measures that had been put in place gradually had the desired effect by subduing those involved and the United Irishmen began disbanding, but still remained strong in counties Antrim and Down. One last push for freedom from the English was needed and a plan for action was hatched in 1798. An uprising was to take place on Thursday, 7th June. As part of the plan some of the rebels were to congregate at Dr. Agnew's Inn in Templepatrick. This may refer to the area of the present day Moat Inn at Donegore (not the original building which was burnt down), which is now a private dwelling.[25] [26]

There is much evidence to suggest that Edward was more than just sympathetic to the cause. He made no secret of the fact that he gave the Larne branch £100 towards the cost of two cannon and indeed, he was thanked publicly for this in the newspapers. It was also not uncommon at the time for landlords to coerce their tenant farmers to join a yeomanry. Edward was no different from the other landlords and he raised a local militia though this may not have been such an arduous task since many of the tenant farmers had an affinity with the United Irishmen.[27] He was a popular figure in the area and that alone would have been enough for the Government to have cause to be suspicious of him. In fact in the list of Grand Jurors for County Antrim in 1797, he was marked, *Disaffected*.[28]

The rebellion came one year before Edward lost his County Antrim seat and this too, may have helped put paid to the end of his parliamentary career. He made no secret of his sympathies towards the United Irishmen and since he also mixed with the parliamentary elite at the same time, it is more than likely that his charismatic personality allowed him to remain popular with both sides. This was obviously well known and coupled with his local popularity, was enough to stop harm coming to him when he made his way over to Ballygally Castle to visit his cousin Henry Shaw in the midst of the rebellion. The following is Edward's own account of the rebellion in the form of a

---

[25] For a complete description of the Donegore Moat please refer to O'Laverty, 1981, pps. 209-211.

[26] The house sits beside St. John's Parish Church. In the grounds of the church stands an obelisk on the right-hand side of the graveyard. The obelisk in grey granite, is dedicated to Thomas and Samuel Agnew and on one side, shows Somerled's eagle (part of the Agnew Coat of Arms) and the date of 1876 inscribed under it.

[27] PRONI, D2095/18.

[28] Stewart, 1995, p.99.

memorandum, which he penned at Kilwaughter House at the end of November 1798.[29]

"What happened in the Late Rebellion as I saw it on the 7th and 8th of June, 1798.

The days of the late rebellion were very eventful in these parts of the County from Carrickfergus to Ballycastle. On the 7th day of June last I rode over to visit cousin Shaw at Ballygally and to exchange our views on the great events at hand. At Glenarm I had been informed by my worthy servant John Hunter, the rebels were in arms thousands strong, and that Mr. Achison, the Dissenting Minister, had been removed under a strong guard of the Tay Fencibles and the Yeomanry. On reaching Gilbraith's cross roads, I encountered some forty or more of the rebels, some of whom I recognized as my own tenants, dressed in their Sunday best clothes, two had green tailed coats cut in military fashion with brass buttons and yellow facings, and nearly all wore green ribbons. I saw some firelocks and pistols but well burnished pikes were much in evidence. Two men whom I did not know came up to the near side of the cross and ported their pikes across the road and ordered me to dismount in a very military fashion. I left the saddle and on coming to the horse's head one said, 'You are Squire Agnew?' to which I replied in the affirmative. 'You are held to be a level-minded man' said he 'And may I ask what has you here in these 'Troublous (sic) hours?' I replied that my business was only a friendly call on Squire Shaw. The two men joined the others, and in a few minutes they hailed me to mount and pass, 'All's well (in) the name of the Republic'.

I reached Ballygally about four by the clock in the afternoon and found cousin in his parlour with Mr. Devenny,[30] the priest and Mr. Boyd of Mount Edwards. All of them were in grave mood. I was only seated when a messenger arrived with the news

---

[29] Ibid, p.98.
[30] No-one knew at the time that Devenny was a Government informer. (Stewart, 1995, p.101).

that the rebels had taken several persons from Larne and were going to shoot them on Bellavie Hill if the Fencibles and Yeomen did not give Achison the Minister of Glenarm and William Coulter and Hugh McCoy both of Glenarm, which they held at Lord Antrim's house.

One of the Larne men was said to have been Samuel Baillie of the Larne Yeomanry. We took speedy counsel and it was decided that the priest and I would ride over to Lord Antrim's house which we did.

The officer in command of the Fencibles, an easy Scot, whose name I did not catch at the time, agreed to parley with the rebels for an exchange of captives, and so it was that Mr. Achison and Coulter and McCoy were exchanged for the Larne men.

After a glass of punch with the agreeable officer, we returned to Ballygally and were given the pass by all rebel posts on the way. Cousin Shaw and I visited the rebel camp at Bellavie (Bellair) before 7 o'clock next morning and were well received. He and I were always on good terms with our tenants and were accorded with the greatest esteem. We saw Mr. Achison, then in full regimentals, green jacket faced with yellow, white breeches, black hose and silver buckled shoes. He was in great spirits and was wildly cheered by his little army of more than 2,000 and there were women in the field, some cooking an early meal on the camp fires and others moving around with jugs of fresh milk and oat cake for the citizen army. This was the sight I beheld on the most beautiful morning in June as the sun climbed above the hilltops and the mist lifted like a great white sheet in the valley. I returned to Ballygally with a sad heart as I, like the ancient Greek so deeply pondered on the fate that lay ahead of these worthy common people of this Kingdom.

It all came too true for the rebellion in Antrim, in which the greater rebel army was engaged, was broken by a great military force, but the news of it prevented many of my tenants advancing into battle to meet with the same bloody fate.

This account I shall put away from the eyes of man for a generation, when no one can come to any harm thereby, and

may I add that in my house at Kilwaughter and at that of Cousin Shaw the hunted rebels were given shelter and many afforded a safe passage to America.
26 Day November 1798
Edward Jones Agnew."[31]

Edward's account gave a clear description of a very serious situation that had engulfed the area. It indicated the strength of his popularity, that his tenants liked him, that he was allowed freedom of movement in a time when no-one was able to go anywhere without permission from the rebels. The level of Edward's negotiating skills and the powers of persuasion that he used on the Scottish officer were also indicative of a good arbitrator. Abilities well-honed from his parliamentary debating. This is borne out later because when Achison who was a Presbyterian Minister was released, he fully intended to return to the fray, (but this time in the uniform of the United Irishmen) and to take a stand by commanding the rebels at Bellavie (Bellair) Hill. Edward and his cousin saw the futility of this and the gravity of the situation and were at pains to dissuade this from happening, because not only did they fear for Achison's life,[32] but they predicted that the inevitable carnage would result. The gathering there was not small, somewhere between 1,800 and 2,000 people.[33] Fortunately they managed to convince him and not only that, but prevailed upon him that he should try and win over the people sufficiently so that they would disband and thus reduce the tension.[34] The fact that this happened resulting in the saving of lives says much about Edward and his cousin Henry. Not only were they quick to spot a potential disaster, but Achison must have had confidence in their judgement, to agree to try to disperse the rebels. Unfortunately for Henry however, he was arrested after

---

[31] Dickson, 1997, pps.223,224.

[32] The Rev. Robert Achison, the son of a farmer, was born in Clough in 1763. After studying medicine and practising in Coleraine for some time, he retrained for the ministry and became assistant minister to his uncle Thomas Reid at Glenarm. He was arrested and tried by a Court Martial, however, his uncle's importance in the Masonic Order was enough to save him. He died in 1824 at 61 years leaving a wife and six children. (McKillop, 1987, p.33).

[33] Wilsdon, 1997, p.97.

[34] Stewart 1995, pps.136,137.

the rebellion and detained in Market House, Carrickfergus. He died a short time afterwards and was succeeded after much dispute, by his son William.[35]

Edward's description also showed us a man with a heavy heart who thought deeply about the human cost of such violent dissension, who worried about his country's future and who gave great empathy to the people around him who fought for what they believed. In the end he showed his true colours when he gave refuge to those insurgents whose lives were in immediate danger, some of whom he helped escape to America. Sometime though during the winter of 1798-9, Edward's confidence took a knocking as attacks on magistrates were taking place in the hunt for arms. Edward being a magistrate felt that his safety was in jeopardy and took himself off to Bath as his house had been raided.[36]

James Agnew Farrell, second cousin to Edward Jones Agnew

His Role in the 1798 Rebellion

Whilst it seemed that Edward's integrity remained intact, life was not that straight forward for his second cousin. James Agnew Farrell, who had earlier supported Edward in his petition to the King, was born to Margaret and James Farrell. Margaret[37] was the daughter of James Agnew and his wife Margaret who was the daughter of James Wilson. James Agnew (1st of Larne), died in 1784, eight years after his brother William, Edward's grandfather. In his Will[38] (proved 10th February 1784), James who was described as a merchant, requested that most of his estate be sold, apart from a few family legacies including one to his grandson James Agnew Farrell.

James Farrell senior, had married Margaret whilst a midshipman in the Royal Navy. Her maternal grandfather Robert Mearns, was a tanner and had a business in Larne. Their son James Agnew Farrell became an insurgent with the United Irishmen and was considered to be an opportunist with a great intellect.[39] His visions for the North of Ireland extended so far as to enlist the help of John Rennie, the famous engineer in 1808, to carry out a feasibility

---

[35] McKillop, 1987, p.32.
[36] Foy, 1999, p.75.
[37] She was given the nickname of *Handsome Peggy*, (Porter, The Agnews of Ireland, undated).
[38] PRONI, T206/1.
[39] Porter, The Agnews of Ireland. Undated.

study on the possibility of building a navigable waterway between Larne and Lough Neagh. Agnew Farrell had obtained a lease on 290 acres of land in the vicinity from the Marquis of Donegall. Rennie was enthusiastic and carried out his brief, suggesting suitable alternatives.

The cost of the implementation of the canal structure was estimated to be around £168,137.00, but with grant aid from the Government forthcoming and since the farmers would also benefit, it was thought that they would be willing to buy transferrable shares of £50 or £100 per share. Agnew Farrell's enthusiasm was soon dampened as the farmers were not at all keen to part with their money and thus the plans for the canal were thwarted. Not only that, but Agnew Farrell's wallet was much depleted since he had paid out around £800 for a survey which was lost.[40] Unlike his second cousin Edward, James fought from the front in the United Irishmen. In 1792 a new company of Volunteers was formed and James became their Commander. He chaired a meeting of the Larne branch on Wednesday, 19th December that year, seemingly to pass some resolutions and declaration of intent. He wanted to cut down any oppressors and those who wished to corrupt society whether they be *mob or monarch*.[41]

This period was an anxious time in Ulster because the United Irishmen continued to gain support and to build on this enthusiasm. They had much to complain about. Life was harsh for the vast majority of people and the conditions in which they lived were distressing. In earlier times Jonathan Swift had described a harrowing scene of a typical Irish family, *"The miserable dress and the diet of the people the families of farmers who pay great rents, living in filth and nastiness, upon buttermilk and potatoes, not a shoe or stocking to their feet, or a house so convenient as an English hog-sty to receive them"*.[42] It is little wonder then that they felt one last push should be made to finally rid themselves from English domination. The dissenters were keen for rebellion.

At a meeting on 1st June 1798, their Commander-in-Chief unexpectedly resigned his position due to the pressure of the local leaders who were keen to set things in motion. Three names were proposed to find a successor and one of those, *"A gentleman from Larne"*, was thought to have been James Agnew Farrell. As all three were absent from the meeting the decision on how to

---

[40] McCutcheon, 1980, pp.80-81.
[41] PRONI, D2095/18.
[42] McKillop, 1987, p.31.

choose was literally left to chance - the first one of the three to be met, should be the Commander-in-Chief. This selection method bordered on the farcical. It was also decided at the meeting to pass on the decision for pressing ahead with the uprising to the commanders of the various divisions, but a postponement was agreed as the situation was not yet right. More preparation was needed, but just as important, the assurances from the French that they would help, were not yet forthcoming. The decision having been agreed, the attendees of the meeting made their way home through Ballyeaston only to be met by some indignant rebels whom upon hearing that the uprising had been postponed, accused them of cowardice. The outcome was that Henry Joy McCracken[43] of Belfast was now elected the new Commander-in-Chief for the combined strength of all of the United Irishmen in the North of Ireland. McCracken was more to the rebels liking since he calculated that the uprising could go ahead and on 6th June 1798, he declared that the revolt had started and would begin with the march on Antrim town.

Instructions from McCracken were passed on to the various commanders, to attack all Government military posts in their neighbourhood and the hope was to kidnap the Governor (Lord O'Neill) and his peers. James Agnew Farrell the Commander in Larne, together with several other Commanders decided against this and turned informers, betraying McCracken and his plans in the process. Agnew Farrell notified Major General Nugent, the Government's Commander, of the plan of attack. McCracken's followers having little arsenal at their disposal, which reflected both their poverty and lack of organisation, were ill-prepared and lacking guidance, so capitulated to Nugent's army.[44] [45]

Knowing the aggressive stance of the rebels and how keen they were for rebellion, it was a highly dangerous position that Agnew Farrell and his peers were now in. Turning King's evidence at such a volatile time, literally hours before the commencement of the attack, must have posed a great dilemma for him and his like-minded colleagues. If caught, then there would have been no doubt that all would have hanged. Their families too, would have been at risk. Agnew Farrell must have come to a decision to try and stop the rebellion sometime during the day before the assault was meant to begin because he did

---

[43] McCracken was afterwards hanged for the part he played in the rebellion.
[44] PRONI, D2095/18.
[45] Elliott, 2000, p.253.

not turn up at the specific rendezvous that evening which meant that another officer was elected to command the insurgents.

With the action started and with things rapidly getting out of hand, a message was sent to Edward Jones Agnew to come and try and remonstrate with the men. Yet another indication of Edward's influence and standing in the community. This time it was to no avail and he was unsuccessful in preventing the militia from marching on to their meeting place at Donegore Hill. They did though, allow him to return home unmolested.[46]

James Agnew Farrell would have been aware of the futility of this operation. The rebels had no training for the assault and the United Irishmen were badly armed and ill-prepared for the attack. The only weapons they had were better used on their farms – scythes, pitch forks, reaping hooks – than in the battle field.[47] James realised as his second cousin had done at Bellair Hill, that there would be killing on a massive scale, but he knew that it was too late to prevent it and having defected immediately understood that his own life was now in danger. He fled to Scotland with his wife in a ship commanded by Charles Dawson Stewart and remained there until circumstances were much calmer at home.[48]

His part in the rebellion was well known and his exploits infamous because he was thought to have been the main fictional character O'Halloran in a novel written by James McHenry in 1820. McHenry, a Larne doctor, set his story around the 1798 Rebellion, along the coastal area between Larne and Ballygally. The old stone castle off Ballygally Head was the focal meeting point for the United Irishmen in his novel.[49] The rock eventually became known as O'Halloran's rock due to the popularity of the story, but what is also interesting, is that the old castle on the rock was once the residence of one of the Ó Gnímh bards.[50][51]

---

[46] PRONI, D2095/18.
[47] Haddick-Flynn, 1999, p.175.
[48] Porter, The Agnews of Ireland. Undated.
[49] McKillop, 1987, p.35.
[50] Dallat, 1990, p.6.
[51] O'Laverty, 1981, Vol.III, p.207.

Family Life of James Agnew Farrell

The Sale of the Family Home, the Magheramorne Estate

Before the rebellion James Agnew Farrell had married Letitia Armenella Turnly of Drumnasole. The couple eventually had eight children.[52] By 1805 he had returned to Ulster. He eventually re-established himself within the community as is evident not only by the purchase of the Magheramorne estate, but his acceptance in the Irish Division of the Northern Yacht Club, the patron of which was HRH, The Duke of Clarence.[53] The size of the estate was estimated to be about 2,154 acres and contained the quarries of lime.[54] James built a large house on the estate, but sold the property in 1825 to John Irving, an MP from London for £60,000. His businesses were failing and he was in debt, so the house and what little businesses he had left, had to be sold to pay his debtors.[55] From 1789-1823 it seems he borrowed substantial sums of money from various people, including family members such as, Edward Jones Agnew, Francis Turnly, Mary Jones, but all were repaid and their names contained in Certificates of Satisfaction.[56] Afterwards he later moved to Canada where he died in 1835.[57]

Sadly he did not live to see his daughter Letitia form an alliance with another prominent Ulster family when she married Captain Francis Dobbs in Canada on May, 1839.[58] Another daughter Catherine, married Christopher Armstrong, a barrister and died in Kingston, Ontario on 29th September, 1842.[59] James would perhaps, have known about an unfortunate story told concerning his first son and namesake, James Agnew Farrell, junior. He was born in 1793 and joined the Colonial Service in what was then Ceylon. He began work as a tax collector in Magampatoo and was required to engage a bearer to pull the Collector's palanquin. No bearer was available so James insisted that the Headman perform the task instead. The Headman fell after

---

[52] The Canadian Biography Dictionary & Patriot Gallery of Eminent and Self-Made Men, 1880.
[53] The Belfast Newsletter Database, 1829.
[54] O'Laverty, 1981, Vol.III, p.148.
[55] Kindly recounted by Adam Mead, 2024.
[56] PRONI, D1326/2/19.
[57] Porter, The Agnews of Ireland. Undated.
[58] Freeman's Journal and Daily Commercial Advertiser, 1839.
[59] The Bytown Gazette, 1842.

some yards and was beaten by James. He then fell again and was beaten so badly that the Headman died. The death of the Headman was concealed for a time, but this was not possible, the story got out and so James was tried for murder which, if proven, would have meant the death sentence which was mandatory. He was tried by special jury which found the charge not proven and so he was acquitted. The Judge decreed, *"You are restored to your rank and station in society with unblemished record"*. To add to the sham, it was recommended by the Editor of the *Madras Courier* that James sue for punitive damages from the *Calcutta Journal* for libel.[60] James died in 1843, aged 50 years.

James Agnew Farrell seeks to prove connections with the Lochnaw Family

There is an interesting letter from James Agnew Farrell, senior, written from Camstradden in Scotland, to Sir Andrew Agnew at Lochnaw Castle, dated 1818. He was obviously interested in his own family history, their origins and connections to the Lochnaw family, and tried to pursue this with Sir Andrew, referring to himself as, *"Tenacious"*. Its quite strange that even in 1818, no family stories had come down that indicated the correct descendancy between the Kilwaughter and Lochnaw Agnews, as well as a connection between them and the bardic Ó Gnímhs. James had some knowledge that the Kilwaughter and Lochnaw Agnews were connected, as told to him by Mr. Sinclair, a Presbyterian Minister of Larne who had resided for 30 years with the Old Squire William Agnew at Kilwaughter and had been tutor to one of the children there and visited Lochnaw with his pupil, who was greeted as a relative. Unfortunately Mr. Sinclair could not find any documents to verify this, nor seemingly could James who suggested that written documentation had never been made. James went on to say that circumstantially many facts fitted the theory that the Agnews had possessed the land at Kilwaughter from a very early period and long before the Lochnaw Agnews took possession of leases there. This brings us back to the Ó Gnímh period and perhaps the closest we will ever get to believing that the three families were one and the same.[61] Unfortunately it has not been possible to find the reply from Sir Andrew Agnew to James.

---

[60] Ceylon, A People's History 1793-1844.
[61] The National Archives of Scotland, GD154-687-2-1-00011.

The Magheramorne Estate is sold again

In 1842 Irving sold the Magheramorne estate to Charles McGarel of Larne who, on his death, passed it to Sir James McGarel Hogg.[62] Charles McGarel was a slave owner in present day Guyana and had substantial holdings on other plantations with partners. He also had interests in London companies which were involved in the slave trade. When the compensation scheme was rolled out in 1837, to reimburse plantation owners, McGarel was awarded considerable sums of money running into many thousands of pounds then.[63] He was thus able to buy the large estate at Magheramorne and to give the people of Larne the McGarel Town Hall at a cost of £4,400, no doubt using his new-found wealth from his compensation awards.

The town hall was formally handed over to the Trustees of the community at a banquet there in August 1870. Amongst the guest list were two Agnews - Agnew Farrell and another, James, who was a barrister-at-law in Toronto.[64] It is more than likely that these two were brothers since Agnew Farrell was the youngest child of James Agnew Farrell. The son Agnew was born in 1804 and in 1833 emigrated to Canada, making his way to the township of Dunn on the shores of Lake Erie. Although the area was primitive to say the least, Agnew Farrell wasn't afraid of hard work. He bought a log cabin and began life as a farmer. Like his father before him he had political leanings and involved himself in a rebellion in 1837 that he helped quell. He later became Colonel of the 1st Battalion Haldimand Militia and in 1844 was appointed County Registrar. Seven years later he became County Treasurer. By then his life had become much more prosperous and he lived near the village of Cayuga in a house which had been given the grand name of *The Hermitage..*

Agnew Farrell, the son, seemed to enjoy a good reputation in his adopted country. He was an active member of the Anglican church and became a Justice of the Peace and Notary Public, but sadly for him and his wife, an English woman from Bristol, named Catherine Purnell whom he had married

---

[62] Larne Gazette News, 13th September, 2000.
[63] For more information on McGarel's profile, see the Centre for the Study of Legacies of British Slavery.
[64] Larne Gazette News, 29/11/2000.

on 14 March 1835, they lost all their six children and were left with two grandchildren who remained in their care.[65]

The Kilwaughter Estate continues to Survive

Throughout all the troublesome years that had passed, the financial situation of the Kilwaughter Agnews seemed to have remained undisturbed. James 1st of Larne, the grandfather of James Agnew Farrell, already had a lease on *Drumalis* and the Curran at Larne (that piece of land jutting out into the harbour). He left it to his son William on his death in 1784.[66] William[67] continued to hold this lease and in May 1823 a renewal of the lease on a permanent basis was granted by Lord Donegall. The new arrangement was for the Curran again and all the anchorage in the harbour. Some ten years later the Curran quay was established and was used for the shipment of limestone, but in 1842, a decision was made to improve the harbour by extending the quay, so that it could be utilised better. This was carried out at a cost of £1,350 and the quay was extended to 200 feet long[68]. It was probably a clever investment since the larger quay would give greater anchorage facilities, make loading and unloading easier, thus attracting more vessels which would improve the sale of lime.

When William died in 1828 he left the Curran to his son James. His other son Charles received large tracts of land and money for his *advancement* in the army.[69] James sold the harbour for £9,500 and Charles sold the town and lands of the Curran and *Drumalis* for £10,500. All were sold to James Chaine, the son of a wealthy County Antrim linen merchant.[70] Chaine also purchased Cairncastle Lodge and estate at Carnfunnock in 1865, which had been the home of James 1st of Larne.[71] [72]

---

[65] The Canadian Biography Dictionary and Patriot Gallery of Eminent and Self-Made Men, 1880.
[66] PRONI, T808. p.59.
[67] His son was a naval Captain and earlier officer of the *Hynd*. (PRONI, D2095/18).
[68] McCreary, 2000, pps.3,4.
[69] Kindly recounted by Simon Elliott, October, 2006.
[70] McCreary, 2000, p.12.
[71] History Guide Carnfunnock County Park, Undated, pps.1,2.
[72] McKillop, 2005, p.184.

Kilwaughter – The Unknown Castle

Edward Jones Agnew begins to Renovate Kilwaughter House

With Edward Jones Agnew no longer a member of the Irish Parliament and the 1798 Rebellion quashed, his thoughts turned to the management of his estate and his home. In 1807, he decided to have Kilwaughter House refurbished. This had come about from having seen the work done on the Stewart family home at Killymoon Castle (the Stewarts were his cousins). William Stewart had employed John Nash, one of London's foremost architects to rebuild his home in 1802. On what was Nash's first Irish project he took only a year to complete the alterations at a cost reputed to have been £80,000. Edward's father Valentine had died in 1805, just two years before Edward thought about modernising his home. He and his siblings had been heirs to a fortune from their father's various businesses and he must have acquired a substantial inheritance from him which would have gone some way towards the payment of the Kilwaughter's transformation,[73] but it is also thought that his sister Margaret paid for some of the rebuilding work and the purchasing of more land.[74] She is thought to have had independent means financially and according to her grandfather William, regardless of whether she married or not, she would, *"Still have £7,000 of her own money even if she married Jock the Fool"!*[75] Margaret's mother Ellen who was the widow of James Ross, would presumably, have inherited a large legacy from him on his death. He was from a wealthy family and had been highly successful in his business pursuits including those of part ship-owner, the vessels being used to transport slaves. Having only two remaining children, Edward and Margaret, Ellen will have bequeathed substantial bequests to them. Knowing how their father made a considerable part of his fortune, it might be prudent to suggest that Kilwaughter's refurbishment, came about simply through money earned by the sweat of the slaves.

John Nash was duly employed to design a more modern and substantially enhanced building from the plantation house of the previous century. Some local builders were used, in particular, John Gingles, junior of *Red Rock*. Fred and William McClarty from Cushendall were instrumental in constructing the

---

[73] It remains a source of great disappointment that Valentine's Will (the elder), cannot be found.
[74] Porter, The Agnews of Ireland. Undated.
[75] Ibid.

large tower at the Castle.[76] Nash also enlisted the help of architects Miller and Nelson of Belfast to oversee parts of the work.

Kilwaughter Castle was similar in design to Killymoon with tower and turrets. It was built in typical Scottish style for that period. One of the Castle's most interesting features were the sandstone windowsills that had fanciful designs on the outside which were very attractive. The late Professor Jope thought these may be the work of the O'Shea brothers who were Irish carvers. They can still be seen today.

In 1810, Edward enhanced his estate by adding an artificial lake. (An ice house was created close to the lake). The lake extended over 5 acres and contained various waterfowl. Whilst the garden was thought small, the Castle grounds were considered to have been extensive and aesthetically pleasing and thought to be the work of the landscape gardener and architect, John Sutherland. He is known to have designed the grounds of five houses that were all designed by Nash.[77] The trees were mainly ash, beech, elm, fir and larch. The main entrance to the Castle was gained through a stone gateway which had an octagonal tower on either side and was some distance from the main building.[78] The entrance gates to the Castle were designed by Nash, but the gate lodge circa 1835, is thought to be the work of Miller and Nelson.[79] (The field in front of the Castle was originally called *The Smoothing Iron Field*, by local inhabitants, simply because it resembled that laundry aid).

Along with the elevated position of being the main landowner in the parish, came the responsibility of motivating others and of helping them see the necessity of continually improving the area. Edward was also required to hold petty sessions from time to time to administer justice to those involved in any transgression of the law. These sessions were held at the Castle, but by 1840 however, a court room had been established in Larne within the new market house to deal with these.[80]

---

[76] The Corran, 1977, No.4.
[77] Dictionary of Irish Architects.
[78] Day, McWilliams, Vol.10, pp.108,109.
[79] Register of Parks, Gardens and Demesnes.
[80] Day, McWilliams, 1991, Vol.10, pps.116,117.

The Tenants on the Estate

During Edward's time the tenants who inhabited the more fertile sections of the estate, were said to have lived in comfortable and clean cottages. They had two rooms with the same number of windows letting in some light. The cottages were certainly warm inside as there appeared to have been an abundance of fuel for the fire in the form of turf which was not surprising considering how much bogland surrounded them. Potatoes and flour played a large part in their diet and the people were recognised as dressing well. They seemed somewhat seriously minded and didn't indulge in any significant pastime. This was probably something to do with their religious attitudes or maybe even from physical exhaustion. Those labourers however, who lived in the more remote and outer areas did not enjoy the same quality of life. Life was much harsher for them as it continued to do so for the cottiers who lived in houses of a very poor standard and seemed unaware of the need to keep them clean. They had only one small room and a kitchen.

For those lucky enough to live close to Kilwaughter Castle, there was both a corn mill and a flax mill and working there would have provided a further source of income for them. When Edward died he left a bequest of £50 to be paid in April each year, to the poor householders to help them buy flax seed. He was seen as a good Landlord and in a letter addressed to him on 17th June, 1815 by Robert Thompson, pertaining to the destruction of a farmhouse by fire, caused by arsonists, who wrote on behalf of several tenants, he implored Edward not to think of them all as criminals. Robert Thompson described Edward in the highest regard and esteem, mentioning his, *"Unostentatious acts of benevolence and friendship"*. In Edward's reply two days later, he thanked the tenants for their compliments of his character with, *"Warmest acknowledgements"* and was pleased that the tenants were dealing with the savage act and had put up a reward to find the culprits. (Interestingly after signing his name at the bottom of the response, he puts his address as Kilwaughter House, even though the refurbishments had already taken place and turned the dwelling into a Castle).[81]

Whilst the soil in the parish of Kilwaughter was considered to be poor and of a boggy nature, the lower areas were more fertile. Potatoes, oats, barley,

---

[81] PRONI, D2453/63.

wheat and some flax were generally the crops grown in the area, but lime too was plentiful and this was both quarried and burned.[82] Various kilns for the burning of lime were dotted around the region, but gradually the larger kilns at Glenarm and Kilwaughter took over production. The burning of lime was considered added income to the tenants and as the limestone rock appeared plentiful, the farmers would take a cartload of it to the kilns. A process would begin of burning limestone and peat together and the fire would then be allowed to die out. After two days the residue of lime that was left, was then collected for distribution.[83]

The Kilwaughter area was almost two thirds mountainous. On the highest point of this mountainous region was Agnew's Hill, originally part of the Ó Gnímh estate and somewhat of a misnomer because the *Hill* rose 1,558 ft. above sea level. It sat almost central in the parish. Agnew's Hill would probably be most famous for catching fire in 1826, in what was considered then to have been one of the driest summers. The fire began about 1,500 ft. up on the Hill and no conclusion was ever reached, as to whether it was started accidentally or maliciously. Since it was covered with heather and light bog, the flames soon took hold and spread rapidly as the undergrowth was so dry. The fire was said to have been seen for miles around as it lit up the evening sky. Many methods were employed to quench it and a number of men were employed by Edward to try and stop its progress, but to no avail and as it spread to the next mountain (Shane's Hill), the heat of the fire, coupled with the summer sun, was said to have been so intense that the anxious farmers moved their livestock to safer pastures. The fire burned all summer, consuming around 100 acres of land but as the harvest approached so did the rain and it was eventually extinguished leaving a thick pall of smoke and vast tracks of ash-covered land which would have taken several years to recover sufficiently to be used as up-land grazing.[84] [85]

Edward Jones Agnew attempts Marriage

Edward's personal life which earlier seemed to have revolved very much around politics and the refurbishment of his home, must have left him little

---

[82] Day, McWilliams, 1991, Vol.10, pps.106,111,112,115.
[83] McKillop, 1987, pps.46,47.
[84] Day, McWilliams, 1991, Vol.10, pps.106,108.
[85] McKillop, 1987, p.38.

time to socialise. His sister Margaret saw to it that she remained the chatelaine of Kilwaughter and prevented any plans he had for a married life. His cousin Kitty to whom he was betrothed, was his first and serious love and when she, Edward and his sister Margaret on travelling to Dublin began talking about the changes that Kitty would like to make in the Castle, Margaret was furious and an argument ensued. Needless to say the engagement was broken off.[86] Kitty went on to marry someone else, but died a short time afterwards and Edward was grief-stricken. His next romantic liaison was with the daughter of W. Kerr of *Redhall*, but this too was stopped.

Scandalous Behaviour

Edward never married, but on 30th October 1824, when he was 57 years old, he became a father (just one year older than his own father had been when he was born). His mistress Eleanor Galbraith gave birth to a son whom they named William. The Galbraith family had rented a property on the Kilwaughter estate but had been ejected due to non-payment of rent. Their next property rent was being paid by Edward as he did in some circumstances for his tenants when they couldn't, but a dispute had arisen about it with the collector who was furious with having continually to deal with *pauper rent* and Eleanor (or Nellie as she was called) had been sent to the Castle to sort out the problem with Edward. Nellie returned home crying, complaining that Edward had become somewhat familiar with her. He suggested an arrangement for the two of them which was sanctioned by Nellie's mother. The story goes that when Nellie's mother found out that Edward liked her daughter, she was said to have told her, *"Go and get a pair of shoes on and return to the Castle!"*[87] Whether or not this was true we will never know. The Rev. Classon Porter who penned the story in his 19th century notes, would have been judgemental to say the least, on a couple having a relationship outside marriage, but Nellie's mother probably saw the benefits of her daughter being involved with the wealthy landlord and sanctioned the relationship in a letter. Thus began an affair that lasted several years.

---

[86] Porter, The Agnews of Ireland. Undated.
[87] Ibid.

Edward Jones Agnew becomes a Father to two Children

Their son William was not born in the Castle or in Nellie's home, but in the old bawn which was called, *The Barracks* and which was situated at the back of the Castle near the graveyard. William was taken to Cairncastle church for a perpetual christening by the minister, the Rev. Ralph Ward, who is said to have known perfectly well, the name of the baby's father.[88] The relationship continued between Edward and Nellie and two years later on 31st May 1826, another child was born to the couple, this time a daughter whom they called Maria. A third died in infancy.

For the Squire of Kilwaughter Castle to have two children outside marriage must have sent rumours abounding in the area. He was a popular man and a member of the Presbyterian Church in Larne[89] so the moral implications at the time for both him and Nellie, would not have been ignored, but he took responsibility for his children and acknowledged them officially as his. Margaret though, was extremely unhappy about the relationship between the pair and during a trip abroad with Edward in 1828 which they took to try and dampen down the stories of the licentious relationship, she proposed sending Nellie away. If Edward agreed with this, then he could have the two children brought to the Castle and be reared there. Sadly this was the case and the children lost their mother. We don't know just how close Nellie was to the children as she mostly did not rear them and perhaps the exciting thought of a new country made things for her less difficult. On 30th September 1830, Nellie and some members of her family arrived in America and were sent on to Baltimore, Maryland and she never saw her children again. At the same time Edward revoked the £45 per year that he had bequeathed to her in his Will though some stipend was arranged for a period. Why Baltimore? It could be that a relative of Nellie's was already living in Baltimore, but a more convenient explanation occurs. Edward's agent William Adair was already established in Baltimore which was a well-known port in the slave trade suggesting that Edward too, had slave business there. The Adair family of Mount Vernon in Belfast had been trading in Baltimore for some time and were connected with the Baltimore Packet Ships, frequently making the

---

[88] Porter, The Agnews of Ireland. Undated.
[89] Stewart, 1995, p.99.

journey from Baltimore to Belfast, so it would be convenient for Nellie and her family to be domiciled there as arrangements were easily made.

The two children were initially looked after by Jennie Betty Nelson and Martha Kyle, but when William was five years old and his sister only three, they were brought to the Castle. It is said that the children were both reluctant to go in, the surroundings were unfamiliar to them. William was more hesitant than his sister, but Edward brought him a dog to play with and that seemed to pacify him. They were handed over to their father and the Castle became their family home.[90] Although we know nothing more about Nellie, a strange letter survives that is written to Edward from Baltimore and is dated 30th May 1832. This letter though, is from Mary Gilbraith *(sic)*, describing her stricken circumstances and acknowledging money that Edward sent for funeral costs, a possible reference to Nellie's death? No name of the deceased is mentioned, but she is imploring him for more money as the cost of living is higher than her financial state. She does enquire after the two children and mentions a third child who seems to have suffered ill-health, so she was obviously aware of the situation. [91] We don't know if the unknown woman received any help.

The children had a Governess, Miss Debille who educated them initially, but William then attended a local school for a short time where he was taught by the Rev. Stephen Gwynn. This was followed by another tutor Thomas Collyns Simon,[92] but he left in 1839 and for six weeks during the summer the Rev. Classon Porter was given the task of educating William.[93] He was a Presbyterian minister and historian from Larne who resided in Ballygally Castle which, in 1820, had been purchased by Edward Jones Agnew for the sum of £15,400. This Castle of course, was familiar territory to Edward as he had frequently referred to *Cousin Shaw* who owned it. Henry Shaw died in 1799 leaving his son William (who at the time was only 6 years old), as his heir. [94] Unfortunately some time later, William in attempting to become a merchant, failed in a business project in Belfast and fell on hard times. Edward came to

---

[90] Porter, The Agnews of Ireland. Undated.
[91] PRONI, D2095/6.
[92] He later married William's sister Maria much to her aunt's dismay.
[93] Porter died on 27th May 1885, leaving an estate valued at £12,398 3s. 6d. (PRONI, D300/1/5/862). He is buried in St. Patrick's cemetery at Cairncastle.
[94] Porter, 1901, Vol. VII, No.2, p.10.

his rescue by purchasing the Castle.⁹⁵ Ballygally Castle eventually passed to the Moore's who had intermarried with the Kilwaughter Agnews. Just before the First World War it was inherited by Lt.-Col. William Agnew Moore and his wife, also a Moore (their great grandfathers were brothers).⁹⁶ After the war Moore was elected in 1919, as the Official Unionist Candidate for East Antrim. He gave his address then as Kilwaughter Castle, Larne.⁹⁷

Porter added mathematics, Greek and Latin to William's normal subjects, but he thought him *A dreamer though* admitted that once William had learnt something it was there for ever. Both children were later taken to England where William attended a private religious school. He did not have any further education.

The children must have been well loved and looked after because their aunt, Edward's sister Margaret, wrote them both an endearing letter in 1832 when they were just 8 and 6 years old. In that she pointed out to them that they were born *"natural children"* and being so would have to strive for exemplary behaviour and modesty in their ways. She penned that if they conducted themselves well, then the illegitimacy of their birth would soon be overlooked. Margaret let them know that they should look after their father in old-age and to remember that regardless of their birth, they were well loved and looked after by both their father and aunt. ⁹⁸

When Margaret wrote this letter to the children she could not have foreseen that she would become much more involved in their lives, because their father had only two years left to live. At the time Edward was not so caught up in family life that he neglected his political role. A week before Christmas 1832, he chaired a meeting concerning the installation gates which were to be placed at the entrance to Larne town. The turnpikes were to be placed at various entry points to the town, but the idea was not well received by the people of Larne and the surrounding parishes. One of the inhabitants, Archibald Barklie, suggested that the meeting had been called under the guise of an attempt at electioneering, though this was hotly denied. Edward's relative, James Agnew Farrell, maintained that the Bill for erecting the tall gates had been *smuggled* through Parliament without the knowledge of the local

---

⁹⁵ McKillop, 1987, p.21.
⁹⁶ Agnew, 1926, pps.275-277.
⁹⁷ The Times, 1919.
⁹⁸ PRONI, D2095/14.

committee and another, R.W. Johnston suggested that it was just an excuse to claim local taxes and reduce local trade. It was also argued that it would disrupt the flow of goods in and out of the harbour since everything would have to be carried. In the end a resolution was passed that a petition be drawn up to resist the erection of the gates and the Committee was given full powers to stop the Bill going through.[99]

Edward Jones Agnew Dies

On Tuesday, 18th March 1834, at the age of 67 years, Edward died suddenly of typhus. His obituary printed in the Belfast Newsletter a week later, on 25th March 1834,[100] described him in glowing terms:

"At Kilwaughter Castle on Tuesday last the 18th inst. of Typhus Fever, Edward Jones Agnew, Esq. of Kilwaughter. The decease of this excellent man has occasioned a general sensation of sorrow in this neighbourhood, where his valuable qualities have been long known and acknowledged. His immediate friends and his tenantry feel the privation in a still more distressing degree from the suddenness of the unexpected catastrophe. The private and ostentatious virtues of benevolence and charity were invariably exercised by this good man in no common or stinted measure.

In public life, he was always a consistent patriot and he lived to see the principles he had earlier maintained as representative of this County in the Irish Parliament consolidated by the reform in the institutions of the state so recently accomplished.

He was indeed a life of the greatest integrity and simplicity, he was imbued with the mildest and purest dispositions – always intent on doing the greatest good, to the greatest number, within the sphere of his influence.

The remains of Mr. Agnew were interred on Thursday last in the burying ground of Kilwaughter Demesne and Parish, in the rear of his mansion, accompanied by the sorrows of his tenantry, and the deep grief of his friends and relatives."

---

[99] The Belfast Newsletter Database, 1832.
[100] Belfast Newsletter, Linen Hall Library, MIC/1834.

With Edward dead, the children were left in the care of their guardians when just 10 and 8 years old. Their sense of loss and confusion must have been overwhelming, not only had they lost their mother, but their father was now also gone.

By the time of his death Edward's Will[101] of 1825 was 18 pages long and comprised four codicils. It appeared very thorough in its execution. He appointed his sister Margaret as one of the Trustees and John Montgomery Casement, the Rev. Ralph Ward and his sister were also appointed as guardians to his two children. Unlike his predecessors Edward was much more financially robust judging by the enhancement of his land purchases and property due to an inheritance from his father and help from his sister Margaret. His land bank was already well established and he added to this by purchasing land and property from Andrew Tullis McCulloch Crowe of Corkermaine, Cairncastle. Crowe was the son of a Scottish stone mason and was famous for his whiskey drinking. After selling his property to Edward in 1811 for around £6,500, he emigrated to America, then Canada where he died in Montreal.[102] [103] Edward also bought the town and lands of Ballygally in 1820. By the third codicil in July 1830, he had added a corn mill, kilns, water rights, the bogs of Mullaghsandal[104] together with access and water rights, quarries and their royalties, as well as lands in Ballyfatten, County Tyrone. On 9th May 1833 one year before his death, he made his final codicil and had acquired the lands of Ballyviland and Carnreal in County Antrim. By then he was a man of considerable means.

Edward's sister, Margaret Jones, was tasked with securing the estate for his son William until he attained the age of 25 years when he would inherit all.

Maria for her part, was initially left £4,000 by her father however, this was revoked in 1829 to £1,000 as her aunt Margaret was bequeathing her the original amount in her Will. (It is interesting to note that Maria was referred to in her father's Will, as his, *illegitimate or reputed daughter,* unlike William who was accepted in Edward's Will as his son without doubt).

---

[101] PRONI, LPC, 1040.
[102] McKillop, 1987, p.36.
[103] McKillop, 2006, p.42.
[104] A connection with Mullaghsandal had been established earlier when the Earl of Antrim leased land to Edward's grandfather William, in 1738 (McKillop, 2006, p.74).

Whilst the children were minors the interest from money left to them per year was to help finance their needs and also to be used for their education. Edward made sure that the children's correct dates of birth were entered in his Will. No doubt this was intended to stop disputes occurring over the ages of inheritance.

From what we have learned about Edward, he would have thought considerably about his Will and the circumstances of each individual, but five months after his death a letter from Baltimore was sent to Margaret Jones. It came from Rachel Galbraith. This lady would appear to have been the mother of Edward's mistress as she described her daughter's death though did not name her. She was imploring Margaret to continue with the remuneration of £25 per annum that had been established by Edward, as she found herself in difficult circumstances and was keen to save for her passage back to Ireland. It is not known if she ever returned or if her allowance was continued.[105]

---

[105] PRONI, D2453/9.

Chapter 6

Margaret Jones, sister to Edward takes over the Estate

Edward's sudden death thrust his sister Margaret, unexpectedly into the role of custodian of Kilwaughter Castle and the estate. She had been born in 1764, three years before her brother and when he died she was already 70 years old. Not only was she now abruptly called upon to oversee the day-to-day running of the estate and household, but she had also become a surrogate parent to her nephew and niece, who were still young children. A difficult role one might assume for an elderly, unmarried lady, but that did not stop her accompanying them to reside in England for a time in 1841, so that William could further his education.[1]

Her new responsibilities cannot have been effortless, but she would not have come to the task completely inexperienced. She was, after all, the daughter of a man well practised in the art of business and she was part of an extended family that had been prominent in both politics and in helping to restructure the society in which they lived. Propinquity within the family seemed to have been important to Margaret as evidenced in the Drennan/McTier letters which tell of the many occasions that Margaret spent with her relatives, not only those living locally, but travelling to visit her cousins the Stewarts, at Killymoon Castle. Part of her time would also have been spent discussing the various problems surrounding the estate. As a result she would have been familiar with what skills were required to look after the Castle and its affairs.

When Margaret inherited the Castle and estate in Trust for her nephew, it was in the relatively early stages of the nineteenth century. Ulster then was a

---

[1] Porter, The Agnews of Ireland. Undated.

well established, male-dominated society and the role that women played was unimportant outwardly. Societal attitudes were such that female views about life and their thoughts of a career were deemed irrelevant and a woman's place was most definitely within the family boundaries, largely focussed on the caring of others - husband, children and elderly parents. These views were particularly prevalent in rural Ireland. Marriage was seen as the ultimate objective for women at the time because to remain a spinster may have placed a woman amongst the lower level of respectability.[2] Society's view of spinsterhood however, did not seem to have troubled Margaret to a great extent because she never married. It was not for the reason that she lacked suitors because that was not the case. William Drennan proposed marriage to her in 1785 when she was 21 years old, but she turned him down.[3] He was not deterred however and remained assiduous in his pursuit of her for a long time afterwards. He would pester his sister often for news of her and would try and glean some scrap of interest from his sister's letters that would indicate to him that Margaret cared about him. In one such letter William must have felt particularly wounded because he discovered that she was rather disposed to the charms of a barrister named William Saurin who was the son of the Rev. James Saurin (cousin of the Mussendens).[4] The attraction did not seem to be reciprocated which must have given him some reprieve at least.

Margaret appeared to have been well liked and popular amongst her friends. She was regarded by them as having an enquiring mind and of being receptive to new ideas. This open-minded attitude no doubt stemming from her upbringing since we know that her father was a great liberal thinker. She obviously had a good sense of humour and once related a story of a young man whom she had asked to dance and then began to tease. The young man, a shoemaker, appeared shy, but Margaret only saw that as a challenge and tried to engage him in conversation. She broached the subject of marriage and suggested to him that he ought to consider it since it could be recommended. (Somewhat strange since Margaret wasn't married herself). She was not afraid to ask the most personal questions either and continued quizzing the shoemaker if he had ever been in love. Realising though that the conversation was getting somewhat out of control and having felt that she had embarrassed

---

[2] Hill, Pollock, 1999, p.8.
[3] Agnew, Luddy, 1998, Vol.1, p.68.
[4] Ibid, 1998, Vol.1, p.102.

him enough, Margaret decided that she should try to recover some of her dignity and his too, because she ended the conversation by promising to buy some shoes from him.[5]

Her unmarried status was obviously of great interest to those who knew her because in April 1785 rumours abounded that she had fallen in love yet again. This time the person of her desires was George Bamber, the youngest son of Richard Brown Bamber of Belmont, County Down. The young couple's behaviour was much remarked upon and the basis for the rumour.[6] (This was the same year that she received Drennan's marriage proposal which must have unnerved him greatly). Nothing however, came of her, *Bamber period* and Drennan's sister suspected that a match would eventually be made for Margaret with one of her Stewart relatives. With this in mind she urged her brother William, to make known his desires to Margaret by writing her a very personal letter which he did.

In reply to this genuinely warm and thoughtful declaration, Margaret's retort was terse and to the point. Her lack of empathy was obvious, that she had no intention of marrying him.[7]

Needless to say William must have found her response disappointing and perplexing. Her curt response left him with no doubt that nothing further could come from this friendship and it seemed to put an end to his longing.

In 1797 Margaret's love-life was again under scrutiny. This time a brief reference was made about her involvement with Robert Williamson of Lambeg.[8] After that, and perhaps due to her flirting, she seemed to drop out of favour with William Drennan and his sister because she no longer appeared within their social group.

Margaret changes conditions for the Tenant Farmers

Having taken possession of the Castle and the estate, Margaret set about changing routines by establishing various conditions for her tenants. She would not permit them to sublet any of their land, neither would she allow a farmer to have more than one labourer or cottier for help.[9] On the one hand

---

[5] Ibid, p.130.
[6] Ibid, p.200.
[7] Ibid, pps.235-237.
[8] Ibid, 1999, Vol.II, p.300.
[9] Ordinance Survey Memoirs of Ireland, 1991, Vol. 10, p.113.

she wanted them to work the land, on the other she limited the amount of help that her tenants could use. This must have been a very harsh way of reducing their aspirations and it could well have forced labourers off her estate. All rent that accrued had to be paid to her. The average size of a farm then in the Kilwaughter parish was 20 acres and a farmer would pay rent of two pounds per acre if the soil was fertile and half of this if it was in poor condition. The cottiers paid one to two pounds per year for their house and garden. The leases for the land had previously been granted by Edward for a term of 21 years and two lives, but on his death this was reduced to 21 years only.

The tenant farmers had to be hard working people to survive. They kept a mix of livestock on their small farms and grew the main crops of the parish which were potatoes and oats. Some of the houses they inhabited were more comfortable than others (around a dozen homes in the area had two storeys), but most contained only three to four rooms and had dirt floors. Labourers who worked for Margaret were paid one shilling per day and the women received half of this amount. Her liberal thinking did not seem to stretch so far as to offer equal pay to the women.

The only politics which the people seemed to be interested in were those that dealt with the two main religions that had been the main cause of many years of strife, though strangely, the Kilwaughter parish did not have any place for its inhabitants to worship. Instead they had to travel to Larne or Ballygowan. Like her grandfather William, Margaret kept one old tradition alive, that the tenants gave *duty days* to their proprietor and in Margaret's case this meant that they brought her turf, the amount dependent on the number of acres of land that they farmed.

The people of the area appeared healthy, a sign that they were relatively well nourished and seemed to live a rather peaceful existence since little or no crime was reported.[10] Following the introduction of the education system in 1831, children were able to go to school. One of the school houses at Mullaghsandal had been supported by Edward who contributed £10 towards the cost of the building.[11]

---

[10] Ibid, p.116.
[11] For more information on Mullaghsandal School, see McKillop in The Glynns, Vol.32, pps.91-94.

The Great Famine

Whilst Margaret appeared tight-fisted with her tenant farmers, she was more generous with the few exceptionally poor people in her area. At Christmas time she would distribute clothing and money to them and in between she also gave money to those in need who would venture up to the Castle on a Saturday for some help.[12] In 1845 however, she was called upon to do more than give clothes and money to the needy because that year saw the beginning of the Great Famine in Ireland. There had been famines before, but not like this. The blight on the potato caused by a fungal growth, saw the whole crop fail, resulting in the starvation of an entire country. In County Antrim as in other parts of Ireland, the inhabitants not only had to contend with starvation, but many of them suffered from disease, particularly dysentery, brought on by their weakened immune systems.

Some affluent landlords such as the Earl of Antrim and the Marchioness of Londonderry[13] initiated relief schemes for their tenants. In this way they helped provide money and food for those who suffered hardship, but others simply emigrated because they had no way of tackling the misery. It was totally beyond their meagre resources. Soup kitchens were opened around the country to try and eradicate some of this, but it was reported that these were not attended as much as they ought to have been. The people may have been ill and weak with hunger, but their self-inflicted principles of dignity and honour were more powerful forces for them than their physical symptoms.[14] Nevertheless, the soup kitchens in County Antrim and in particular around the Glenarm area flourished and were considered to be the most successful, probably due to the diligence of the churches working together.[15]

As famine and disease continued its aggression, another mass wave of emigration left Irish shores to escape the wretchedness. America was the favoured destination for the million people who decided that their future lay elsewhere. Ships that normally only sailed the Atlantic in spring and summer

---

[12] Ordinance Survey Memoirs of Ireland, 1991, Vol.10, pps.109,113-117,120.

[13] In 1848 the Marchioness of Londonderry commemorated a large block of limestone (known as, *The Famine Stone*), to the famine victims. The stone, inscribed in their honour, was placed on a rock along the Antrim coast road. (Dallat, 1990, p.25).

[14] McKillop, 1987, pps.52,53.

[15] Elliott, 2000, p.309.

were now so oversubscribed that they had to sail through the autumn and winter storms in order to satiate demand. In the end some five thousand vessels made the long journey to America during the famine period. Safety on many of them was suspect and conditions on board were very primitive. The people succumbed to disease because they were so weak and malnourished. In the end the vessels became known as *coffin ships* because of the large number of deaths on board. The Irish travelled exactly as the poor slaves had done before them on the very same ships only this time these travellers must have hoped that they were leaving their tortuous lives behind them.[16]

The famine lasted around seven terrible years, but County Antrim was one of the more fortunate counties in that it lost no more than ten per cent of its population.[17] Kilwaughter Castle did not remain aloof from the tragedy because buried in a hollow, beside the small graveyard at the rear of the Castle, lies a mass grave of famine victims. (An added significance is that the name Kilwaughter means, *Upper burying place*). Poignantly the bushes that provided the branches to carry the coffins, still grow beside the hollow.[18] Sadly when Margaret died many unfortunate and cruel changes were brought about by her heirs during this difficult period of famine. Whilst her nephew William was the main benefactor, the Kilwaughter estate from the beginning, had been complicated. Successive proprietors had given entails and reversions of the estate, to their relatives in order to keep the estate within the Agnew family and in turn, some sold their birthright for an annuity. This made the entire Kilwaughter estate ownership structure incredibly complicated. Some of the leases had been altered and revoked through the years and unfortunately when Margaret died, several of the heirs began rescinding her benevolence to her tenants. Not only that, but they cleared out Kilwaughter's smallholders, cottier weavers and labourers. In fact the area's population declined by 36.4% in the ten years between 1841 and 1851. Such was the enormity of this that by 1851 almost a third of the families at Kilwaughter had disappeared, half of whom had lived in the worst dwellings.[19]

---

[16] Laxton, 1997, p.7.
[17] Elliott, 2000, p.307.
[18] Manko, 1994, p.21.
[19] Crowley, et al., 2012. p.427.

Margaret Jones Dies

Margaret's Will dated 19th October 1847[20] was straight forward and contained only one codicil which was made at the same time. She fulfilled her late brother's wishes by naming her nephew William as the main benefactor whom she described as, *"My reputed nephew William Agnew"*. His illegitimate birth still appeared to remain significant, although she endowed him with the Castle and estate and all her lands including new lands purchased from the Trustees of the late Patrick Agnew which included Ballyhacket, Drumahoe, Rorysglen, Boydstown, the Brae and Lealies. At the time of his aunt's death, William was 24 years of age, but Margaret still appointed five Trustees to help implement her wishes. These were, James Agnew, son of William Agnew, of Cairncastle, (Margaret's mother and his father were full cousins); the Rev. Ralph Ward, the local Minister; Edward Jones Smith, her nephew from Belfast; James Bristow of the Northern Bank, Belfast (he had married the grand-daughter of Margaret's half-sister Jane Galt Smith); and Edmund McGildowney Casement. They were each left £50, seemingly as fees for their labours.

Margaret made the same stipulation in her Will as her brother and grandfather had done before her, namely that anyone who inherited the Castle and estate after her, had to take and use the name Agnew, thus continuing the unbroken line in the Castle's history.

By now her niece Maria had married Thomas Collyns Simon. She was bequeathed the £4,000 previously mentioned in her father's Will, plus a further £4,000 which was added to this to be used for the education of her children. Margaret also remained close to her extended family throughout her life and her Will reflected this. She made provision for various family members but unlike Edward though, she did not divide the monetary value of the estate into shares, but left her beneficiaries a sum of money, or in Charles Agnew's[21] case, certain lands. In the complicated structure of the Kilwaughter estate, this would have proved helpful to the next owner. She did not forget her maid or servants, the poor of the parish or indeed the *Asylum* for the blind, deaf and dumb in Belfast, as they were all rewarded.

---

[20] PRONI, T1009/390.
[21] He was the second son of James Agnew, one of her Trustees and had been born in Kilwaughter Castle. (Porter, The Agnews of Ireland. Undated).

Kilwaughter – The Unknown Castle

In another bequest, £30 was left to a gentleman named John Hay Lambert who resided at Kilwaughter. John Lambert had been yet another of William's tutors who had come recommended by Sir James Emerson Tennant a politician.[22] (He was later referred to as agent in the 1851 Census). At the time of Margaret's death he was due to leave, but having nowhere else to go William decided to retain his services and Lambert indeed, remained with him as his companion to the end of his life.

Margaret lived until she was 84 years of age, so must have enjoyed good health,[23] though earlier in 1785 when she was 21 years old, she succumbed to a serious fever. The fever was so grave that her father thought she might die. Margaret didn't die until 2nd January 1848 at 8.00 p.m. after an illness which lasted only two days. She was buried four days later in the Castle graveyard next to her brother.[24] As a popular young woman, she took pleasure in a vigorous social life and was not short of male friends, yet she never married. It is tantalising therefore to ask, in a culture so accustomed to women marrying, why she did not, but she was financially independent and that may have had something to do with it. Her father Valentine may also have had some say in the matter, knowing that the estate would be well looked after if she kept a steadying hand on her brother Edward.

By the time Valentine died in 1805, Margaret was already 41 years old and past the normal age for child-bearing. She presented herself as someone confident and assured; appeared to possess a strong character and was a clever business woman as she proved when she took on the serious task of administering the Castle and estate – and this, at a time, when she probably thought that life would become somewhat quieter. Instead, at 70 years of age, she found herself not only with this responsibility, but with the daunting task of rearing two young children through their formative years to adulthood. It seemed that she rose to the challenge successfully and was able to hand on the Castle and its lands intact, to yet another generation of Agnews. Sadly though, she could not have foreseen that the future of Kilwaughter Castle was about to enter a lengthy period of uncertainty which would eventually bring about its sad demise.

---

[22] Sir Emerson Tennant was a friend of Charles Dickens. Porter, The Agnews of Ireland. Undated.
[23] Agnew, Luddy, 1998, p.225.
[24] Porter, The Agnews of Ireland. Undated.

The Illegitimate nephew of Margaret Jones becomes Heir

When William became proprietor in 1848 he was 24 years old. In the post-famine era which followed Margaret's death and when he took over the estate, changes had to be accommodated and the Kilwaughter tenant farmers like all the others in the country had to begin the slow process of recovery. The farmers though, were very quick to change their ways of working from grain to livestock and benefited from this since livestock prices rose more rapidly. The number of labourers and cottiers had fallen substantially during the famine years, which brought not only a shift in the social structure of the rural classes, but meant that farmers were elevated to a much more important status, both in terms of their role and resources as the size of their farms increased. People began to marry later in life which meant a decline in birth rates and there was still continuing emigration.[25] William's life will have changed immeasurably too, from being a relatively carefree young man, to becoming the landowner of an estate in a country undergoing a metamorphosis. It would have been a very worrying time for him because during the famine the non-payment of tenant rents had caused more than ten per cent of landlords to go into liquidation.[26] The fact that his estate had survived probably said much about the shrewd business acumen of his aunt during the famine, but at the same time he had to contend with the struggle for Tenant Rights which had begun during that time. This attempted to legitimize the Ulster Custom that had been put in place to compensate tenants for any improvements they had made on their land, during their tenure. The compensation was frequently used to help those who wished to emigrate.[27] In 1876 William owned just under 10,000 acres which were valued at £5,845.[28] (This had increased to 13,000 acres by 1892, the year after his death).[29]

William also made donations to various causes, £20 towards purchasing coal and blankets for the poor at Cairncastle[30] and he gave money periodically to such places as the Connor Parochial School (£10) and the Irish Church

---

[25] Lee, 1979, pps.1,3,4,10.
[26] Ibid p.36.
[27] Eliott, 2000, p.318.
[28] Land Owners in Ireland Register 1876, p.183.
[29] Manko, 1994, p.35.
[30] Dublin Evening Post, 1850.

Mission (£8).[31] In 1848 the Marquis of Donegall appointed him to the Commission of the Peace for the County of Antrim.[32]

William Agnew moves to France with John Hay Lambert

Around 1852 William became an absentee landlord when he decided to move to France with his former tutor John Hay Lambert. William concerned himself enough with his estate in Ireland, to oversee its future and he did return from time to time to check on it as is evidenced by various committees that he sat on and he also participated in the showing of livestock at agricultural shows.[33]

He left the estate in the capable hands of his agent, Edmund McGildowney Casement.[34] Edmund held the agency at Kilwaughter for 37 years having succeeded to the post after his father John Montgomery Casement, JP.[35]

William and John lived in Villeroy and then Boissy-St-Leger outside Paris, where John purchased Château des Pins. Before leaving Ireland, William made a Will on 17th April 1851, which was a simple affair.[36] (The 1851 Census showed that William had nine staff living with him at the Castle at that time – his agent, butler, footman, housekeeper, cook, three housemaids and a kitchen maid).[37] By then he had acquired more land, Tullynamullen, Ballymacrea and Bog, and Inverniskey. From this Will it is clear that he felt little responsibility other than the disposal of his estate and personal effects to just a few people.

On 8th September 1883 he altered his original Will and his niece, Maria Augusta Simon became the beneficiary of his estate. Three further codicils were put in place, but most of the changes were subtle.

Throughout William's adult life he remained close to John Lambert his earlier tutor and later agent. In all changes that were made in the Wills, Lambert was priority and his loyalty to him never wavered. That same arrangement also stood for Lambert because in his Will, apart from a few small bequests to his four nieces, he left everything to his friend William and

---

[31] The Belfast Newsletter, 1863.
[32] Coleraine Chronicle, 1848.
[33] Information kindly recounted by Lorenza Gatti Balzani.
[34] On Casement's death in 1876, Malcolm McNeill of the Curran replaced him as agent. (Porter, The Agnews of Ireland. Undated).
[35] McKillop, 2005, p.122.
[36] PRONI, D300/1/5/244.
[37] Irish Census, 1851.

also appointed the same trustees as William had done. John Lambert was born in Kent in 1815, the son of a baker. Lambert died on 21st May 1888 leaving assets of £10,050.[38] After his death, William bequeathed the Château to his niece who was then, the Countess Augusta Balzani, but it is not known if she ever came into possession of this legacy because it was needed to be sold to pay off William's debts. (An Affidavit was made for the Inland Revenue in John Lambert's name for £10,000).[39] The property was sold to a banking family, the Baron of de Bethmann, son-in-law to the Hottinguer bankers. Its fate after that was sadly to be demolished in 1926 to make way for housing.[40]

An interesting point emerges from both Wills and that is how John Lambert could have afforded to buy the Château? He doesn't appear to have come from a wealthy family, his job as tutor and then agent would probably not have brought in enough money to buy a large property in France. It may be that it was bought in his name by funds from William, for tax purposes either in France or Ireland?

Another interesting point concerns the emergence of friends in Paris of both William and John, the Magniers. They befriended Mlle Marie Catherine Armance Magnier who was born in the Somme on 8th December 1823 to Pierre François Magnier and Marie Françoise Porte-Bois. William and John left Armance a substantial legacy of 100,000 French francs though it is not clear exactly the nature of their relationship with her. She died on 24th February 1910. Legacies were also left to her nephews George and Lucien Morand, alias Magnier (why their surname changed is not known). John Lambert was buried in the Père Lachaise Cemetery in Paris together with the Magniers.

Maria Agnew, Sister to William. Marriage, birth of Daughter and Death

Several years before, William's sister Maria had married his tutor, Thomas Collyns Simon on 16th May 1844 when she was just 18 years old, in St. Leonard's Chapel in Hastings, Sussex. Thomas who was much older, was born in 1811. He was of Huguenot descent and was the son of Peter Simon. The

---

[38] Will of John Hay Lambert, dated 8th October 1886, Rockwood Museum.
[39] PRONI, T502/68.
[40] I am very grateful to Corinne Durand for the information on William's life in France.

family home was in Cork, Ireland. Thomas attended Oxford University, but did not finish his degree due to ill-health, nevertheless he went on to become a writer of both scientific and philosophical books. He had two brothers – Henry Andrews Simon who was called to the Bar in 1841 and William Frederick Simon who was editor of the *Carlisle Patriot* newspaper.[41]

Maria's aunt was shocked and dismayed at the marriage, probably because Thomas was much older than his bride and he had also been a staff member of the household. We can take it for granted therefore that she did not attend the wedding, but Maria's brother did and acted as a witness for her.[42] The contentious nature of the marriage must have remained unresolved some years later, because on her deathbed, Margaret had still not been informed that Maria had given birth to a daughter on 3rd November 1847, in Queenstown, Cork,[43] a county, which like the rest of Ireland, was still in the grip of the famine. They named the baby Maria Augusta and she was to add a wonderful new dimension to Kilwaughter's history in the coming years. Sadly however, Maria was not to live to see her child grow up because she died, just three weeks before her thirty-first birthday, on 9th May 1857, at Ballysax Rectory in County Kildare whilst visiting friends, leaving her young daughter motherless at 10 years of age. The death was unexpected (after just two days), as she had caught scarlet fever having nursed Augusta through the same illness.[44]

Maria was buried in St. Paul's graveyard at Ballysax and was remembered by her brother who placed a plaque inside the church at the front of the nave facing the sanctuary - *"Sacred to the memory of Maria the beloved wife Thomas Collins (sic) Simon Esq. She died of Scarlet Fever taken in her devoted attendance upon her child. It was on the 9th May 1837 at the Rectory House of the Parish in the 30th year of her age that her generous spirit was withdrawn to the better world from the sorrows and disappointments of the present one. This tablet was placed by her brother William Agnew Esq. of Kilwaughter Castle in the County Antrim as a tribute to his love for an affectionate sister"*. (The error in the year of death is probably due to someone erroneously, making good the faded date on the stone).[45]

---

[41] Obituary St. Sepulchre's Cemetery.
[42] Certificate of Marriage, 16th May 1844, No.102.
[43] Grave paper of Maria Augusta, kindly donated by Alessandra Gatti.
[44] The Times, 16th May, 1857.
[45] Information from Rev. John Marsden who kindly gave his help in finding Maria's grave.

Her death was announced in The Times.[46] Later Augusta and her father moved to England and in the 1861 census they were living in Somerset. Five years later Thomas was awarded an Hon. Doctorate of Letters by Edinburgh University. After this they moved house again since an Indenture dated 15th April 1878 made between William and his niece Maria Augusta for the sum of £12,000, with regard to the purchase of certain estates, gave their address as, *Kensington in the County of Middlesex*.[47] Thomas died in September 1883 and was buried in St. Sepulchre's Cemetery, three days after his granddaughter Nora was born in his house.

With William living in France and his sister living elsewhere, there was no immediate family member to look after the well-being of the estate or live in the Castle,

In 1876 he granted a site for a new burying ground. After a meeting at which a deputation gathered to ask for this since the old graveyard behind the Castle was full, William acceded immediately and a Trust was formed representing all denominations as William wanted all communities to be involved. Mr. Cobain was appointed the Chair.[48] Records show that in 1865 the deaths of two children occurred at Kilwaughter Castle, Mary Bell aged five years who died on 4th November and her young brother Adam, aged one year, who died just two weeks later on 18th November. Both were the children of William Bell who must have been a staff member and looked after the estate.[49]

William does not seem to have been as diligent as his elderly aunt. Indeed, it could be argued that he might have been somewhat of a spendthrift because his outgoings failed to match his income, but he may also have had to cut his losses with his tenants. After an initial reduction of their rents he gave them a second one for his tenantry in Kilwaughter, Ballygally, Cokermaine, Ballyruddow and Ballymulloge estates. This, together with the first reduction amounted to twenty-five percent, plus he paid a large amount of money for the draining of their farms.[50] since he gave them a ten per cent reduction on their May rents, possibly to encourage them to pay the remainder.[51]

---

[46] Death announcement of Mrs. Maria Simon, The Times, dated 16th May 1857, page 1.
[47] PRONI, D1326/2/6.
[48] New Burying Ground at Kilwaughter, 15th July, 1876.
[49] Rutherford, 2004, p.141.
[50] Dublin Evening Post, 1850.
[51] Belfast News Letter, 1886.

In a Declaration dated 8th April 1892, (one year after William's death), from his sole surviving Trustee and Executor Henry Thomas McNeale of Regent Street, London, to solicitors, it is stated that a £30,000 loan secured by a mortgage on the Kilwaughter estate, had to be raised to pay off Wiliam's debts, legacies and other commitments. At the time the Declaration gave his address as, Boissy-St. Leger, Seine-et-Aise, France.[52]

William Agnew Dies

William died on 10th January 1891, leaving assets of £7,317 0s. 2d. and was buried in Boissy-St. Leger, outside Paris.[53] An unfortunate tragedy occurred to Malcolm McNeill his agent who, on travelling to Paris to attend the funeral, caught scarlet fever and died there on 9th February 1891. He was buried beside William.[54]

Whether William's overspend resulted from an elaborate lifestyle in France or not, it signalled the start of an insecure future for the Castle and the whole estate, for it marked the beginning of the end of what had been a family home for the Agnews since the 1600's. Throughout the different centuries of all the problems of civil unrest in Ireland, of famine and illegitimate births, of safeguarding the estate, the family had still managed to hold on to their legacy for future generations. Now however, that continuous line had finally been severed and although Maria Augusta would go on to inherit the property, due to her Italian marriage and even though she was an Agnew herself via her mother, she would never live in Ireland and as a result this would bring to an end the association between Kilwaughter and the Agnews that had lasted four hundred years.

---

[52] PRONI, D1326/2/6.
[53] The Times, 13th January 1891.
[54] Rutherford, 2004, pps. 175,176.

Sir Andrew Agnew, 9th Sheriff of Galloway
(Courtesy of Sir Crispin Agnew)

Sir Andrew Agnew, 10th Sheriff of Galloway
(Courtesy of Sir Crispin Agnew)

Sir James Agnew, 11th Sheriff of Galloway
(Courtesy of Sir Crispin Agnew)

Valentine Jones (the Elder)
(Artist's impression by Linda Hooke)

Margaret Jones
(Courtesy of Alessandra Gatti)

Edward Jones Agnew
(Courtesy of Alessandra Gatti)

William Agnew
(Courtesy of Alessandra Gatti)

Maria Simon's Grave
(Author's own collection)

Count and Countess Balzani (L) with John and Bessie Galt Smith (R) (Courtesy of Alessandra Gatti).

George Kennedy Galt Smith at the front entrance of Kilwaughter Castle (Courtesy of Shipley-Bringhurst-Hargraves Family Papers, Special Collections, University of Delaware Library, Newark, Delaware, USA).

Villa Balzani, Rome
(Author's own collection)

Graves of Maria Augusta, Ugo and Nora Balzani, Rome
(Author's own collection)

Guendalina and Guido Valensin
(Courtesy of Lorenza Gatti Balzani)

Graves of Guendalina, Guido and Giorgia Valensin, Florence
(Author's own collection)

One of the surviving windowsills at Kilwaughter Castle
(Author's own collection)

Chapter 7

A New Era – The Balzani Family

Disastrous as that may have sounded, something entirely new and culturally different was about to happen to Kilwaughter, for it heralded the arrival of a family of some distinction from Italy that would become woven into the Castle's rich historic tapestry. On 24th April 1878 Maria Augusta Simon married Count Ugo Balzani at St. Mary Abbot's Church in Kensington, London.[1] They were both 31 years old, his date of birth being 6th November 1847, just three days after her own birthday. At the time they lived in 1 Albert Street, Pimlico, London. The couple are said to have met in Rome where Augusta and her father had gone to hear the Italian writer and philosopher Count Terenzio Mamiani speak and where Ugo was also present.[2] That month of April was a busy one for Ugo because he travelled extensively to London, Florence, Bologna, Padova, Milan, Turin and Paris.[3]

The Balzani family came from Bologna in northern Italy, but the progenitor of their family is said to have been a Scottish soldier named Corrado Murdoch, who arrived in the thirteenth century. He gained a reputation for originality and with his swashbuckling ways, he was initially given the name of Bordocchio, which meant *Crazy*, though this was later changed to Balzano.[4] He soon embraced the Bolognese culture and eventually joined the army in 1249, becoming a Captain.[5] Over the centuries the family had produced several distinguished people amongst whom were the painter

---

[1] The Times, 1878.
[2] Kindly recounted by Lorenza Gatti Balzani and Alessandra Gatti
[3] Kindly recounted by Alessandra Gatti.
[4] Ibid
[5] Villa Balzani information, 2003.

and sculptor Giovanni Girolamo (1658-1735); the poet (yet another) Bordocchio Balzan *(sic)* and of course Ugo who was an Italian mediaeval historian and writer. The family was bestowed with a hereditary title of Count in 1587 and the title continued through the male members until recent times[6].[7] Villa Balzani, their home at Zola Predosa near Bologna, and still owned by the Balzani descendants, was refurbished in 1860 by Ugo's father, Andrea, a lawyer. The building is said to have been sympathetically refurbished including the attached oratory which has had many of its original features restored. The oratory is opened to the public every three years to celebrate the festival of Saint Trinita.[8]

Count Ugo Balzani was a prolific writer and historian and indeed was so esteemed by Oxford University that he was awarded an Honorary Doctorate in Literature. Amongst his many exchanges was one with Max Muller, the Anglo-German philologist and Oscar Browning, the English writer. Browning, originally a master at Eton College where he had been educated, later became a lecturer in history at his alma mater, Cambridge University. He too, was a scholar of Italian history and through this mutual interest it would seem that he and Ugo met. Ugo's correspondence with Browning still survives and it tells us that they became good friends and enjoyed each other's company as is clear from one of his letters to Browning, *"I hope you are in Rome for some time, but to make sure my seeing you, would you be so good as to come and dine with me very quietly (no evening dress, please). Thursday evening at half past seven. You would give me great pleasure. Faithfully yours, Ugo Balzani".*[9] (The Countess Balzani was then ill in bed and expected to remain indisposed for some time).

A month later Ugo, in declining Browning's invitation to Chair a lecture on 24th April 1895, informed him that the date was his wedding anniversary and he described it as, *"A kind of sacred day for us, which we keep always in selfish seclusion".*[10] By then the Countess was sufficiently recovered enough that the couple hoped to take a break in the country for two weeks. Judging by Ugo's comment above to Browning, they appeared to have had a happy marriage.

---

[6] Enciclopedia Storico-Nobiliare Italiana, Vol.1, pps.492,493.
[7] Kindly recounted by Alessandra Gatti.
[8] Villa Balzani information, 2003.
[9] King's College Library, OB/1/84/A, letter dated 26th March 1895.
[10] Ibid, letter dated 3rd April 1895.

Their first daughter Guendalina was born on 3rd October 1882 when they were living in Rome. They did not stay there long but returned to England the following year in time for the arrival of another daughter Nora Lucia Malvina Beatrice (known as Nora), on 21st September 1883. Nora was baptised three months later in St. Giles Anglican church in Oxford. Their address then was 10 Norham Gardens, Oxford, the home of Augusta's father. [11]

When Augusta inherited the Castle and estate in 1891, it must have disrupted their lives substantially and far from being a welcome legacy, would have brought its own set of problems for a couple residing both in England and Italy. Augusta's knowledge of Ireland and its politics would have been limited and not first-hand. Though born in Cork, she had never lived at Kilwaughter, so would have had no experience of what was required to maintain the Irish Castle and relatively large estate. Looking after tenants and being the main land-owner in the parish would have involved much pastoral work. Added to that the couple had two small children by the time Augusta's uncle died. She appointed Mr. Henry Morgan Byrne of Kinvarra House, Larne as her new agent, to replace the late Malcolm McNeill. Augusta decided to let the complete property and grounds from 1st November 1891, including the corn mill and kiln, the flax and saw mills, together with the horses and the grazing land. She instructed Byrne to place an advertisement in the local newspaper. The Castle and demesne were described as, *"One of the most beautiful residences in the North of Ireland"* and was to be let either furnished or unfurnished by private contract.[12] Fate however, was also to intervene and bring a helping hand to the Count and Countess Balzani that would go some way in resolving the problems of being an absentee landlord, which although common in Ireland for centuries, was nevertheless, still unpopular.

The Galt Smiths add an American Dimension

On 1st June, 1886 a marriage had taken place in Delaware, America, between Elizabeth Bringhurst and John Galt Smith (2)[13] who by then was an Irish linen exporter travelling between Ireland and America, where his business premises were located at 44 White Street, New York. He was also the agent in America

---

[11] Kindly recounted by Alessandra Gatti.
[12] The Belfast Newsletter, 1891.
[13] Hereafter known as John Galt Smith (2).

for William Kirk from Keady in Co. Armagh who was a famous manufacturer for Irish linen. The wedding was conducted in accordance with the Society of Friends ceremony. Galt, as he was known, was born in Newry, County Down and the son of Samuel Smith and Marianne Bryan. How Bessie and Galt met is not clear, but since part of his business was carried out in New York, where Bessie's family also owned a property, that would have given them the opportunity to meet.

The Quaker wedding was described in The New York Times as the, *"Social event of the season"* and Bessie as, *"A prominent society belle".*[14] As befitting such an auspicious occasion, the guest list was littered with high society people from New York, Philadelphia and other out-lying regions. The reception was held at the bride's home and the honeymoon was spent on the, *"Baronial estates of the groom's family in Ireland".* Both families were wealthy and Bessie's sense of adventure was probably attractive to Galt. [15] Bessie was 23 years old and almost twenty years younger, but she was not Galt's first wife who had died leaving him with two children, Kennedy and Florence. She was Cornelia H. Knapp, daughter of Cyrus Knapp and his wife Catherine Terheun. The couple married in 1873 and it was also a society wedding. The bride wore diamond adornments which had been given to her by the groom and the wedding presents were considered to be, *"Magnificent"* and valued at $5,000.[16]

Galt had had various careers beginning with that of a tax collector in his native country, working in an office next door to his uncle who was a solicitor, a profession which he later embraced, before finally entering the linen trade.[17] His uncle was George Kennedy Smith, who was descended from the Kennedy family of Cassilis of Scotland. The Kennedys had first appeared in Ireland during the reign of Charles II when one, the Rev. Gilbert Kennedy facing persecution against the Presbyterians had fled his homeland in Girvan, Ayrshire. George was descended from his son who was also called Rev. Gilbert Kennedy.[18]

---

[14] The New York Times, 1886.
[15] Ibid, 1892.
[16] Description of the Smith Knapp Wedding, Irish Emigration Database, 25th December 2015.
[17] Manko, 1994, pps.17-18.
[18] Merrick, 1991, p.156. The Kennedy name was familiar with the Agnews as Sir Patrick's wife was Margaret Kennedy, daughter of Sir Thomas Kennedy of Culzean Castle.

Elizabeth Bringhurst Smith

Bessie was born in 1863, the eldest of four children. She was the daughter of Edward Bringhurst and Anna James Webb. Her three siblings were, Mary, Edith and Edward, who was born 21 years after Bessie and to whom she acted as a surrogate mother. Her father Edward was a wealthy man and a Board member on many financial institutions. He also owned a pharmacy business. Although well integrated into the American way of life by the nineteenth century, their original roots lay in Leicestershire, England, from where William Shipley, a devout Quaker, had left in 1725 to seek his fortune in Pennsylvania. The move to America was an inspired choice for William because his wealth and career flourished in time and he became the main founder of the town of Wilmington in Delaware which attracted other Quakers to join him. The family had aspirations and all their hard work soon began to pay dividends as they were able to purchase several mills that they ran with great success and created a solid family business.

William's great grandson Joseph Shipley who was the great uncle of Bessie's father Edward, developed important connections involving Anglo-American trade that evolved after he decided to visit the land of his great grandfather's birth. He sailed for Liverpool in 1819 intending to stay for a brief period, but this turned into thirty-two years by which time he had abandoned his strict Quaker faith in favour of more earthly pursuits such as fancy dress balls. His lack of interest in his faith would have dismayed his great grandfather whose reputation as an influential Quaker had enabled the family to acquire much wealth. Joseph's time in England though, was not spent in complete self-indulgence, but in studiously pursuing his business interests and as someone who was well experienced in the nature of American trade, he became a popular man as his opinions and advice were much sought.

By 1850 at the age of 55, Joseph was tiring of the English way of life. Added to that he had developed gout and that helped make up his mind to return to Delaware and spend his retirement in a climate that was much kinder to his condition. It was in the following year that he decided to build a house of some prestige for himself, which he named *Rockwood*. The house was designed in the style of a rural Gothic villa and in fact, remained the only major Gothic-style house built in Delaware in the nineteenth century. Only the best materials were used – solid oak, granite and mitred woodwork to allow for corners and various patterns in the design; cast iron and plate glass were brought over from England. The interior was furnished in the Victorian style and somewhat unusually, had gender-defined rooms, denoting various masculine or feminine features. No expense was spared either in landscaping the surrounding grounds. Joseph was a keen gardener and took on much of the work himself with the help of some staff and it was this expertise, that helped him become elected as second Vice-President of the Delaware Horticultural Society in 1852. Even outside the property, visitors were reminded just how important the Shipley's had become because to approach the villa, they had to travel along Shipley Road to gain access.

In 1867 Joseph died and left *Rockwood* to his three sisters and it was on the death of one of them, Hannah, that at public auction *Rockwood* and some of its contents, became the home of Bessie's parents.[19] The advent of the Bringhursts brought new ideas and they added a completely new wing to the house, much in the same style that Joseph had liked. The family brought their own heir-looms, but set about acquiring more artefacts to furnish their home and with their travels around the world, the house soon took on the appearance of an eclectic style of interior design with a great penchant for the orient.

The family was quite unique in one particular aspect of their home, for when it came to the contents, they catalogued everything so that it could be found quickly and easily. They obsessed in making lists of all the items and this extended to diagrams of cupboards and cabinets where articles should be stored. There were even detailed lists of their clothing. Shelves were also numbered and a further numbering system was used for their correspondence which was to prove a great help to Bessie during her years residing at Kilwaughter Castle. Bessie used the system time and time again with great effect to obtain things from *Rockwood*. She was able to pinpoint exactly where the various items were stored and even gave instructions when a letter should be destroyed, though this wasn't always adhered to.[20] The family also used a code system when sending telegrams to reduce the number of words and thus save money.[21]

---

[19] Romantic Rockwood, Booklet 1982.
[20] Letter, dated 1891 to Mother.
[21] Manko, 1994, p.22.

Bessie became an avid letter writer to her family and friends whilst living in Ireland.[22] In all, during her period at Kilwaughter, she wrote over a thousand letters which gave a good description of life in Ulster. She would write every few days giving all the news of her daily life and as was custom within her family, each letter was numbered and logged in her notebook, so she was able to see which letters had gone missing or were delayed in arriving at *Rockwood*. Her writing was descriptive and passionate and she would go to great lengths to build an image of the people she met, describing their clothes, what they did for a living and the kind of houses they owned. She also penned little sketches of clothes she bought and objects of furniture she had acquired. Bessie remained close to her family. Even though she was many thousands of miles from them, they were very much to the forefront of her mind and from time to time she would purchase clothes for them, again drawing little sketches of the items, before she bought them.

The Galt Smiths return to Ireland

Galt brought his new bride back to his home at *Meadowbank in* Whitehouse a suburb some six miles north of Belfast, which he had inherited from his solicitor uncle, George Kennedy Smith, who died in July 1886. The couple fortunately, were in Ireland having returned from what was a belated honeymoon in Scotland, when uncle George died.[23] Unfortunately Bessie was ill during part of it as her rheumatism had caused her problems. When Galt's uncle died Bessie pointedly wrote home that no women would be allowed to go to the funeral[24] as was the Irish custom then and she decided to send home all her clothes since mourning dictated that she wear black for the foreseeable future.[25]

Galt had been the sole beneficiary to his uncle's Will and was something of a property speculator and owned several other properties that he leased to tenants. In time he would look for another property for himself and Bessie, but right now the house seemed perfectly adequate for the couple and Galt's two children, as it had fifteen rooms, a cottage and orchards.

---

[22] Ibid, 1994, p.8.
[23] Letter summary, 13th July 1886.
[24] Ibid, 26th July 1886.
[25] Ibid, 29th July 1886.

August 1886, must have been quite a rude awakening to Bessie as a new bride in a new country because it saw disturbances in Belfast when the Protestant shipyard workers marched through Catholic areas. Buildings were set alight and there was stone throwing. The crowds ripped up the paving slabs and used them as ammunition with great effect, since there were many injured people and the hospitals were full. When the military police arrived to quell the riots, they too, became targets as they were thought to side with the Catholic people. What must have unnerved Bessie, was that she got caught up in all of it, even outside her own home at *Meadowbank* where a young couple was innocently shot. The worsening situation eventually led to a curfew.[26]

Galt was concerned that Bessie didn't mention these riots to her family as this would inevitably have frightened them and they would have feared for their young daughter's safety and as it just so happened, they were leaving Ireland for some weeks anyway, to get away from the workmen in the house who were making alterations to it. They travelled first to Douglas in the Isle of Man to do some sight-seeing, before moving on to London three days later. All in all they were away five weeks by which time Bessie admitted to being tired and had caught a cold.[27] She was also making plans to return to America in October to bring back some furniture (an old round table) for the music room.[28] Galt and Bessie travelled extensively during their first years together, not only between their two homes in Ireland and America, but to Europe also. They visited Switzerland, Italy (that brought to mind for Bessie, a painting at *Rockwood* of Lake Como); and France where they stopped off in Paris.[29] At the same time she was busy with her step-children – finding a boarding school for Florence and choosing a St. Bernard puppy for Kennedy's birthday. She was also busy planning the re-decoration of the New York home at 145 West 73rd Street, Manhattan and wanted her mother to persuade her father to let her have the necessary funds and then leave her to it.[30]

By June the following year (1889), on the way back to Ireland, Bessie was again ill with stomach problems this time. She had to spend the night in Liverpool before making the last leg of her journey to Kilwaughter and was

---

[26] Ibid, 11th August 1886.
[27] Ibid, 14th September 1886.
[28] Letter summary, 18th September 1886.
[29] Ibid, 12th July 1888.
[30] Ibid, 8th September 1888.

looked after by her maids Rose and Celine as well as Galt.[31] The next few weeks were taken up sorting out furniture from *Meadowbank* and finding a new agent to deal with Galt's other rental properties that were now vacant. She also found time to organise another trip to London and Paris and was thrilled to see some of Landseer's original work, since her family had several of his engravings at their home in America. Bessie being a great gossip and after her stay with her friends the Bury's who owned *Branksome Tower* in Dorset, enjoyed telling people that they had been offered, *"Two million"* (presumably dollars), for a painting, by the Duke of Westminster, but had refused to sell.[32] She liked others to know that she had wealthy and influential friends.

As the year was turning to autumn, Bessie began thinking about returning to America for the winter. Galt's children were to visit their grandmother in Hackensack and Bessie was also keen to know about the money her father had received from selling property in Florida. She was always keen to be kept abreast of events happening at home and she wasn't shy about asking the most personal questions.[33]

During the next year Bessie's inquisitive mind kept her occupied. She enjoyed refurbishing her home at *Meadowbank* and also pursuing her hobby of photography and set up a dark room for this purpose. She liked shopping and trips to the theatre and of course holding her infamous dinner parties.[34] At the end of August Bessie and Galt made a visit to Kilwaughter Castle. Galt was now keen to purchase another property and since the Castle was still owned by the Agnews and as a distant relative, may have thought that he could make them an offer, but it was for rent only. Bessie's first thoughts are not known and she makes no mention of it until the following year when she and Galt visited the Castle again.[35] By this time William Agnew had been dead six months and the property was now vacant.

Family Connections

The Galt Smith's were well known within the Kilwaughter history because of the marriage of John Galt Smith's(2) great grandfather to Jane, the half-sister

---

[31] Ibid, 16th July 1889.
[32] Ibid, 5th-6th August 1889.
[33] Ibid, 22nd August 1889.
[34] Ibid, 17th July 1890.
[35] Ibid, 23rd June 1891.

of Edward Jones Agnew in 1765 and the present John Galt Smith(2) was the Countess Balzani's distant cousin. The intervening years had not, seemingly, diminished the relationship between the Agnews and their extended family. Bessie was also proud that Kilwaughter had been in the Agnew family since *"1200 AD"* (that date cannot be verified) because of the history attached to it and it would still not be entirely devoid of a family member since Galt and her were relatives.[36]

At first the couple wondered what they might do with *Meadowbank*. They thought that it could be rented, since Galt already had other rental properties. The revenue would bring in about $5,000 a year, but after thinking things through, they changed their minds and sold the property in August 1891 as they were planning to rent Kilwaughter Castle. [37] [38] By then they must have realised that they would need the profit from *Meadowbank* to help pay for the enormous reparations at the Castle (together with Bessie's small inheritance of $700 from her grandmother), to bring their new home up to Bessie's exacting standards. Bessie was something of a serious social climber and the move to a more prestigious address would have suited her. (In later years her family was to re-name her, *Lady Kilwaughter*).[39] William Agnew's death and the empty Castle provided that opportunity.

Kilwaughter Castle undergoes another Refurbishment

The arrangement also suited the Balzanis and some months later Galt and Bessie signed a lengthy lease on the Castle for thirty years.[40] [41] Moving day for them to Kilwaughter Castle was set for 1st November 1891.[42] The Balzanis were no doubt pleased that both the Castle and estate would be lived in after having been empty for so many years and added to that, there was the bonus of extra income from the leasehold. Galt was to be responsible for the tenancies, crops and livestock and for this, he would share the profits.[43]

---

[36] Letter, dated 15th September 1891 to Mother.
[37] Letter summary, 29th July 1886.
[38] Ibid, 27th August 1886. Bessie later became a property developer after Galt's death and built some homes to let, in the same area as *Meadowbank*. Letter summary, 7th September 1901.
[39] Ibid, 21st April 1901.
[40] Manko, 1994, p.21.
[41] PRONI, D971/9/1.
[42] Letter summary, 13th August 1891.
[43] Manko, 1994, p.22.

Kilwaughter – The Unknown Castle

There was much to do however, before the couple could take up residence. The Castle had lacked care and attention for forty years, so one of the first things that Bessie and Galt did was to enlist the help of an architect to draw up some refurbishment plans and to oversee the work. The plumbing was one of the most important aspects to be tackled. There was an ample supply of water to the Castle and the drain as Bessie described it was, "*So large a man can walk in it*"[44], but the laundry room was below ground level, so rain water which still had to be brought into the room, continually lay under the built-in tubs and Bessie thought this unhygienic. It was decided that it was a relatively simple task to turn the old kitchen into a new laundry room to eradicate the water problem and the boarded-up fireplace in the kitchen could easily be brought back into use.

Bessie delighted in the challenge that Kilwaughter brought and never seemed to tire of making plans. "Galt and I are very busy about Kilwaughter. I have been drawing plans for a new bathroom in the old part, for a dress-cupboard, laundry, etc. which requires frequent meetings with the plumber, architect, builder, painter, etc".[45] Her enthusiasm never seemed to dampen and she was involved in every aspect of the work including the budget and was pleased to note that the cost estimates which had been given for the labour, were coming in well below the anticipated price. She did not spend every waking moment dealing with the affairs of Kilwaughter, but found time during her many shopping trips to keep an eye out for clothes that would suit her mother. In particular, she found, "A Perfect French wrap, in black velvet, trimmed with feathers." She thought this wrap was entirely appropriate as it had armholes and no sleeves. In her usual brusque manner, she told her mother that it, "Would just suit thy fat arms!"[46]

Her mother's response was not recorded.

Both she and Galt suffered with gout from time to time which slowed them down, but this didn't stop them travelling. During Bessie's time in Ireland she visited most of Europe and was not averse to criticising what she didn't like. On one occasion in London where she had gone to see the Crystal Palace Exhibition she was greatly disappointed and made her views known in

---

[44] Letter, dated 2nd September 1891 to mother.
[45] Letter, dated 2nd September 1891 to mother.
[46] Letter, undated, but No. 27, 1891, to mother.

one of her letters.[47] Exploring new places was important for her and she travelled frequently, usually arranging this either en route to America or on her way back to Ireland in the spring. She also took her duties as a step-mother seriously involving herself in Florence's education which was to be in America. Bessie suggested Sandy Point or Ellicott's Mills, but in the end Florence attended a Quaker school in Rockland where she learnt how to do an Irish jig,[48] but when it came to Kennedy it was thought that he would have a much better chance passing his examinations if he had a Yale tutor to coach him.[49]

In between everything else the tourists were a headache for Bessie and Galt. Kilwaughter Castle was on the tourist trail and the couple permitted them to visit the Castle grounds on Mondays only. On one day alone (11th September 1891), there had been forty-five people from Manchester and a party from Aberdeen as well as some stragglers and it was not unusual to have tourists arriving in groups of one or two hundred. Some of the people finding the door to the hall open, had even ventured into the house to have a look around much to Bessie's surprise.

Bessie decided that some of the fixtures and fittings should come from America and began with the window blinds or *shades* as she called them. The windows in the servants' quarters though, made do with white muslin as they were so low down on the walls that blinds were not necessary. She also enlisted her mother's help with some sewing and when she left for America at the end of September, she took the material with her, to be made into cushion covers and sheets.

Auction

Before this and in between all of the work needing doing, a two-day auction arranged by William Baxter, Auctioneer and Valuer at Larne, was held on 15th September, 1891, to clear the Castle of the contents which had belonged to William Agnew and were now the property of his niece the Countess Balzani. The entire household effects were up for sale including a full-size billiard table, first class wines and other alcohol, a valuable collection of books and the

---

[47] Letter summary, 6th September 1886.
[48] Ibid, 17th July 1890.
[49] Letter, dated 26th July 1896.

furniture from all the 13 bedrooms.[50] Augusta understandably, wanted to keep some of the things herself, before allowing the rest to be sold. She chose the linen, plate and pictures and some china - mostly tea and dessert sets, but left Galt and Bessie some old furniture and her grandfather's carriage.[51] All the beds in the Castle were four-posters and the mattresses which had been renewed some fourteen years ago, had not been used as William Agnew had spent only intermittent time in his Irish home. Bessie and Galt wanted to purchase some of the contents as that would make life easier for them with the furniture already in situ, but mindful of the expenditure and their budget they were not prepared to pay over the odds for them. They had some favourite things they wished to buy – the four bookcases in the library, an exquisite side-board and dining table and a gilt chandelier for candles which hung in the drawing room and which was a particular favourite of Bessie's. The two-day auction, was successful for them and they got most of the things they had wanted apart from the dining table which they felt was far too expensive. They purchased other things too – most of the chairs, all of the sofas, two Chippendale card-tables, two solid rosewood tables which had brass trim on the legs and a large centre table to match. Two other tables in black, which had been made from wood on the estate were also bought and a spinet inlaid with brass. Some cut-glass dishes in two sizes with, *"Four square ends",* were purchased too and Bessie thought these perfect for a, *"Brick of ice-cream".*[52]

That first day of the auction had not been without its traumas for Bessie. She and Galt had two men bidding for them – Mr. Gray from Clark's Auctions Mart and William John McCoy who was a dealer in old furniture. Of course, Bessie and Galt entered into the auction game of pretending that they didn't know their bidders. Bessie had cunningly invited Mr. Gray to the Castle beforehand to go over the contents and pick out the pieces she most desired. There was quite a crowd that day, but the people were good-humoured. As the bidding gathered pace, there was some jostling and pushing and plenty of shouting out the bids. Poor Bessie was beginning to lose her temper and resented being nudged about in her own home. She particularly disliked the

---

[50] Belfast Newsletter, 1891.
[51] Letter summary, 13th August 1891. (The carriage was used to take Edward Jones Agnew to Dublin during the time he was a Member of the Irish Parliament).
[52] Letter, dated 15th September 1891 to Mother.

spitting on the carpet and the, *"Rough men"* who were sitting on the side-board that she wished to purchase. Bessie managed to control her temper by disappearing with Galt into his new dressing room for lunch. The couple were hoping to enjoy lunch in some peace and quiet, but that did not happen as very soon afterwards, the door opened and some people walked in for a look around, *"Pipes and all!"* much to the astonishment of the couple.[53]

The auction got off to a good start on the second day too and was to concentrate more on the contents that were upstairs in the Castle. It was a warm and sunny day and as Bessie approached Kilwaughter she noticed how many people were making their way to it in all forms of transport – some in carts and others in cars. There was already quite a crowd as the couple arrived and Bessie being as observant as ever, noticed that some of the people nudged each other, *"There goes Mrs. Smith"* or, *"The Master"*. She was thrilled of course to be thought of as the new chatelaine and not least the latest, important person in the area. Neither Bessie nor Galt attended the second day of the auction as they were not interested in what was on offer. The following month on 22nd October, 1891, a further three-day auction was held to sell the livestock, carriages and other farming implements and utensils.[54]

Lady Magheramorne, who was at the auction, was not quite so lucky. She wanted all the copper kitchen utensils which included scales, two fish kettles, preserving kettles, saucepans, moulds, some of which of course, had never been used in forty years. All were sold for £100 which Bessie thought a good price, but Lady Magheramorne thought that too much and when she eventually changed her mind, lost the whole lot and came away with only a warming pan for the beds.

At the end of September Bessie left Ireland to winter in New York and when she returned again in May the following year, the Castle was in full swing. She had plenty to do indoors and set about continuing the organizing of her new home with some gusto. Being new to the country and its culture did not deter her and she quickly found craftsmen to help her make the place more habitable and to her liking. They assembled furniture, put down the carpets, covered sofas and gilded the chairs in the dining room, but, *"They are all maddeningly slow here,"* is what she said in describing how some material that

---

[53] Letter, dated 22nd September 1891 to Polly.
[54] Belfast News Letter, 1891.

she had ordered for the drawing room curtains failed to appear after it had been promised several weeks ago. (The yellow brocade for the curtains had to be ordered from Paris and Bessie was inordinately proud of them when they were finally hung to her satisfaction). To add insult to injury when the samples of the material finally arrived, they were the wrong ones. *"It is no use to scold, for they are too lazy and good tempered to mind it"*, is all that she could say. It also did not help that the wallpaper chosen for the re-decorating had to come from England which delayed things even more.[55]

She continued to make lists of things to do and kept everyone fully occupied for some time, but Bessie's frustration and impatience began to show in a letter to her mother, but she could not complain too much though, since two of the workmen volunteered to stay all night when the new range which was six feet in length, was being fitted into the kitchen. The original range had been enormous and awkward and was not connected to the water boiler. The fire that was used to heat the water was placed in another part of the Castle and as well as that when the cook wanted to do some baking, yet another fire had to be lit for her to carry out this task.[56] This made life very difficult for the staff.

Brother Galt as Bessie called him (a throw-back to her Quaker ways), left much of the running of the Castle to his wife as she was more than capable, but he too was kept occupied outside erecting fences and Bessie noted that, *"He looked 10 years younger"*. He also found time to escape from the frantic pace and attended the Great Unionist Convention in June 1892 as well as arranging shooting and fishing parties on the estate for Lord Magheramorne's two surviving brothers, the Hons. Gerald and Dudley McGarel Hogg. Galt and Lord Magheramorne shared a game-keeper called, Fricker who lived at the rear of the Castle. Galt was a good shot and one day managed to bag 100 rooks, only missing four. Bessie was proud of his shooting skills even though his shoulder was left badly bruised, but delighted that he continually managed to kill so many rooks and crows since they were deemed a pest as they destroyed the grain.[57] The lake provided an extra bonus too, in that they enjoyed fresh trout for breakfast.

---

[55] Letter, dated 21st May 1892 to Edward.
[56] Letter, dated 3rd June 1892 to father.
[57] Letter, dated 21st May 1892 to Edward.

Court Case

In 1892 six years after Galt and Bessie married, Galt and Kirk were embroiled with the American authorities over the price of linen. On a recent occasion $35,000 of linen goods had been imported, but a dispute had arisen as to the true value of these goods. Less value of the imports meant lower taxes to be paid. The disagreement was so serious that the Government's expert in linens, Alfred C. Dutcher at the Appraiser's Store, was called in to assess the situation. He ruled that the linen goods were undervalued by between 10%-20%. Galt and Kirk appealed against the ruling to the U.S. General Appraisers, but they were over-ruled and in the end this difference of opinion, whether intentional or not, cost Galt and Kirk a heavy penalty of $7,000. This amount must have impinged upon the bill for the forthcoming reparations at Kilwaughter.

During the day and sometimes in the evenings, the couple relaxed in the old oak hall which was one of the original Castle rooms and which they used as a sitting room where they would take tea.[58] In mid July whilst attending the Regatta at Bangor in Co. Down, Galt accepted an invitation to dine on board the German Emperor's yacht.[59] Bessie must have been thrilled. They were a popular couple, whether this was due to Galt knowing many people in the Kilwaughter area or to Bessie's friendly American openness, it is hard to tell, but they were not short of invitations to visit their friends' homes. They spent many occasions with Lord and Lady Magheramorne at their estate in Magheramorne and one wonders if Bessie knew that this estate too, had once belonged to James Agnew Farrell, a second cousin of Edward Jones Agnew. Lady Magheramorne was the daughter of the Earl of Shaftesbury and her mother had been the only child of the Marquis of Donegal who owned Belfast Castle. Bessie thought Lady Magheramorne, *"Charming and a beauty"*.[60]

The Refurbishment is complete and the Galt Smiths begin socialising

In 25th June 1892 the last of the workmen left though Bessie and her servant Mrs. Wheeler were still busy finishing off the curtains for the drawing room

---

[58] Manko, 1994, p.26.
[59] Letter, dated 15th July 1892 to father.
[60] Letter, dated 10th August 1892 to mother.

and preparing the visitors' rooms. Bessie had bought a Wilcox and Gibb sewing machine earlier that month which she put to good use during all of her time at Kilwaughter.[61] It is clear that both Bessie and the people she enlisted to help her renovate the interior of the Castle, worked hard, since much had been achieved in the few short months from their arrival. Bessie was delighted with the result and even if Kilwaughter had not been lived in for forty years, she felt it was in wonderful preservation that needed little improving. She loved the fact that it was so, *"Old and lovely"* and declared to her mother, *"If I had all the wealth of the Vanderbilts and the whole of the United Kingdom to choose from, I could not find a place I liked better than Kilwaughter"*.[62]

By now the couple were enjoying the country pursuits which this fine place offered. Kennedy, Galt's son, had a selection of ponies at his disposal and there were numerous dogs to play with, including an Irish Wolfhound named, *Banshee*.[63] Later on the dog became so badly behaved that it had to be chained to another, *Gelert* to stop it killing sheep.[64] He and his sister Florence were taught every day at the Castle by their teacher Miss Bird. They seemed to enjoy their lessons, but whether this was to do with Miss Bird's teaching skills or the fact that she was a strict disciplinarian, was open for debate. Nonetheless, they turned up promptly for lessons each morning at 8.30 a.m. to the school room.[65]

The visitors and guests had already started arriving in May 1892. Bessie was first to sign the new Guest Book and gave both addresses – Kilwaughter and her home in New York, 145 West 73rd Street, which ran from Central Park to the Hudson river.[66] Trips out, around the local area and walks through the garden, past the bowling green to the lake, were popular places to take her guests. Bessie was in her element however, when at the end of June, *"A gorgeous turnout of coachman and footman in top hats and breeches"* appeared at the Castle door. The visitors were Mr. and Mrs. Smiley of *Drumalis* and Bessie explained excitedly in a letter to her father, that Mrs. Smiley used to be called, *"The Nugget"*, because of her enormous wealth and was the only child of Mr. Clark

---

[61] Letter summary, 7th June 1892.
[62] Manko, 1994, p.2.
[63] Letter, dated 15th June 1892 to brother Edward.
[64] Letter summary, 10th June 1893.
[65] Letter, dated 7th June 1892 to mother.
[66] Kilwaughter Guest Book.

of Paisley, the, *"Linen thread man".* [67] [68] Mrs. Smiley's father had probably been known to Galt as they were involved in the same business, but it is just possible that Bessie knew that the Clark home at *Cairndhu* had previously belonged to Robert Agnew who had sold it to Mr. Stewart Clark in 1878.[69] She was a frequent visitor to *Cairndhu* and the house seemed to impress her because she described it in a letter to her brother, that it, *"Had about fourteen bedrooms that we saw. And the magnificence of the silver toilet articles! Handkerchief boxes and glass boxes, hand glasses, mirrors; brushes and brush trays, all of heavy, superb silver. And this is the toilet table of Mrs. Clark and each of her four daughters. They just roll in money, millions and millions".*[70]

She also liked the fact that their yacht was anchored in the small bay beside their house. This was not just any old boat covered in barnacles and rust that was used for cruising along the Lough on a peaceful summer's day, but it was a large yacht capable of accommodating sixteen people, not including crew and other staff. The bedrooms were decorated with heavy brocades and luxurious tapestries and the blue and yellow satin quilts on the beds were wonderfully comfortable as they were filled with down. There were open fires in the main rooms and even electric light in the chandeliers. There was a piano for entertainment and to top it all, the chef was a very accomplished cook and prepared delicious meals for the Clark's guests. Of course, Bessie had to explore it all and was quite astounded when she discovered that when Mrs. Clark wished to bathe, her maid had only to lift a lid up which was on the floor, to reveal a beautiful marble bath for her Mistress to step into – and there was both hot and cold running water.[71]

Entertaining the local elite was important to Bessie – Mrs. Chaine (another linen family), *"Whose husband was buried standing on his feet that he might look out over the town of Larne"* and the McGarel Hogg's, brothers of Lord Magheramorne, were some of the people who visited Kilwaughter Castle in the early days. She went to endless trouble to make sure that her guests were well cared for, including picking cherries for lunch for them from the garden.

---

[67] Letter, dated 28th June 1892 to father.
[68] The Smiley's had purchased *Drumalis* when James Chaine died in 1885 (McKillop, 2005, p.153).
[69] *Cairndhu* later became a convalescent hospital until it was taken over by Larne Borough Council in 1995 (McKillop, 2005, pps.184-185).
[70] Letter, dated 10th August 1892 to mother.
[71] Letter, dated 14th September 1892 to mother.

In all of this she was helped by her faithful servant Mrs. Wheeler of whom she was very fond and of her own sister Mary who was two years younger than Bessie and who stayed at Kilwaughter for lengthy periods.

Mary and Galt's daughter Florence, each had their own room decorated in blue and white whilst Kennedy's room was somewhat bizarrely decorated in pink. The couple's own bedroom was shaped in a half-circle with an extra section used as Galt's dressing room. The bed was so high that it needed three steps to assist the occupants to climb into it however, Bessie, *"Generally jumped in"*. As it was a four-poster bed it had sumptuous red damask curtains around it trimmed with red and gold fringes. Their bedroom faced the lake and they enjoyed watching the swans swim in and out amongst the little islands.[72]

Bessie was quite judgmental in her approach to people, but seemed to like most and in particular, the clergyman. *"Our clergyman is Mr. Phoenix of the Kilwaughter Church*[73]. *He is a most amusing and entertaining man: thoroughly Irish".*[74] The tiny little church had only twenty pews and six half-pews and was frequented often by Bessie and Galt.[75] On one occasion when they were there, the church bell as usual stopped on the stroke of 11.30 a.m. for the service to commence, but that day there was no sign of the Minister or the choir. After a, *"Full ten minutes"* with everyone waiting and wondering what had happened, in scurried the choir followed by the clergyman and no explanation was ever given.[76]

At the end of the first week in July 1892 the artificial lake which Edward Jones Agnew had introduced in 1810, had to be fixed. The lake had developed a leak the previous summer and was now quite dry. The Countess Balzani had seemingly, arranged for it to be dealt with, but this had not happened. By now Bessie had developed the patience needed for dealing with Irish workmen and she saw the funny side of it. When referring to the long delay in fixing the lake, she wrote to her father, *"That gives you some idea of the rush people are in here".*[77] She was a hard worker and very effective with it; she had planned,

---

[72] Letter, dated 21st May 1892 to Edward.
[73] Mr. Phoenix died on 23rd November 1901 and was replaced by Mr. Story. (Letter summary, 23rd November 1901).
[74] Letter, dated 30th July 1892 to father.
[75] Letter, dated 10th August 1892 to mother.
[76] Letter, dated 16th August 1892 to Edith.
[77] Letter, dated 6th July 1892 to father.

organized, overseen and done much of the practical work needed to make Kilwaughter the home that she desired, but it was beginning to take its toll on her and she was exhausted. In the same letter she admitted, *"I have really worked hard these past eight weeks and I am beginning to wish for a rest!"*

Life though carried on at the same frenetic pace and it was soon 12th July, the day on which the Protestants celebrated King William III's victory at the Battle of the Boyne in 1690. Galt was a firm Unionist [78] and Bessie obviously supported his point of view. She was also very much influenced by a cousin of Galt's, Frances McTear, whom Bessie always referred to as, *Cousin Frances*. Frances was a middle-aged woman and a strong supporter of Unionism, so much so, that when the Ulster Women's Unionist Council was formed in 1911, she became one of its first members.[79] Although women did not get the vote in Ireland until 1918, this did not stop them being politically aware. There were several other female organizations such as the Women's Suffragette Movement (established 1876), the Ladies' Land League (established 1880), that gave a voice to women.[80] The Ulster Women's Unionist Council was initiated to oppose Home Rule and attracted members from the Protestant upper-classes.

Kilwaughter's gardener who was also called William, decided that he should contribute towards the celebrations and thought that a profusion of orange lilies on the dining table would help enrich the day. Having found some wonderful lilies, he then proceeded to enhance the arrangement by adding blue snap dragons and white candy-tuft. The arrangement that he ended up with was so appalling that Bessie, who was a real perfectionist, was dismayed, but she managed to control herself and it did not spoil the day completely.

Her days at Kilwaughter were filled almost to overflowing, but she and Galt also found time to continue their joint hobby of photography which they had started at *Meadowbank* and liked to process the photographs themselves. This was a hobby that she also enjoyed with her brother Edward.[81] She was also constantly organizing her staff, entertaining her many guests, fulfilling local engagements and frequently travelling to Belfast on shopping trips. The

---

[78] Bessie later became a member of the Ulster Women's Unionist Association. (Letter dated 18th August 1914 to mother).
[79] Manko, 1994, p.74.
[80] Luddy, 1995, p.239.
[81] A selection of Bessie's photographs is held in the University of Delaware.

odd trip to Dublin which Bessie loved, was also on the agenda. She adored the way the landed gentry in Dublin wore dowdy clothes and looked down on the, *"New rich"*. What also amazed her was the internal décor of their houses which comprised various different styles of furniture, covered in worn and moth-eaten upholstery.[82]

The Galt Smith's not only entertained, but they received many invitations too. Bessie soon became a popular guest and visited amongst others, *Redhall* at Ballycarry, the home of Mr. and Mrs. John Macaulay.[83] She was greatly looking forward to this and intended going to bed early to get some, *"Beauty sleep"* as she would have to look her best. As it turned out Bessie had a thoroughly good time at the Macaulay's home and thought the couple, *"Lovely people"* though the servants at Kilwaughter thought differently, since they were aware of Mrs. Macaulay's, *"Fearful temper"*.[84] [85]

By July 1892 Kilwaughter Castle's guest list was growing because that month saw the arrival of the Bancrofts, old friends from Delaware who were arriving on the second of the month, in time for breakfast. Bessie and her staff were still finalising some of the details of the Castle's interior – making lampshades, fixing the dressing rooms and adorning the four-poster bed with luxurious material. The pink and white washstands which they had brought from their old home, *Meadowbank* were used again in various rooms at Kilwaughter and the ever-resourceful Bessie also rejuvenated some old *Meadowbank* curtains for the dining room, by dyeing them red.[86]

Undoubtedly however, Bessie's favourite entertaining room in the Castle was the drawing room and she used every opportunity to promote it as, *"The very prettiest I have ever seen"* – from the polished inlaid floor to the Sheraton tables and the gilded old chairs from Dublin.[87] (These chairs had an interesting history and once belonged to a previous Duke of Leinster. Bessie had only managed to get four out of a set of eight, from an elderly lady, called Mrs.

---

[82] Letter, dated 1st June 1892 to Unknown.
[83] John Macaulay was a leading flour merchant, but moved to Cheltenham in 1900 where he died in 1912, aged 89 years. (Rutherford, 2004, p.46).
[84] Letter, dated 7th June 1892 to mother.
[85] Mrs. Macaulay was Jane Callwell Agnew. She died on 26th June 1899 aged 71 years and was buried in St. Cedma's Parish Church, Inver. (Rutherford, 2004, pps.45,46).
[86] Letter, dated 3rd June 1892 to mother.
[87] Letter, dated 1st July 1892 to mother.

Stephanie Geale whom she had purchased them from at a cost of £12. Mrs. Geale was a cousin of the then Duke of Leinster).

The room really shone for her on 19th July 1892, when she held what she considered to be, her first real dinner party. It was a circular room with three windows on one side of a fireplace and two doors, one leading into the library and other into the hall. The infamous yellow brocade curtains hung at the windows and the same material had been used to cover the upholstery on the gilded chairs. The mirrors were framed in green ribbons with bows on them and the mahogany tables were inlaid. Her favourite gilt chandelier with fifteen candles which, when lit, brought the room to life[88] and this was helped also by the light of some old lamps with finishing touches of vases of yellow flowers to match the rest of the décor. Bessie didn't forget the library that evening for it too, was lit with six lamps and filled with yet more flowers. The oak hall, main hall and billiard room all dazzled and fires were burning which gave off a very cosy glow. Bessie's attention to detail were well rewarded that night and she felt that the dinner party which was rounded off with a sing-song had been perfect.

The Countess Augusta Balzani was determined to be very much involved with the estate and the day after the party on 20th July 1892, a month before she and her husband visited, she sent her Trustee, Henry Thomas McNeale to Kilwaughter to talk to Bessie and Galt to find out how things were. Bessie thought McNeale, *"A very pleasant gentleman, about 45, who has lived mostly in Paris"*.[89] They seemingly got on well and the visit was a success.

The Balzanis visit Kilwaughter

The following month Augusta and Ugo paid the first of many visits to the Galt Smiths at Kilwaughter, accompanied by their two young daughters and their niece, Andreina who was looking after the children.[90] Andreina Alessandra Balzani had been educated for a time at Queen's School in Reading and was very close to Ugo and Augusta, calling them, *Mama and Papa*. She was 25 years old when she accompanied them to the Castle, with her young charges who were then just 9 and 10 years old. Andreina was a lively young

---

[88] Bessie later purchased another chandelier from the Duchess of Montpensier's Palace of St. Elmo, which she described, was in, *"Perfect order"*. (Letter summary, 17th December 1902).
[89] Letter, dated 23rd July 1892 to father.
[90] Manko, 1994, p.27.

woman considered beautiful and a talented musician. Her mother Maria Stefanoni was the great grand-daughter of Prince Lucien Boneparte a younger brother of Napoleon I. Maria married Count Annibale Balzani, but Andriena's parents had separated, one was living in Rome and the other in Naples, so she spent much of her time with Ugo and Augusta. Four years later she married Sir William Malcolm Hailey (later Lord Hailey), from Buckinghamshire, in Bombay, on 24th December, 1896.[91] Hailey was an Oxford scholar who spent most of his working life in Africa and India as a senior Civil Servant. (He was Governor of the Punjab, 1924-8 and of Agra and Oudh, 1928-34). The couple had two children, Alan and Gemma. Their daughter died in 1922 from appendicitis and their son Alan, who was in line to inherit his father's baronetcy which had been conferred in 1936, was killed in action in the Middle East on 1st February 1943. After this Andreina's health took a downturn and she suffered greatly from her loss. By this time her husband was very successful in his profession and was in line to be appointed Viceroy of India, but due to the ill-health of his wife could not take up the post.

Andreina died in 1939 after a heart attack.[92] [93] A funeral service was held for her in St. Paul's Church, Vicarage Gate, London on 2nd February 1939 and was attended by her many friends, amongst whom was Augusta's daughter Guendalina Valensin.[94] After the cremation her ashes were taken to Shimla in India for burial. Her obituary paid a glowing tribute to a woman who spent much of her time helping others and supporting her husband in his work. She was thought to have saved his life with her care and attention, after he caught a serious infection.[95] Lord Hailey died in 1969 in England and his ashes were taken to be buried in the family vault in Shimla, India. There is a memorial tablet to him in Westminster Abbey, London.

The Balzanis stayed for a week and the visit was one of the local highlights that summer and amongst other things they did, was attend a bazaar in Larne Town Hall which had been organised by the Larne and Kilwaughter Old Presbyterian Congregation. Augusta was asked to declare the bazaar open, but before doing so the Chairman, Mr. H.H. Smiley explained to the crowd some

---

[91] The Times, dated 1896.
[92] Kindly recounted by Alessandra Gatti.
[93] National Biography, 2004, Vol.24, pps.471-474.
[94] The Times, 1939.
[95] Ibid, 1939.

of Augusta's Agnew history, stating that she, *"Belonged to the oldest family in that neighbourhood"* and, *"Who had always taken a deep interest in the affairs of that congregation and had helped the Church in many ways"*.[96]

Although the couple had never lived at the Castle their popularity was such that the tenant farmers wished to acknowledge their visit and arranged for a reception for them to be held in Larne. Galt however, thought it more appropriate that the entertaining should be done at the Castle which was after all, their Irish home. On 12th August 1892, ninety-two of the 370 farmers from Kilwaughter were presented to the Balzanis. The Countess wore a dress in grey brocade, which, according to Bessie matched her hair.[97] Speeches were made to welcome the couple and Augusta responded in kind, speaking emotionally which brought tears to many eyes. She told them that she regretted that it was not possible for her and Ugo to live at Kilwaughter. At the end a whiskey toast was proposed and a photograph taken to celebrate the occasion and to record their visit.

The taking of the photograph was quite an ordeal for the tenant farmers, some of whom knew nothing about photography. Most of them were disappointed with the whole procedure since they believed that they would be able to go away with a photograph to show their families. One even said to Bessie, *"Mistress dear, it's the first time I ever had me picture took, what wull it be loike? (sic)*. *"Ah"*, said Bessie, *"You don't know how good looking you are, until you see that picture"*.[98] It was easy to see from her response, just how well Bessie related to people and why she was so popular. Her good humour was innate.

Augusta conscious that the Castle had not been lived in for forty years and of being an absentee landlord, took time to talk to the farmers to see if anything further could be done to help them, but she need not have worried because all seemed happy and content.[99] By all accounts the reception was a great success. Before leaving Ireland for their home in Italy, the Balzanis visited their friends, the Macauleys at *Redhall*. Bessie, as already mentioned, knew the Macaulays and actually thought that Mrs. Macauley (Jane Callwell Agnew) was Augusta's cousin[100], but in fact she was not. Jane's father

---

[96] Belfast News Letter, 1893.
[97] Letter, dated 13th August 1892 to father.
[98] Ibid.
[99] Manko, 1994, p.27.
[100] Letter, dated 7th June 1892 to mother.

Patrick[101] had been a cousin of Ellen Agnew, Augusta's great grandmother, but the family had continued to maintain the contact with the Macauleys years later, as indeed, they had done many times before as we have seen, with other extended members of the family.

The Countess Balzani was a clever woman who spoke six languages and although her husband was also a linguist (he spoke five languages), she translated many of the books that he wrote into English, for him.[102] She was also popular in Ireland and showed concern for her tenants. For the next three years until her early death, she and Ugo visited Kilwaughter regularly each summer to see how the estate was progressing and to iron out any problems. They did not always stay at the Castle though, but at one of the local hotels in Larne, presumably because they did not want to impose unduly, on the Galt Smith's. One of Augusta's main concerns was for the widows of the parish because she wished to build them each a home. She involved Bessie in the task of establishing each widow's circumstances to see what could be done to help.[103] Bessie liked the Countess a great deal and described her as, *"A charming woman, very tall and thin in appearance"*.[104]

The Countess Balzani Dies

By now the couple were again living in Rome because Ugo had been appointed historian to King Umberto I and would soon become President of the Government Libraries there (1901-1907).[105] [106] He knew the King and his wife Queen Margherita well and thought her a brilliant woman who was an avid reader. Bessie described Ugo as, *"Fair, talkative and a perfect gentleman in his manners. Speaks English very well, is a friend of Gladstone[107], though not approving his politics."* [108] They had moved house several times in the city, but by 1896 had

---

[101] Kindly recounted by Paul Robinson, January, 2005.
[102] Agnew, M.V., p.276.
[103] Manko, 1994, p.33.
[104] Letter, dated 10th August 1892 to mother.
[105] Manko, 1994, p.27.
[106] Direttori della Bibliotecca Vallicelliana di Roma.
[107] The Liberal Prime Minister of Britain. Gladstone was also known to Sir Andrew Agnew of Lochnaw, the 7th Baronet whom he wrote to in 1849, supporting Sir Andrew's stance on the Sunday Observance question. (National Archives of Scotland, GD154-921).
[108] Letter, dated 10th August 1892 to mother.

settled at 5 Via Vicenza in the district of Termini.[109] Their magnificent patrician villa with internal marble columns still stands, but is now a hotel.[110] Sadly Augusta died on 3rd July 1895 in Rome, aged 48 years, after having been ill for several months.[111] She left her daughters without their mother at the ages of 12 and 13, a similar situation to that which she herself had faced as a young child of 10.

Although born in Cork and the owner of an Irish estate, Augusta had never lived in the Castle, but nonetheless she seemed to have made her mark in the area. She took responsibility as far as she could for her tenants and in Bessie and Galt seemed to have found a couple who assumed the further pastoral care of those tenants. She was popular with the local people as was seen by various receptions held for her and was considered to be a charming and intelligent woman by Bessie. Neither was she forgotten in her adopted country of Italy, where she was also known for her good works. When she died a dispensary for sick children was named the, *Dispensario Augusta Balzani* in her honour.[112] The Countess Balzani was buried in the fascinating, but overcrowded Cimitero Acattolico, widely known as the Protestant Cemetery, in the Testaccio district of Rome.[113] Regretfully there is no indication on the gravestone, of her distinctive Irish background. Her marriage to Ugo had been a blissfully happy one and he was distraught for a lengthy period after her death.

The Countess Balzani's responsibility for the Castle was now at an end, but her husband wished his wife to be commemorated and decided to do so, by having a small school built for the local children in her honour. On 2nd May 1896 he bought back part of a lease of some land (which was adjacent to the road and just a short distance from the Castle), from one of the farmers to build the school.[114] The school for both boys and girls, became known as, *The Countess Balzani Memorial School*. In 1931 it was purchased by Antrim County Council and maintained and used as a school until the summer term, June

---

[109] North-Eastern Education Board, Indenture, dated 2nd May 1896.
[110] The Hotel Villa Delle Rose, Rome.
[111] Obituary of Countess Balzani, The Times, dated 12th July 1895, p.10.
[112] The Belfast Newsletter, 1896.
[113] Cimitero Acattolico di Roma, Stone Number 1532.
[114] North-Eastern Education Board, Indenture, dated 2nd May 1896.

1983 when it closed. The building has since been converted into two private dwellings, but the Agnew/Balzani plaque on the wall can still be seen.

Count Balzani and his Daughters

The Castle and estate were held in trust by Ugo for his two daughters, Guendalina and Nora.[115] Two Trustees were nominated, William Osborne Christmas and Archibald Constable. It was fortunate that the Galt Smith's had leased the property for so long because with his wife's death, Ugo must have lost much of his enthusiasm for it.

In 1905 a happier statement was made by Ugo who announced the betrothal of his eldest daughter Guendalina to Signor Guido David Valensin. The couple were married in Rome on 11th June 1905 when Guendalina was 23 years old. Her husband Guido was born in Florence on 5th July 1877 and was five years older than his wife.[116] This marriage introduced yet again, another remarkable international link to Kilwaughter's already colourful past.

Guido was the son of Emma Lumbroso and her late husband Giorgio Valensin, an esteemed and well-known, composer of music, in particular opera. Guido had a sister Maria Luisa who married Ferdinando Balbo di Vinadio and they had two sons. She died in 1977. Guido's mother, the daughter of Grasiadio Lumbroso, was born in Alexandria, Egypt. At the time of her son's marriage she had re-married to Count Carlo Canevaro who was born in Lima, Peru and the son of the late Count Guiseppe Canevaro.[117] The Canevaro's had been a family of some importance and wealth. Guiseppe, who was also the Duke of Zoagli, married Luisa Ridolfi, the first of his two wives.[118] In 1900 he purchased an enchanting palazzo in Florence which became known as the *Palazzo Canavaro*. The building had been constructed during the previous century by the architect Guiseppe Poggi. It comprised some magnificent features including a ballroom with elaborate frescoes, an imposing great staircase and impressive carved doors. There had been several previous owners of the palazzo before Guiseppi purchased it and at one stage from 1865 to 1870, it had been used as the French Embassy. Between the two world wars it became renowned for the extravagant entertaining of various

---

[115] PRONI, D971/9/1.
[116] Istituto Araldico Coccia, Florence, 2003.
[117] PRONI, D971/9/1.
[118] He later married Dianora Guicciardini.

royal princes and other distinguished people. In 1947 Consul Walter W. Orebaugh purchased the building on behalf of the US Government. Since then the building has been used as the US Consular Office in Florence.[119]

Although Ugo held the Kilwaughter estate in trust, when Guendalina married, she was able to withdraw some revenue from this to the value of £10,000 as part of her dowry. Her father also arranged for her to have an annual contribution of £400. The marriage settlement stated that as well as Guendalina's contribution, the properties owned by her husband Guido would also form part of the settlement. Added to that he would receive a yearly income through various Italian bonds, from his mother and stepfather.[120]

Guendalina and Guido begin Married Life

The couple began their married life living with Guido's mother and her husband at their home in Tredozio, just outside Florence[121] and four years later Guendalina gave birth to a daughter Giorgia, in Rome on 6th June 1909. The family moved constantly between Rome and Florence.[122] Guido, a law graduate, was a professor of geography and author, but owing to his Jewish faith he was forced to relinquish his position during the second World War, this in spite of him having converted to Catholicism previously.[123] He died in Trevozzo in the Province of Piacenza on 18th February 1947, aged 70. His wife survived him for ten years, but died in Florence on 15th January 1957, aged 75.[124] Their daughter Giorgia moved to Naples on 18th April 1964 where she worked for NATO.[125] Giorgia like the rest of her family was a clever linguist (including Chinese) and it is thought she worked as an interpreter there. She remained unmarried and died in 1969.[126] She was buried with her parents in the cemetery in Settignano close to Florence.

---

[119] Official USA Embassy, Florence, 2003.
[120] PRONI, D971/9/1.
[121] Via Marsilio Ficino, No. 3.
[122] Istituto Araldico Coccia, Florence, 2004.
[123] Kindly recounted by Lorenza Gatti Balzani.
[124] Istituto Araldico Coccia, Florence, 2003.
[125] Kindly recounted by members of the Balzani family.
[126] Istituto Araldico Coccia, Florence, 2004.

Nora becomes sole Heiress

With the death of Guendalina and her daughter Giorgia, Nora, Ugo's other daughter, now became sole heiress of Kilwaughter Castle. According to a present member of the Balzani family who met her, she was an elegant, pretty woman, dressed in silk and her apartment reflected her many travels.[127] Nora led an interesting and exciting life mixing with the nobility and a story is told of her having driven by car with Prince Scipione Borghese from Paris to Pechino in 1905.[128] [129] She was a friend of the Prince's wife, Princess Anna Maria Borghese who sadly drowned in Lake Garda in 1927.[130] She was also a member of the Board of the Italian Save the Children Fund and presented a paper, *"Training for Social Work in Italy"*, at an International Conference of Social Work in the early 1900's. (It is more than likely that this took place at the John Hopkins University International Centre in Bologna, founded by Walter W. Orebaugh, the American Consul who purchased Palazzo Canevaro in Florence from Count Giuseppe Canevaro many years later). In this, Nora described the work involved in setting up proper institutions for the training of social workers as this was yet to be fully addressed in Italy.[131] She became the President of the Italian Red Cross and helped as a translator in the British Embassy.[132] Nora never married and died on 17th November 1975. She was buried with her parents in Rome.

At the time of Guendalina's marriage, Ugo had moved house yet again from his large Italian villa in Termini, to Via Virginio Orsini, No. 12. He was then 58 years old and had been a widower 10 years. After his wife's death he continued to work and keep busy, but the black edging on his calling cards reflected his sad circumstances. Three years later he returned once more to England and lived at 58 South Hill Park, Hampstead, but by 1902 he was again in Rome and was occupied with the forthcoming International History Congress which was to take place there the following spring.

---

[127] Kindly recounted by Alessandra Gatti.
[128] Ibid
[129] Two years later Prince Borghese was to win the famous Peking to Paris automobile race.
[130] Kindly recounted by Lorenza Gatti Balzani.
[131] The Alan Mason Chesney Medical Archives, 2004.
[132] Kindly recounted by Alessandra Gatti.

The Congress was to be opened by the King on 2nd April 1903. Ugo wishing his friend Browning to come wrote to him, "France and Germany will be largely represented and we should like that England, should not remain behind in these meetings of historians. You must be our Whip for Cambridge."[133] Ugo was heavily involved in the arrangements for the Congress and immediately after Christmas he wrote back again to his friend asking for the names of various dignitaries who should be invited – members of the Royal Historical Society; the vice-chancellor of Cambridge University (the vice-chancellor of Oxford University had already indicated his acceptance); representatives from Cambridge University library and the Bodleian. Things though were not as straight forward in Rome with the internal arrangements because the Government could not quite make up its mind as to who should attend. "I believe it is a thing that must be left to our Foreign Office. Our present Ministro Degli Esteri is rather a touchy gentleman and we must keep him in a good temper as he is helping us in many ways".[134] Ugo obviously did not want to disturb the peace.

The organisation of the Congress was substantial because by February the following year, there were already one thousand delegates registered and they were to be welcomed by Prince Prospero Colonna. With so many people coming to Rome and with the Emperors of Russia (Nicholas II) and Germany (Wilhelm II) visiting the city immediately after Easter, Ugo was very worried about accommodation for his English friends. In fact such was his conscientious nature that he decided to take matters into his own hands and secured rooms for them in the home of his daughter's niece.[135] There was no further reference made in his later correspondence with Browning as to how the Congress was received. In late summer that year Ugo made his last visit to Kilwaughter Castle.

In 1912 Ugo contacted his old friend again to tell him, *"I was called suddenly to Naples by the death of a dear brother of mine, an event which has greatly saddened me"*. In the same letter however, he berated the expansionist factions in Italian politics. *"What is sad, is the amount of mischief that these people make. To estrange England and Italy from each other is a curse and they do all in their power to reach that end. They call themselves peaceful and they do all they can to bring about a position which*

---

[133] King's College Library, OB/1/84/A. Letter, dated 18th December 1902.
[134] Ibid. Letter, dated 30th December 1902.
[135] Ibid. Letter, dated 26th March 1903.

would lead Europe to war".¹³⁶ Ugo's prophecy was quite profound. By then he was staying a month with his daughter Guendalina at her home in Tredozia, just outside Florence, which she normally occupied during the summer. Ugo moved house once more and was now residing at 9 Via Po, Rome, with his other daughter Nora.

One year later he was still keeping up his correspondence with Browning who visited Rome frequently and would spend time with his friend over lunch or dinner discussing the various books that Browning was writing. Three years after, Ugo died in Rome, on 27th November 1916 aged 69 years of age and was buried there alongside his wife. Their large headstone is aptly divided in two with a biblical verse carved in English under Augusta's name and the same in Italian for Ugo. There were local Irish condolences and a letter was written to Nora Balzani by the Minister of the congregation of Larne and Kilwaughter church conveying sympathy to her and her sister on the death of their father who was held, *"In the highest esteem in our town and neighbourhood and indeed wherever he was known.* Interestingly the letter makes reference to his late wife's, *Old Irish family whose name is recorded with honour in ancient Irish Literature"*. ¹³⁷ A possible reference to the original bardic family of Ó Gnímh, still remembered by the local people.

---

¹³⁶ Letter, dated 23rd September 1912.
¹³⁷ Letter dated March, 1916.

Chapter 8

The Galt Smiths Entertain

Long before Augusta's death, the autumn of 1892 and the end of the Galt Smith's first year living in the Castle, was fast approaching. The estate had taken on a new and different appearance and Bessie thought it, *"Looking just lovely now. I never saw a lovelier place. The hay is all in which leaves the place so green and beautiful"*.[1] The Galt Smiths had kept up a busy pace all year and there had not been one minute spare, but Bessie had always found time for one of her favourite hobbies - the entertaining of guests at Kilwaughter which she relished. She loved to gossip with them and to see what the people were wearing and talking about and was always staggered in disbelief by the amount of jewellery and diamonds that some of the women wore to her dinner parties and which sparkled around the room in the candlelight. Her husband though, whilst humouring Bessie, was more concerned with running the estate and as the refurbishment of the Castle interior was progressing satisfactorily, his thoughts turned to the outside fabric and he began by bringing the stables up-to-date, the floors of which were Staffordshire brick. He enlisted the help of Musgrave's in Belfast to make all the iron fittings and Bessie described Musgrave's as the, *"Greatest stable fitters in the world"*. Quite a high accolade, but she was not far wrong because their clientele included the Prince of Wales, the Duchess Medina-Celi of Spain and Emperor Franz Joseph of Austria – and they were just the customers that she knew about.[2]

The autumn brought fine weather for Bessie and Galt to enjoy, but it was tempered by the scare of cholera which had swept along a few of the coastal

---

[1] Letter dated 10th August 1892 to mother.
[2] Letter, dated 3rd September 1892 to father.

towns. It didn't seem to worry Bessie unduly as she rationalised that it really only affected the immigrants, such as the Russian Jews and Germans that had arrived in Ireland. Invitations continued to arrive for the couple and one day they made the journey to Garron Tower, the Castle home of Lord Herbert Vane-Tempest. Bessie of course, was in her element to see the inside of yet another magnificent house. When they arrived, they were shown over the building by Mrs. Todd who had been the housekeeper for many years. There were 150 beds for guests and whilst this impressed Bessie, it was nothing compared to what she saw next - a substantial supply of silver and gold plate. Some of the gold cups were two feet high and were studded with amethysts, rubies and aquamarines. Then there were bowls made of gold which had been presented by the Shah of Persia and glasses that were decorated with emeralds and rubies; cameos too, which had been given by the Emperor of Russia to the Marchioness of Londonderry, Lord Herbert's grandmother. After seeing all this, Bessie's main concern, was that the only security in the house was elderly Mrs. Todd and two maid servants.[3]

As the end of September drew near, the couple had to begin preparations for taking care of the Castle whilst they were in America over the rest of the autumn and the winter. They were due to sail on 12th October 1892 and so as usual Bessie began planning what to do. She decided that she would take charge of packing up the house on this occasion herself, as it was the first time that it was being done. That way her housekeeper Mrs. Greer would know what to do in the consecutive years. Fires were to be kept lit to keep away the damp and a seamstress was required to come and sew covers for all the furniture and carpets. Bessie was insistent on that because the *'soft'* coal made so much dust. The only carpet that she wanted lifted was the stair carpet.[4]

The Servants

At the same time some of the servants were also going with Bessie – Mrs. Wheeler, Boyd and Rose - so they too, were engaged in their own packing. The couple had thirteen servants and around twelve grooms and gardeners, then of course there was Fricker the game-keeper and Sams the Coachman. Their days were very regimented – dusting the main rooms by 6.30 a.m. before

---

[3] Letter, dated 7th September 1892 to Edith.
[4] Letter, dated 17th September 1892 to Edward.

having their breakfast at 8.00 a.m. Then cleaning the library and oak hall which would have to be done before the Galt Smiths descended for their breakfast at 9.00 a.m. For the next hour or so, the two senior maids would wait on people, fetching hot water, running baths and bringing tea.[5]

A new member of staff had joined them in June that year as John the Footman had left. His name was McCormick and he was about thirty years old. Galt had known McCormick for years and thought very highly of him and he and their butler Boyd had known each other too, since childhood and got along very well together. McCormick was also a butler, but as there was no vacancy at Kilwaughter, for that position, at the time, he agreed to come as, *Second man*. He was very keen to move to America to try his luck and thought that by working in Kilwaughter for an American Mistress, his chances for emigrating would be much improved. As it turned out he was right because Bessie believed that he would make an excellent butler for her parents at *Rockwood*. She liked him and thought him, *"Quiet* and *Nice looking"'* and as he liked the countryside, that made him popular with Bessie. There was an extra bonus too, because he was placid and never complained and what was even more important, he never lost his temper with Boyd who, as the head butler, was a hard taskmaster with a fiery temper.

Bessie thought the world of Boyd[6] and described him as, *perfect*, but the servants were not quite of the same opinion. They had to work quickly for him and not make any noise and his standards were high. Nonetheless, Bessie believed that if McCormick could work with Boyd all summer without a cross word then he was definitely worth hiring as a butler. She arranged with her parents that he would be paid $25 per month and that he would have a free passage across the Atlantic. He decided to leave his family behind until he was sure that this new life would work out. Fortunately it did and his wife and two children followed him after a year. He remained at *Rockwood* until the 1920's by which time he was old and infirm and couldn't do any heavy work. His son helped him and eventually took over his father's position.[7]

Another employee, Mrs. Brennan lived in a little grey stone gate lodge at the rear of the Castle still in existence. She had the key to the gates and

---

[5] Manko, 1994, p.43.
[6] Bessie sent Boyd to New York to learn first hand from the manufacturer, how to maintain the new boiler at the Castle. (Letter summary, 14th June 1893).
[7] Letter summary, 1st October 1922.

absolutely no-one could get in without her say-so. Bessie didn't mind this because the result meant that they were not bothered with trespassers.[8] [9]

Life continues at Kilwaughter for the Galt Smiths

The long journey back to Ireland in 1893 was uneventful. Bessie was thankfully, not seasick, but kept to her room nonetheless, reading or sleeping whilst her servants entertained themselves with the servants of the Vanderbilts. They all had a table together, in the dining room and Boyd the, *"Life and soul of the party"*, kept the Vanderbilt's German maid amused.[10] That same year, just two years after Bessie and Galt had signed the lease for the Castle, Gladstone introduced a second Home Rule Bill for Ireland. One wonders what Bessie must have thought of her newly adopted country that was continually at war with itself. The in-fighting between Protestants and Catholics had continued on and off through the centuries since Sir Patrick Agnew had first arrived at Kilwaughter and Bessie must have thought how difficult it was to understand the nature of their grievances. She had much to learn about the culture and traditions of this foreign land, but was not undaunted by any of it and continued to absorb herself in the Irish way of life, mixing with the most wealthy people she could find.

There were various wives of MP's, Lady McCalmont, Lady Adair and Lady Chichester; who were just some of the wealthy people that frequented Kilwaughter Castle and much to Bessie's delight, all thought her pride and joy, the round drawing room, delightful. The decorating though, was still taking time, but Bessie didn't mind too much as the decorators were not being paid hourly. She always kept a shrewd eye on the family budget and this was particularly brought home to her as her friends the Magheramornes, had bankrupted themselves, having lost a huge racing debt ($3,000,000). They had had to shut their house and get rid of their staff.[11] This would have appalled Bessie and it is hard to imagine it happening to her since she was in such control where possible, over all areas of her life.

---

[8] Letter, dated 16th August 1892 to Edith.
[9] Some of the Castle Gates were later given for use to a B&B establishment in exchange for a pony. Kindly recounted by the late Frank Ferguson, July 2002.
[10] Letter summary, 8th June 1893.
[11] Letter summary, 14th June 1893.

The couple enjoyed picnics and trips around the countryside and Bessie helped Galt at times around the estate, but they had other responsibilities too, to care for their tenant farmers and the widows. The couple took their pastoral duty seriously and visited those in need. Bessie gave away clothes and presents and attended country bazaars, though was never very keen to purchase anything unless she had to, since she felt that her style was somewhat more sophisticated.[12] On 24th July, 1893, the couple invited 80 children from the local school to visit the Castle and enjoy themselves playing in the grounds. They sailed in the lake, played football and tug-of-war. During the day one of the boys became ill and Galt taking pity on him, thought that he was doing the right thing by helping him. It turned out though that the boy had made himself ill from smoking. Galt felt foolish and embarrassed and it didn't help that the other children began to make fun of him.[13] It didn't help either, that various other guests were also there, including his uncle George Kennedy Smith and the local rector of the parish, Mr. Pheonix.[14] At the end of the day Bessie made them sing the National Anthem, at the same time commenting," *No Home-Rulers or Fenians allowed here!*" Giving no thoughts obviously to her biased views. (A few years later she was to embarrass herself by showing her ignorance when she wore a green outfit to the 12th July celebration of the Battle of the Boyne. She had to hurriedly redress the balance by pinning a bunch of orange lilies on to it).[15]

In July Bessie was busy as usual being entertained – by the Wards at Bangor Castle. She reported everything that happened in her letters home, from the food served to the clothes worn by all. She was also waiting for her Steinway piano to arrive from her New York home. This was just one of the many pianos which were dotted around the house.[16] Galt celebrated his birthday later that month and received a Landseer engraving that had once belonged to his mother who died in America. This engraving had been rescued from her personal affects before the rest was auctioned and both Bessie and Galt

---

[12] Manko, 1994, p.34.
[13] Letter summary, 25th July 1893.
[14] The Belfast Newsletter, 1893.
[15] Letter summary, 15th July 1896.
[16] Ibid, 14th July 1893.

regretted not being at the auction where they could have tried to salvage more of his mother's possessions.[17]

Public Duty and more Travels

At the beginning of August a small fire broke out in the basement of the Castle, but fortunately Mrs. Green discovered it before it had taken hold. A couch had caught fire and had spread to some linens which were damaged, but the oil in the couch feathers had caused the worst damage as it had smeared itself all over the room, which meant that much cleaning was needed.[18] During that month Galt gave his first public address in Larne for the benefit of Kilwaughter church. He was responsible for the church and decided that on the first Sunday of every month, the collection would go to the organist, Mrs. Besant, whose husband a sea captain was missing. He had sailed for China three days after their marriage and never returned. Although Bessie thought Mrs. Besant played the organ badly, the poor woman needed the money.[19]

In October she was proud to be asked to open a bazaar at the Cliftonville Presbyterian Church, but did not want to speak and only wanted to declare it open. She also did not take offence when the Chairman, Dr. King Kerr, referred to Galt as her, *"Better half"* – and then went on to expound on how great a debt was owned by America to Ireland because of the, *"Shiploads of stalwart men and women who had left Ireland's shores and taken up their homes in the great Western land"*.[20]

The following year went by like the others – continued talk about Kilwaughter's refurbishment. The ceiling in the dining room was of particular interest as it had cut out shields of oak leaves and fleur-de-lis. Then there was the usual travel – to London where Bessie had to hire a Victoria carriage to be allowed into the park since common carriages were not permitted. (Her financial outlay was rewarded since she saw the Princess of Wales).[21] This was followed by trips to Paris and Scotland. She also involved herself in the day-to-day activities of family life at *Rockwood* – the vast distance meant nothing to

---

[17] Ibid, 29th July 1893.
[18] Ibid, 2nd August 1893.
[19] Ibid, 6th September, 1893.
[20] Letter summary, 25th October 1893 (newspaper cutting).
[21] Ibid, 4th August 1894.

her as she could control family affairs by letter from afar. She approved of her young brother Edward being punished for his nail biting and was keen to learn how he was progressing with his swimming lessons. She also suggested that he should practise piano daily for one hour. Although she was quick to give her disapproval of the new décor in *Rockwood's* music room and described the fringing there in black and gold as, *"Glaring"*, she offered suggestions for the carpet and how it, the wallpaper and fringing should all match.

Bessie wasn't slow to judge people either and was very open with her views. She described her grandmother as, *"Queer"* and believed that because of this, it was easy to understand the behaviour of her father and sister Edith. [22]

In August that year, two of Galt's eleven horses that he had entered at the Larne Horse show, came first and another two were runners up. At the same time he was one of the Larne Horse Show Society's vice-presidents. The others were Lord Magheramorne, Sir Daniel Dixon, Captain McCalmont and George McFerran.[23] (Their gardener won first prize five times over for his vegetables[24]). Horses were important to Galt and he regularly entered them in the Dublin and Larne horse shows and Bessie was to keep this up, even after his death. A year later Galt received another accolade, because in October he was made a Justice of the Peace. The Warrant arrived on a large piece of parchment stamped with the Queen's seal in green wax.[25] Bessie would have been inordinately proud of him for it also raised her standing even higher in the community and would have kept her aligned with her important friends who may have had the honour already. For her birthday that year, Galt also bought her a ring. She already had some turquoise stones and he had arranged for these to be set into the ring with diamonds added on either side. Bessie was pleased with it.

Summer Return to Kilwaughter

In June 1895, the couple once more, returned for the summer to Kilwaughter. This time Bessie brought her young brother Edward with her. Edward enjoyed the journey onboard ship, but when he got bored and lonely, and wanted to sleep on the floor of Bessie's room, he discovered that Galt could

---

[22] Ibid, 16th September 1894.
[23] Belfast Newsletter, 1894.
[24] Letter summary, 4th August 1894.
[25] Ibid, 4th October 1895.

be a somewhat authoritarian figure and he wasn't allowed. On arrival at Kilwaughter though, he settled down quickly and enjoyed playing in the vast open spaces around the estate with the animals. He did incur Bessie's wrath when he thought that she should pay for everything he wanted, even though he had been allotted his own money, but he quickly learnt on that score, that it wouldn't happen. He celebrated his eleventh birthday in Ireland and was determined not to miss a moment because he rose that day very early at 3.00 a.m., washed and dressed himself and then decided to waken everyone else in the house by banging on a gong. Edward was lucky that day since the sleepy occupants including Galt, decided to humour him and gave him his presents of pictures of Kilwaughter and later there were fireworks.

At the end of the following month it was Galt's turn to have a birthday and this time Bessie presented him with a silver knife tray. Edward was still with her, teasing Florence and being frequently chastised for it. When things got so bad he would take himself down to the lake and attempt to kill the larger rats with his slingshot,[26] but when Galt's son Kennedy arrived, he had a new playmate to occupy his time. Edward continued to stay at Kilwaughter at various times and Bessie took him with her on her many travels. She looked after him very well and engaged tutors to educate him.

Bessie had opinions on everything, including child-rearing. She and Galt never had children of their own, but that did not stop Bessie giving advice on various aspects concerning their upbringing. She must have felt that her experience with Galt's children and her much younger brother helped her understand their development. Her parents must have regarded her as sensible enough to look after their son for such long periods and Edward was bound to have seen his sister as a substitute mother because the bond between them was strong and maternal. She admonished her parents at one stage for, "*Ordering*" Edward around and told them firmly that now he was getting older, they would have to alter their parenting skills to match that.[27] Child-rearing experts would no doubt, have regarded Bessie's advice as visionary in its day. In later years Edward became a great source of comfort to Bessie after Galt's death and she didn't hesitate to claim that she found her young brother,

---

[26] Letter summary, 13th August 1895.
[27] Ibid, 23rd August 1896.

"Courteous and companionable". Unlike Kennedy whom she regarded as the opposite.

The rest of the year continued in the normal way – entertaining frequent visitors and looking after the children. In September it was time for Edward to return home to *Rockwood*. He had become accustomed to living with his sister and was sad to leave, but he gave presents to all, buying them with his own money.[28] Before Bessie left Ireland that year she began a Benevolent Society which meant that she started making clothes for the poor. She was able to purchase the material at wholesale prices which kept the clothing cheap and Galt offered to look after the financial side of the Society for the first year.[29] Bessie had a good heart and was clever at sourcing out the needs required within her community.

Bessie's Brother Edward Visits

The following year in June, Edward was back with Bessie and Galt at Kilwaughter once more. Yet again the main focus was his birthday and this time he had a midnight game of hide and seek throughout the Castle. He was becoming much more sensible with his money but ran into some difficulty when he underestimated the price of developing some photographs, however, he was able to redress this and save some money by not riding his pony for two weeks.[30] In July Galt bought both him and Kennedy, a small boat that they could have on the lake. This gave Bessie some peace and quiet and she used the time to catalogue her many books. She and Galt were avid readers and had around 3,000 books, including some recent collections by Robert Louis Stevenson and Charles Dickens.[31]

In all Bessie's letter writing she never gave up control of what was happening at *Rockwood* and the family obliged her by including her in their plans. She was charismatic and gave the impression of having knowledge and experience, so it was easy to see how they came to depend on her. Bessie was also quite brave and lanced an abscess on her tooth herself, with a needle,

---

[28] Ibid, 18th September 1895.
[29] Ibid, 12th October 1895.
[30] Ibid, 15th July 1896.
[31] Letter summary, 26th July 1896.

without giving much thought to it, but unfortunately this did not stop later attacks of toothache.[32]

In the middle of October Bessie's grandmother died suddenly and although Bessie observed mourning rituals from Ireland, she was the ever resourceful and practical woman and saw the death more as a closure of a life that had been, *"So useful and so honoured"*. Edward had returned to *Rockwood* in time to see his grandmother before her death and this gave Bessie the opportunity to talk to him about mortality and thoughtfully to remind him to be sensitive to his parents' loss at the time.[33]

Before returning to America that year Bessie managed to fit in some more philanthropy as she made red flannel jackets for patients at one of the hospitals in Belfast. She cut the patterns and arranged for some women in Larne to stitch the garments. Galt was also involved in this as he agreed to pay the ladies for their work.[34] In 1897 he had been invited to a meeting in connection with the leaving arrangements of two royal visitors, the Duke and Duchess of York who were departing Ireland from Larne Harbour. After some deliberations it was decided to illuminate the royal party's departure and Messrs. Clark and Smiley agreed to adorn their yachts and escort the royal party for some distance.[35] Bessie must have been elated that her husband was involved in such a prestigious committee, but Galt was active in many local pursuits including the Masonic Order. He was also an *Orangeman*, belonging to a local lodge, LOL No.22 Larne.[36]

In 1897 Galt and Bessie were still enjoying their honeymoon period, going for scenic drives in the Irish countryside and Galt was buying and selling horses and appeared, *"Jubilant"*. They attended a Ball in Belfast which was given by Col. Williams and the officers of the North Staffordshire Regiment. The room was decorated appropriately with red, white and blue and there were huge pyramids of ice covered with flowers and vines, which was meant to, cool the atmosphere. All this impressed Bessie and she enthused about the menu and the uniforms the soldiers wore, some of the men having come from Dublin. She did notice that the men were much better looking than the

---

[32] Ibid, 2nd October 1896.
[33] Ibid, 25th October 1896.
[34] Ibid, 28th October 1896.
[35] Belfast News Letter, 1897.
[36] Ibid. 1899.

women, whether that meant in their dress or otherwise is not clear, but Bessie wore her black dress embroidered in silver.[37]

John Galt Smith Dies

The intervening years from Augusta's death had brought changes to the Balzani family, but the estate at Kilwaughter had still flourished under the watchful eyes of Bessie and Galt. What had begun however, as a wonderful social adventure for both of them, was brought suddenly to an end in 1899. Whilst at their home in New York, where they continued to spend every autumn and winter, Galt suddenly became ill and died on 26th April of that year, from peritonitis. He was buried in the Brandywine Cemetery at Wilmington. Three months later Bessie made, what must have been a very painful journey for her, back to her Irish home at Kilwaughter. She was accompanied on the, *Lucarnia,* by her father, Kennedy, Cousin Hattie and her brother Edward. Bessie was heartbroken, but continued to keep up her correspondence with her family at *Rockwood,* only now she wrote on mourning stationery and continued to do so for the next seven years.

The marriage seemed a happy one and the couple worked well together with Bessie in charge of the inside of the Castle and Galt involved in the farm, animals and grounds. At one stage though, she did complain that Galt was, *"Getting hard to manage".* He wasn't always compliant to her needs and when Bessie wanted to visit the Chicago World Fair several years before he died, Galt refused to accompany her. It would seem that her father was financing her trip and this upset Galt. Whilst she was writing a letter home, he intervened and penned his own comment in it. *"My reason for declining to send Bessie, is I quite expect you to send us both, just for once let us see a little of your generosity, it would do me good".* [38] This was a rather terse sentence with a very clear meaning and one wonders what his in-laws thought of it and also why he wrote it? It is surprising that Bessie allowed him to interject in this way, which permits us to think that she was slightly more wary and respectful of Galt than she appeared in public. Bessie was very aware of her constant use of *I* and *My* and she mentioned it in a letter to her sister Edith, that she really should say, *Our* more.

---

[37] Letter, dated 2nd July 1897 to father.
[38] Letter summary, 10th October 1893.

[39] Nevertheless, she embraced Galt's culture and made a comfortable home for him. She had also taken on the management of his two children and since Bessie had no children of her own to draw experience from, this must have been difficult at times. Galt's obituary in the Northern Whig described him in glowing terms. It spoke of his many mercantile connections and of him owning a, *"Gigantic"* establishment in New York which dealt with a variety of trades in the dry goods line; that he was a member of the Masonic Order and was the Commissioner of the Peace for County Antrim.[40] Probate was granted to Bessie.

Bessie's Relationship with her Step-Children

Bessie struggled with Florence's behaviour and thought her a, *"Compulsive liar"*. She was often unwell and it would appear that Bessie believed that her illnesses were mostly imaginary though the girl suffered from seizures which were obviously real enough. Bessie also got fed-up with Florence's banter and would complain about her in her letters home.[41] At one stage she stated that Florence's, *"Mission on earth, tis to furnish excitement for the household"*. This probably came about because she had spent too long sitting on a chamber pot. It had broken beneath her and had cut her enough to require stitches.[42] Earlier before her father's death, she had presented them with another problem. Sams had knocked down a little boy whilst driving the cart on 9th August 1898. Unfortunately the front wheel of the cart had gone over his back, which must have been very painful but the child was soon carried to Mrs. Rea's boarding house nearby and Dr. McNinch and his assistant Adrian were fetched. As he appeared to suffer no ill effects, the doctor declared him fine. Sams took him home afterwards, but Florence proceeded to tell his mother exactly what happened, even though she had been asked not to and this left Bessie and Galt worried that a lawsuit would now ensue.[43] The event was reported in the local newspaper, so it would have made no difference to poor Florence (who no doubt, received a good telling off), whether or not she had kept quiet.[44]

---

[39] Ibid, 11th August 1894.
[40] Northern Whig, 1899.
[41] Letter summary, 20th July 1900.
[42] Ibid, 22nd July 1893.
[43] Letter summary, 2nd August 1893.
[44] Belfast News Letter, 1898.

Later on in 1904 she suffered from a serious eye condition that necessitated surgery which was successful.[45]

Sadly the relationship between both women never improved. Bessie may have seen Florence in competition with herself for Galt's affections, but it must have been rather sad for poor Florence to first, lose her mother at such a tender age and then have a difficult relationship with her step-mother.

Bessie's relationship with Kennedy was always much better, although she still considered him, *"Boorish, selfish and conceited"*.[46] Her main interest seemed to be for him and her young brother Edward to become firm friends which they did, though whether or not they tolerated their friendship for Bessie's sake and a quiet life is unknown. Kennedy had already started Yale University before his father's death. After this he went off to the military college at Aldershot.[47] He passed his examinations on 2nd November 1901 and received his commission at Enniskillen.[48] He left the following year for Africa.

With the lease of the Castle still twenty-two years left to run, Bessie's dreams of sharing this wonderful historic home with Galt and of being part of the established elite, must have been shattered. She now had the whole burden of responsibility for the household and estate to run herself, without his help. Bessie at the time of Galt's death, was 36 years old and it would have been understandable if she had wanted to return home to her family, but she was a practical woman with a great inner strength and although the thought must have occurred to her, she couldn't renege on the Castle lease. Galt's effects were valued at £3,788 17s. 9d.[49] which was a princely sum then, but probably not enough for Bessie to continue to live a comfortable life and to be able to travel frequently, with some of her staff, which she liked, so she needed the estate revenue.[50]

Bessie's Father and Edward visit Kilwaughter

There was much to do and not least to sort out Galt's business interests and belongings. At that time Bessie shrewdly reclaimed her American nationality

---

[45] Letter summary, 8th April 1904.
[46] Ibid, August 1900.
[47] Ibid, 23rd July 1899.
[48] Ibid, 7th December 1901.
[49] Information from the Will. Centre for Migration Studies, Omagh.
[50] Letter summary, 2nd March 1904.

so that she could act as Trustee for his American estate.[51] She was able to deal with the Kirks, Galt's business partners who came to Kilwaughter for lunch, but when it came to sorting out his personal effects, that was another story. It was just too much and she was lonely, so she invited both her father and her brother to join her at Kilwaughter, saying that, *"The house needed a man's presence"*.[52]

That summer the weather was warm and life was kinder for Bessie because everything to do with the Castle, the estate and its tenant farmers prospered. She realised that Kilwaughter would have to earn its keep. She began to learn all about the buying and selling of stock and felt that the tenant farmers considered her now quite an astute business woman.[53] In Ireland's male oriented society it must have been quite amusing for the farmers to deal with a woman – and a foreign one at that, who knew little about Irish culture, but a strong female presence had already been part of Kilwaughter's history when Margaret Jones took over the estate after her brother Edward died. Bessie even became a property developer and organised for some houses to be built for rent, beside her old married home of *Meadowbank*.[54] Part of her income was also coming from her New York home which was rented out for $300 per month.[55]

In the autumn her father and brother left Kilwaughter for home. Although her father had been homesick, he still managed to travel throughout England on a sightseeing tour. He was impressed with Kilwaughter and that pleased Bessie enormously.[56] Bessie followed soon afterwards in November accompanied by Edward. She spent the time travelling around America with her mother and fulfilling the obligations she had with her step-children. The distance between Bessie and Florence was as great as ever and its interesting to note that very little is mentioned of Florence in Bessie's letters through the years unlike the stories about Kennedy. Florence's forthcoming wedding in 1904 did nothing to help that since Florence refused to have her wedding at Kilwaughter and whilst Bessie was in America she removed all her belongings

---

[51] Ibid, 23rd December 1915.
[52] Manko, 1994, p.42.
[53] Ibid, p.45.
[54] Letter summary, 7th September 1901.
[55] Bessie sold her New York home in April 1911.
[56] Letter summary, 7th August 1899.

from the Castle.⁵⁷ She married George Wilkinson from New York who was much older than her at 65 years. Later on she was to demand money from Bessie which was probably her share of the New York house. She eventually received $3,000. Florence never did allow her husband to use any of her money and was said to be unpopular with her neighbours in Canada where the couple had moved.⁵⁸ She died on 14th April 1911, still owing Bessie $8,000 which Bessie hoped to claim from Kennedy. The animosity between Bessie and Florence may have been self-generating. It was obvious in all Bessie's correspondence how fond she was of her brother Edward and stepson Kennedy and Florence must have felt rejected. The upsets though did not stop Bessie showing some sensitivity to Florence on one occasion, when she sent her a black lace shawl and other personal effects which had belonged to her mother.⁵⁹ Bessie's attitude of Florence though, had caused damage, since it rubbed off on Edward and when he heard of her death he exclaimed, *"What a riddance".* ⁶⁰

Bessie meets King Edward VII and Queen Alexandra

On 23rd July, 1903, a glittering event happened in Ireland that must have surpassed anything Bessie had ever experience before, because she was presented to King Edward VII and Queen Alexandra in Dublin Castle. It doesn't take much imagination to understand the preparations that Bessie would have gone to, to look her best. In a letter to her father she went to great lengths to describe what she would be wearing for this auspicious occasion. She drew a picture of the gown which was, *"Old satin and lace"* in a cream colour. She carried a fan of, *"Pearl sticks and Irish lace"* and had three feathers in her hair which was covered by a veil. Afterwards supper had been served on gold plates which had been brought from Buckingham Palace.⁶¹ One year later she met the Prince of Wales and in 1905 she was invited to Malta to attend a costume ball of some 2,000 of the most politically astute and wealthy people of Europe. On that occasion Bessie dressed as the Queen of

---

⁵⁷ Ibid, 14th June 1907.
⁵⁸ Ibid, 7th December 1910.
⁵⁹ Ibid, 28th October 1908.
⁶⁰ Ibid, 14th April 1911.
⁶¹ Letter, dated 24th July 1903 to father.

Lorraine.⁶² She liked her costume so much that she had her portrait painted wearing it. The painting now hangs in the reception room at Rockwood Museum. During that year also her father purchased a car and Bessie, showing her usual involvement, insisted that he should make sure that the car had, *Skidding tyres* put on it. Bessie was always up-to-date with the latest technology. It turned out that the car was for Edward who by now was a clever young man and had begun travelling just as much as his sister. He had adopted Bessie's habit of seeking out only the most illustrious people to mix with and in this of course, he was strongly supported by his sister. At the time Edward got his car, he was soon to visit Cuba and about to take his entrance examinations for Harvard on 14th October, 1905.

One of the interesting aspects of Bessie's loyalty was shown in the way she maintained contact with the Lochnaw Agnews who had long since given up their responsibility for Kilwaughter Castle. She visited the Scottish Agnews on 17th November 1903 and again in the autumn of 1908 and indeed offered them her hospitality at the Castle on several occasions.

Bessie had continued to make the journeys from America to Kilwaughter at sporadic intervals since Galt's death, although she was absent for nearly two years from 1908 to 1910.⁶³ She always suffered terribly from seasickness during the sea crossings and would sometimes spend all the time in her cabin existing on water melon.⁶⁴ She utilised the planning of her trips well, stopping off where she could to visit her friends around Europe, the Ysenbergs, Prince Solano and the Duchess of Baden and Countess Erbach in Germany, Lady White in Gibralter and another friend, Countess Sophie. She even managed to involve the King of Belgium in conversation.⁶⁵ On one occasion during a visit to Baden-Baden she had to be treated for severe headaches, possibly migraine, by Dr. Frey-Dangler. At the same time she admits that she, *"Has gone to pieces"* and has to stay in her room.⁶⁶ In 1911 she again spent time in Europe, but this time with her brother Edward who was suffering from tuberculosis. During that summer she managed to earn some extra income by

---

62 Manko, 1994, p.53.
63 Letter summary, 7th September 1910.
64 Ibid, 4th July 1903.
65 Ibid, 2nd February 1904.
66 Ibid, 19th October 1910.

sub-letting the Castle to the Elliott's who took up residence at the end of June.[67]

Bessie's Father Dies

In 1912 her father died and the following year she seemed to suffer from depression. She visited a doctor in London who suggested some rest. Bessie decided to travel to Aberdeen in Scotland for a period. She said that her, *"Nerves were all gone to pieces"* and complained that she spent most of her time in bed, but this incapacity did not keep her from sending orders to her mother or discussing the servants' wages.[68]

Bessie returns from America

She returned to Kilwaughter in the middle of 1914 which was to become a year of turmoil, not only in the world, but also in Ireland. She had decided to sublet the Castle to her friends the McCalmont's. Bertie McCalmont was an MP and a Commander of the Central Antrim Regiment of the Ulster Volunteer Force.[69] The UVF was a Protestant and pro-British organisation that was preparing to take action against the third Home Rule Bill, but it was taking so long to come to fruition that it had to be postponed due to the outbreak of the First World War, though was due to be enforced when the war ended. The Protestants were against Home Rule and wanted their part of Ireland to remain within the rest of Britain. The Unionist population began to organise themselves against this enforcement because they feared being trounced into a Catholic Ireland. They began in 1912 by arranging for a signing of a covenant by all those who wished to remain a part of the British Empire, but the Volunteers did much more than that. They organized supplies of food, clothing, transport and infiltrated the communications' system. Far more serious however, was their ability to find and purchase mass quantities of arms for they were prepared to defend their sovereignty.

When Bessie was making her journey to Ireland on board Cunard's, *Aquitania,* she was undoubtedly aware of European events unfolding, but may not have foreseen just how serious it was becoming in Ireland. She arrived at

---

[67] Ibid, 17th June 1911.
[68] Ibid, 11th March 1913.
[69] Manko, 1994, p.86.

Kilwaughter – The Unknown Castle

Kilwaughter at the end of July 1914 and was pleased with what she found. Her servant Rose had the Castle looking *"clean"* and the garden was *"beautiful"* and everyone was busy outside bringing in the hay. Bessie loved her garden which not only produced cherries, but an ample supply of figs and strawberries. It was a mature sanctuary as the conifers planted when Edward Jones Agnew refurbished the Castle had grown tall and thick. There was also lots of brushwood that had helped Galt and his friends hide, at their shooting parties and the lawns were immaculate and closely cut. The lake of course was full of ducks and swans. Flowers hadn't been forgotten either and a gardener from Aberdeen, Mr. Laing who had arrived at Kilwaughter, probably in Edward's time, had been responsible for instigating the flowerbeds that held the profusion that blossomed now. Mr. Laing, a small man whose weather-beaten features indicated his love of the outdoors, was a fine horticulturist and considered to be one of the foremost gardeners in that part of Ireland. In Edward's time he was probably responsible for a rare beech tree that had four different kinds of leaves on it, or more than likely four different species of tree that had been grafted on and had grown into a fine specimen which was much talked about.[70]

Bessie immediately thrust herself back into her busy life. She met people that she hadn't seen for a long time and had a meeting with Mr. Bristow her lawyer.[71] Things had understandably changed for her since Galt's death and she was still lonely. She had lost two of her favourite staff, Sams who had died earlier that year and his wife Martha who, although still alive and still helping out by making cheese and butter, was no longer around Kilwaughter.[72] Rose too, was unable to keep up with Bessie's pace and she told her mother somewhat abruptly, *"Thy anxieties would not all be imaginary if thee were here alone entirely in this big house with not a single relation to do a thing for thee"*. She continued, *"I miss Sams and Martha every minute, for all the people here are very slow and some rather stupid and none are into my ways"*.[73] It was clear that Bessie was feeling abandoned and that Kilwaughter was beginning to lose its appeal, albeit not for long.

---

[70] Larne Times, 29th November 1951.
[71] The Bristow's had intermarried with the Agnews in earlier years and one, John Bristow, became a solicitor who dealt with their affairs.
[72] Manko, 1994, p.87.
[73] Letter, dated 31st July 1914 to mother.

Bessie was all too aware now of the local political scene, but the trouble that was brewing was in Dublin and still too far away to cause her any real concern. She was much more scared of the events that were happening in Europe and that were, *"Frightening everybody"*. At times she felt that Kilwaughter Castle was exposed due to its closeness to the coast, but she remained optimistic that no German or Italian ships would penetrate the seas around the south of England. She did not stop though to consider that the war might have an impact on her plans to sublet Kilwaughter. These were suddenly changed when she received a visit from Mrs. McCalmont who had come to tell her, that if war was declared and England drawn into it, then they could no longer lease the Castle. This rather upset Bessie as she had gone to great lengths to prepare Kilwaughter for the arrival of the McCalmont's and now her plans were thwarted. She was aware though, of the sense of anxiety which prevailed at the impending war. Bertie McCalmont had been called back to the House of Commons in London, to play his part in the vote as to whether or not England should involve itself. The McCalmont's were still hopeful that they could lease Kilwaughter as Bertie McCalmont felt that the war would be short and if Britain became entangled, it would be to guard the Belgian Frontier in France thus ensuring Belgium neutrality.[74]

Circumstances were changing in Ireland too, but Bessie still felt no fear for the serious events which were unfolding. She noted with great glee that she witnessed, *"A wonderful parade of the Volunteers of Ulster. It was only one division, that of North Belfast and it looked to me like an Army. They were not even Reservists, but just the shop men and mill workers of North Belfast. They looked so well and marched so well, but one missed the uniform of the soldiers. They wore all colors (sic) and kinds of clothes, but all had rifles and a belt. Some had caps and one company had the soft felt hat worn by the Rough Riders. I was greatly impressed by their discipline and by their quiet serious faces."*[75]

Bessie hears about the 1914 Gun-Running

Bessie though, had missed a remarkable occurrence that had taken place in the spring of that year whilst she was in America and which was described to her in some detail by Helen Barklie who ran the post house and therefore

---

[74] Letter, dated 3rd August 1914 to Edward.
[75] Ibid.

knew everything that was going on, not least because she had been ordered by the Government to open all mail.[76] Bessie listened intently as the story unfolded and later re-told it with some relish because of the secrecy surrounding it. Helen told her that one day in April, Lucy McNeill had been approached by William Chaine. He had an unusual request. Could she feed nine hundred men that night? This was a tall order for anyone, but Lucy sensing that it was important agreed to do it. She was told not to mention it or ask any further questions. Lucy enlisted the help of two neighbours and got on with the task in hand. She decided to use the laundry room in her house for the food preparation because although she trusted her servants, she did not want anyone finding out and informing the police.

The three women began the massive organisation needed to feed nine hundred men and bought all the coffee they could find in Larne together, with a thousand eggs, six hams and five hundred loaves of bread. It is difficult to imagine in the small town of Larne how all these purchases could have been kept secret, but most of the inhabitants were sympathisers to the cause and knew not to ask too many questions. They had also seen a contingency of Volunteers guarding the harbour the previous night which would have given them an idea that something was about to happen. Help was also forthcoming from other places – the local restaurateur provided the crockery and cutlery.

All provisions were taken to Lucy's home which was conveniently situated at the harbour and the three women began the daunting task of cooking for so many people. They toiled all day, boiling eggs and hams and making sandwiches and must have been exhausted. As nightfall came, nine hundred Volunteers suddenly appeared as if from nowhere, to take charge of the harbour and the Curran. They also commandeered the telephone exchange and the police station. Such was the precision of the organisation that already around five hundred cars began to gather – car after car from as far back as Kilwaughter to Larne, each with its owner and chauffeur. The cars were filled with rifles and ammunition and left as quickly as they had appeared having received orders where to take the contraband. Within six hours, 25,000 rifles and approximately 3,500,000 rounds of ammunition were unloaded and moved away.[77] The guns had been purchased in Hamburg and its not difficult

---

[76] Manko, 1994, p.103.
[77] The guns remained unused because of the outbreak of the war. Some of them were found during the 1970's Northern Ireland Troubles, (Barzilay, 1978, p.147).

to see the irony of this situation when taking into account, the fact that Britain stood on the very edge of declaring war with Germany. To add to this bizarre affair, some distance further south from Larne, in the town of Banbridge, County Down, German horse dealers were doing the rounds of the fairs and purchasing vast numbers of the best horses (as many as 600 in one visit), to be shipped back to Germany in preparation for the war, during which they would be used to pull cannons.[78]

What Bessie did not know as she related this tale, was that when the, *Mountjoy* (or *Clyde Valley* as the ship was renamed), slipped into the harbour that evening with its forbidden cargo, it was commanded by another Agnew - Captain Andrew Agnew from Magheramorne. Captain Andy, as he was known, had led an interesting life. He was a member of the Magheramorne Masonic Lodge together with two of his brothers and came from a sea-faring family. He was born in 1869, the son of David, a sea captain and Mary Agnew and worked for the Antrim Iron Ore Company, most frequently as Captain of the, *SS Glendun*. In 1895 he had been presented with a gold medal by the then American President, Grover Cleveland, for saving the crew of the *Maggie Dalling*. At that time he was chief mate aboard a windjammer vessel named the, *G.S. Penry*. He was later appointed a Member of the Civil Division of the Order of the British Empire, in the New Year's Honours List of 1st January 1920. This was awarded for his services to the British Navy during the First World War. During that war it was said that he had led a charmed life because throughout it, he never missed a journey with his ship and sailed through seas that were teeming with mines and enemy submarines. Yet whilst other ships around him went down, he and his crew always managed to escape unscathed. He married Agnes Maria Davison and the couple had six children. When he died in 1932, he was survived by his wife and three children – a daughter Isobel who was the Divisional Welfare Officer in Larne, a son David who was a bank official and his youngest son James who followed in his father's footsteps and became a master mariner. [79] James became a naturalised American citizen settling in New York and captained the first ship into Toulouse Harbour in France during the second World War. He later commanded vessels belonging to the United Fruit Company in New York.[80]

---

[78] Blair, 2007, p.90.

[79] Unattributed newspaper obituary, 20th August 1932.

[80] Information courtesy of the late Nancy Agnew Ferns, Nova Scotia, granddaughter of Captain Andrew Agnew.

Chapter 9

Outbreak of World War 1

The outbreak of war had scuppered the McCalmont's plans for leasing the Castle, but another idea unfolds with regard to their motives for wanting the lease in the first place which may not have been quite as innocent as it seemed. Bertie McCalmont had begun to think that the Volunteers should be armed and had said so to Lord Carson who was the Unionist leader at the time. Kilwaughter Castle, had he leased it, would have been exactly the kind of place he needed in order to co-ordinate his UVF operations. It had many good features which made it ideal – plenty of land that could be used to lodge the large numbers of Volunteers and it was in close proximity to Larne and the harbour. Although Bessie knew of McCalmont's activities in the UVF and that he had been an officer in the Irish Guards, it is not clear whether she knew of McCalmont's intentions.[1] In any event the declaration of war stopped the plans that McCalmont had and saved Kilwaughter Castle from being associated with the UVF.

Things in Ireland were still no better and many of Bessie's friends who had visited Kilwaughter, now began turning their grand homes into hospitals. *Drumalis* had twenty beds and Lord Shaftesbury had forty beds installed in Belfast Castle.[2] They were against Home Rule and knew that carnage would result for the people should the British Government push through the Bill. For now there was no suggestion from Bessie though, that she would be doing the same and making ready her glorious Kilwaughter that she had invested so much time and energy in, to be muddied by strangers. There was also

---

[1] Manko, 1994, p.87.
[2] Letter, dated 3rd August 1914 to Edward.

frightening news about the imminent world war. Bessie began to prepare in her ubiquitous fashion. Planning ahead, organizing a supply of oil for the lamps to be delivered from Liverpool because that was one of the things that would run short - and obtaining some gold. With this she had a severe problem because all the banks were closed for a week and no-one could get any money, not least the tourists who were now stranded without funds. Bessie was different though and had friends in important positions that she could call upon. She contacted her solicitor Mr. Bristow who had a cousin in the Northern Banking Company and through him, she was able to get the gold she needed. Gold of course, increased its value during war and was a worthy commodity to have. Her complacency when she told this tale was all too obvious, but she did feel grateful when it came to food as she had her own sheep, pigs and cattle and an abundant supply of vegetables on the estate should she and the staff need them. She noted too, that if everything got used, then, *"I can have the lake netted for trout."* [3] Bessie as usual was thinking ahead.

Kilwaughter Castle although close to Larne, was nevertheless, remote and it nestled snugly under the mountains. It was a quiet place and Bessie, even though she had been initially worried about German bombardment, still felt secure that she was, *"In the very safest corner of this Eastern Hemisphere"* [4] but Ireland was preparing for war and Irish troops were on their way to France and Belgium under the British colours. Barbed wire had gone up all around the coast. At the same time some contemptible person had tried to contaminate the local water supply by putting cholera bacilli into the reservoir though fortunately he had been caught. The ever resourceful Bessie was glad that she had her own water supply – but she rallied her staff at Kilwaughter and they were soon making clothes for the troops. A frenzy of rumours was circulating, that the German navy might be able to sail around northern Scotland and attack Ireland and that unnerved her. She told her brother Edward, that apparently the German Emperor, who was described on posters as the *Mad Mullah of Europe,* was said to have been planning this war for years.[5]

She began to think that she would not be able to leave Kilwaughter as usual in October for the sojourn in America, but wars both in Ireland and in Europe were not enough to stop Bessie leading her normal busy life and at the

---

[3] Letter, dated 5th August 1914 to Edward.
[4] Letter, dated 18th August 1914 to mother.
[5] Letter, dated 9th August 1914 to Edward.

beginning of August she decided to spend a few days in Dublin. On her journey there an incident happened which amused her greatly. Having had to move out of her first-class carriage to allow for some army military corps to use it, she managed to find another seat in a carriage marked *Engaged*. The gentleman who had reserved the carriage was taking boxes of gold to Dublin. Six heavy boxes made of wood, secured with iron bands, which took two men to lift each one, covered the floor of the carriage. These companions absorbed Bessie's interest and when her carriage was met in Dublin by six bank officials her pride was evident as she felt so important and, *"Well guarded"*. [6]

More Servants Exploits

Back in Kilwaughter Bessie had hired a new butler called Broomfield. The servants that Bessie engaged through the years at Kilwaughter are worthy of mention because of their capers and individuality. Rose Rafferty the housekeeper, was a stubborn woman, but was one of Bessie's favourites. As she grew steadily older and found it difficult to walk and was much less able, Bessie was very patient with her. She referred to her as Kilwaughter's, *Vicereine*, but although slow, it did not deter Rose from keeping a sharp eye on the rest of the servants. She was, nonetheless, popular with them and her authority was never challenged. She kept the Castle pristine and knew absolutely everything that was going on, but she didn't much care for the head housemaid. Rose thought there was a s*tiffness about her* and she was, *clartie* (slovenly), but Rose's biggest grudge against her was the housemaid's perceived laziness. Whilst the other servants Lily and Majorie were up and about their tasks by 6.00 a.m., the housemaid didn't appear until one hour later.

Lily and Marjorie were sisters and good servants. They were also enthusiastic in carrying out their duties around the Castle, but Lily had aspirations and dreamed of travelling and moving away from Ireland. She had found a position for herself in Scotland and was due to leave in mid September to take up the post, but Rose, backed by Bessie, had other ideas. She liked Lily and liked having her around the Castle – even to the extent that Lily could rest in her bed, should she feel tired. Rose decided that a spot of match-making with a local farmer named Apsley who originated from Scotland, might be

---

[6] Ibid.

enough to make Lily change her mind and stay. To that end she began bombarding Lily with stories about Apsley – how rich he was, *"Has the weight of himself in gold in the bank, besides houses he rents out in Larne"* and what a good *catch* he would make. Bessie of course was right behind Rose in her scheming, but for her own reasons. She liked Apsley and she trusted Lily, so felt that the couple, together with Rose, living in Kilwaughter would be an ideal situation to have whilst she was in America as she could relax in the knowledge that the place was well looked after.

Marjorie the younger of the two, was the third housemaid and an excellent worker. She also did most of the sewing which was a particular favourite hobby of Bessie's, so she was popular because of that too. This soon aroused jealousy with a temporary servant named Sarah Edwards, but Rose, who obviously got fed up with the complaining, soon told Sarah that Marjorie was permanent staff and she wasn't.

Another housemaid was Emily who helped the butler in the dining room and also did Bessie's laundry, as well as helping Rose sort out the linen. Then there was Mr. Gardener who had been the shepherd at Kilwaughter all his working life, as had his father before him. In October 1914, however, he decided to leave and go instead to *Drumnasole to* work for the Turnly's – not because they had asked him, but because his wife wanted a change. The Gardener's also lived in a remote area on the mountain and this was too far away from the children's school.[7]

Bessie reserved her strongest praise for the cook Mrs. Sands whom she thought the most funny and described her as, *"A red hot Ulsterwoman with a husband and two sons in the Ulster Volunteers"*. Mrs. Sands was so against Redmond's views on Home Rule, that she would rather Ulster was in German hands, but she was a wonderfully talented cook who made delicious food and every day went out to the fields to pick mushrooms. Her thriftiness also impressed Bessie as she was able to make a small chicken stretch to a whole week of evening meals for her, the last one being a chicken souffle made with the darker meat of the bird. Mrs. Sands though, had one spectacular feature that singled her out from all other cooks, because she had no upper teeth. One would assume that this must have been the worst thing that could inflict a cook, but not for Mrs. Sands. The lack of teeth did not inhibit her in any way,

---

[7] Letter, dated 16th October 1914 to mother.

nor did it hold her back when she started to talk because she spoke just as fast and Bessie enthused that it was as though, "*She had a double set!*" Mrs. Sands also felt very elevated and secure in her position as the Castle's cook because she had been, *head-hunted*. This had given her an air of authority and consequently she thought herself more worthy than the rest of the, *aliens* as she described them, apart from Rose. Rose being Bessie's favourite may have had something to do with it.

Broomfield the butler was also a character of some note. He had led an interesting life, having been in the army for thirteen years, five of which had been spent in Africa and the remaining eight in England, so he felt that he had served his country enough. Broomfield was a good-natured man who could turn his hands to anything. Since Galt's death Bessie felt she had no need of a footman or pantry boy and so Broomfield filled many roles. He was willing to do other duties and cleaned the silver and tended to the lamps, fixing those that hadn't worked for years and keeping them replenished with oil. One of his favourite jobs was to fix the Castle bells and Bessie thought him an excellent electrician because the electrician from Larne who had attempted to fix them had not been able to do so. Broomfield was even willing to walk into Larne to the post-office for Bessie and she thought this admirable. His ebullience though sometimes got him into trouble for he felt that it was the house rule and therefore his duty, to offer tea to the visitors and to have them sign the Guest Book - even if they were Bessie's tenants. It is easy to conjure up a vision of the tenants tramping through the house to Bessie's precious drawing room for tea, in their heavy boots and muddy farm clothes. The tenants of course, were not her friends, so should not be offered tea and should certainly not sign the Guest Book. Bessie was quite particular about the Guest Book because of course, its entrants would be exposed to the names of the other important people she mixed with when they came to sign and her tenants certainly did not fit the bill.[8]

Then there was William Shepherd who caused a scandal when his wife accused him of flirting with another servant, Rachel McCullough. This may not have been so unusual were it not for the fact that both servants were then over 90 years old.[9]

---

[8] Letter, dated 2nd September 1914 to mother.
[9] Letter summary, 18th March 1904.

Local Politics

Bessie had an inquisitive mind and the evolving events both at home and abroad had heightened her political awareness. She followed the news - both in Ireland and Europe intently, but she was not immune from trouble at Kilwaughter either. When the sons of some Protestant *home rulers* trespassed in the woods around Kilwaughter, they were unpopular – not only because they were trespassing, but as Protestant *home rulers,* they were, *"The lowest form of creature this world holds".* [10] Bessie referred to them as, *"Dirty Protestant Nationalists".* [11]

From 1914 Bessie's letters to America, now began taking on a different tone. She could no longer write exactly what she liked as the censor opened them. Many of her letters were taken up by the war and she wrote about fund raising and that Lord Kitchener appealed for 300,000 pairs of socks for the troops and 300,000 cholera belts which were mistakenly thought to protect soldiers from this condition. Some of Bessie's letters from America which were held up, were coming through again by the end of August and that summer of 1914, was beautiful with little rain. The favourable weather conditions had helped the garden tremendously and the produce from Kilwaughter had never been better. The vegetables and fruit were wonderful, especially the peaches which according to Bessie were the size of big applies. One of Bessie's gardener's, Crawford, had cultivated a flower – a pink sweetpea with white stripes – that he had named the *Mrs. Galt Smith.* Bessie was thrilled and proud, even though it had not yet gone on the market.[12]

Entertaining Continues

There were still guests to entertain at the Castle and life for Bessie continued on as usual. Ireland unlike England, was not short of petrol as there were still shipments coming in from America.[13] This meant of course, that there was no problem for people getting about. It was also now possible to hire a car in Larne from Mr. Craddocj's who charged, *"18 cents with no charge for waiting".* [14]

---

[10] Letter dated 28th August 1914 to Edward.
[11] Letter dated 24th August 1914 to mother.
[12] Letter summary, 24th September 1914.
[13] Letter dated 18th August 1914 to mother.
[14] Letter dated 24th August 1914 to mother.

She visited the Youngs at Galgorm Castle and the O'Neills at Shane's Castle where she had tea with Lord O'Neill's sister.[15]

The Turnlys of *Drumnasole* were particular friends whom Bessie enjoyed. The Turnly family were old relatives of the Agnews as James Agnew Farrell, a second cousin of Edward Jones Agnew, had married Letitia Turnly. Although this was centuries ago, Kilwaughter's capacity for holding on to its extended family knew no end. Francis Turnly was well known to Bessie and had visited her in New York several times. He had married into the Higginson family and his wife's sister was the famous local poetess, Moira O'Neill.[16] All these people were established landed gentry, the people whom Bessie felt most at home with and whom she could also have at Kilwaughter.

Her meetings with the Ulster Women's Unionist Association also continued. Bessie was on the Council and enjoyed these meetings immensely. No doubt this Council position carried with it some responsibility which would have also pleased her. Lady Londonderry was President and with the other luminaries, such as the Duchess of Abercorn and Lady Dufferin, the meetings were full and interesting.[17]

She was still fascinated by the gun-running event in April past and never seemed to tire of talking about it around the dinner table with her guests especially when Lucy McNeill came to lunch and began divulging some of the stories about it. How Lucy had had to go on board the *Mountjoy* to proffer first aid to a man who had fallen down a hole and how Colonel Chichester had caught two detectives snooping around and had them locked up for two days guarded by some Volunteers and farmers.[18]

It was now early September and the war was a month old, but Bessie's friend Bertie McCalmont was still recruiting people for the UVF and was due to make a speech in Larne on the evening of 4th September, 1914. Bessie decided that all the Kilwaughter male staff should attend. She was proud that her men were in the UVF, but disappointed that most of them were too old to sign on for the war though many young men from the Kilwaughter and

---

[15] Ibid.
[16] Letter dated 18th August 1914 to mother.
[17] Letter, dated 30th September 1914 to mother.
[18] Letter, dated 28th August 1914 to Edward.

Larne areas did.[19] September was usually the time when Bessie began her preparations for moving back to America for the winter months, but she decided that life was much more interesting in Ireland and she would remain there as she was, *"Perfectly safe".* [20] It is difficult to imagine that amongst the uncertainty in Ireland and the tragic events in Europe, that life could follow a normal pattern, but it did just that, especially around Kilwaughter and Bessie continued her socializing.

The 8th September started as a busy day for Bessie at the Castle. She held a luncheon party for eight people, but the previous evening her infamous cook Mrs. Sands, had to leave to see off her son who was going to fight in the war. She was in a dreadful state and as it happened that was the last Bessie saw of her at Kilwaughter because such was her emotional condition that her family did not allow her to return.[21] The rest of the staff and especially Broomfield rallied around to help Bessie out and there wasn't a problem. Later that day she hired a car and her party set off for the Turnlys at *Drumnasole* hoping to catch Lady Antrim in at Glenarm Castle on the way. Unfortunately Lady Antrim was not at home, so Bessie's party proceeded to *Drumnasole* where they were wonderfully entertained chatting with the Turnly's guests from Cushendun and Cushendall and playing tennis and golf.

That weekend saw her off visiting again, this time along the coast for a picnic of soup, sandwiches of egg, salad and minced chicken, followed by cake and grapes - and visiting Mrs. McGildowney[22] en route. The journey home was broken by a stop-off for tea at yet more friends, the Martins, but far from the day being almost over, Bessie then headed off to Coleraine where Sir Edward Carson, the Unionist leader, was to address the North Antrim division of the UVF and she wanted to hear his speech, but she hadn't reckoned that she and her party would need a pass to get into the hall. The ever-resourceful Bessie was not going to let something like that stop her hearing Carson, besides she was also a member of the Women's Unionist Association. She produced her visiting card which had a, *"Magical effect"* and

---

[19] As her elderly male staff left she refused to hire any single man who was young enough to fight at the front. (Manko, 1994, p.98).
[20] Letter, dated 4th September 1914 to Edwrd.
[21] Letter, dated 17th September 1914 to mother.
[22] The McGildowney's were long associates of the Agnews.

they were ushered in.[23] The meeting and Carson's speech were everything Bessie wished and her sorrow was that none of her American friends were there to hear the rousing address because then they may change their minds that, Ireland wanted Home Rule. It had been a long day.

Bessie Meets Edward Carson

The following days saw Bessie and her staff begin to do their bit for the war effort by making bed jackets to keep warm those soldiers who would end up injured in hospital. She was an accomplished seamstress and able to tackle most garments. She had also made most of the lampshades for Kilwaughter and enjoyed showing off her handy work. The women worked in the library and one day a telegram arrived from Bertie McCalmont telling Bessie that her hero Carson would be in Larne in forty minutes and would be making a speech before he left on the boat. Bessie just had to hear him again, so with Broomfield's help they managed to make it in time. On this occasion Bessie was determined to get much closer to Carson and managed to persuade one of the Volunteers to let her go on board so that she could get right up beside the man himself. Not only was she adjacent to Carson, but she was seen by people such as Lady Smiley and Lady Baring and young Mrs. McCalmont, whom she thought, would all be most impressed. Then Bertie McCalmont presented her to Lord Carson and that topped everything for her.[24]

Kennedy joins the UVF

With Mrs. Sands, the cook gone and other staff moved to Scotland, Bessie had to make some administrative changes at Kilwaughter. Apsley had joined the staff and seemed to be settling in well and was popular with them. Rose, even if she was somewhat infirm, was having to take on more duties in the kitchen, but it all seemed to be working well. Kennedy had returned from New York to Kilwaughter, the first time in eleven years, to sign up for the UVF,[25] but in the middle of September he was off to war, though first to the training camp at Clandeboye. He now had a girlfriend named Dorothy who did not come from a wealthy background. Bessie would rather it had been a family of

---

[23] Letter, dated 8th September 1914 to Edward.
[24] Ibid.
[25] Letter, dated 4th September 1914 to Edward.

some standing. Dorothy and her two sisters lived with their brother. The girls had insisted that because of this, there was no need to hire a servant since they would undertake the task of keeping house for him. Bessie thought this commendable and because of that, approved of the match and awaited an announcement of the wedding.[26] She and some of the staff accompanied him to the station at Larne where a band was playing some lively music and there were many crowds of people, all waving off their loved ones. There were also cheers from those Volunteers who were too old to join the swells of young men going off to fight for their country. Colonel McNeill gave each man a packet of cigarettes as a parting gift.[27]

Bessie had crocheted a scarf for Kennedy before he left and she decided that she would do the same for the Kilwaughter Battalion - those men from the local Kilwaughter area who had left to fight. She despatched Apsley to get a list of names (there were initially ten, but two more joined) and she and the staff began the task. She had thought out the whole plan – the scarves were to be, *"Khaki in color (sic) and are 1 yard long by 18 inches around. Crocheted as a tube and closed at each end (drawn up with a tassel). Then they serve as cap at night and scarf by day".* Bessie also persuaded other people locally to help with the knitting and well as her mother in America. She didn't forget the navy either because they also received scarves in navy blue.[28] She made a difference though in the quality of the wool for the officers as she used a much finer garn.[29]

Bessie's War Effort

Bessie was making sure that Kilwaughter Castle played its part during the war, but thoughtful as she was, it didn't stop her doing her usual round of social visits. Formal parties had stopped because of the situation, but there were still parties held in the drawing room. This time she was invited to Sir William and Lady Adair's and was gladdened when she was placed on Sir William's right at the table as she found him a, *"Delightful man",* but the conversation now was no longer of fascinating stories about covert events like the gun-running

---

[26] Letter, dated 18th October 1914 to mother.
[27] Letter, dated 17th September 1914 to mother.
[28] Letter, dated 22nd September 1914 to Polly.
[29] Letter, dated 18th October 1914 to mother.

episode, but of the injured and those known to have been killed.[30] *"Everybody we meet has lost a relative and so many are in black, it makes one ill"*, she said. [31]

Bessie was still enthusiastic to help and used the billiard table at the Castle to cut out material for more clothes. She gave 100 yards of flannelette which helped make jackets, chemises and combinations. [32] Fund raising had begun to help finance the war and of course she was involved with that too. Many of her wealthy friends had donated vast amounts of money and she was very impressed when she discovered that her friend, Lady Smiley, had donated fifty thousand dollars and Mr. Chaine and others had given large amounts of money. The Dowager Lady Dufferin had allowed part of her estate to be used as an army camp.[33] Bessie still had no idea however, when she would be able to leave Kilwaughter for America, but she was much too caught up in playing her part for the war effort that she didn't seem to mind.[34] Food remained plentiful and rationing had not begun. For one of her luncheon parties at Kilwaughter for seven people she provided a robust meal of soup, cold salmon mayonnaise, roast grouse and chicken, cold ham and salad, 'tipsy' cake, jelly, crackers and cheese, grapes, peaches and coffee.

The Irish political scene had taken a back seat because of the war going on, but Kitchener was called to Dublin. The Nationalists there had put up posters announcing that nationalist Volunteers should not enlist in Kitchener's campaign for more soldiers, since England was the enemy and not Germany. Kitchener had to address this intimidation and Bessie had high hopes that he would. *"He is the one man everybody is afraid of – even the Germans included"*, she states. She later went on to detest Lloyd George and Churchill, blaming the latter for the Dardanelles and Antwerp disasters.[35] War tragedies were beginning to make their way to Ireland's shores when forty Belgian refugees arrived, including two children and rumour had it that the children had had their hands cut off. [36] This proved to be untrue, but the rumours were damaging nonetheless. When Bessie was invited to tea with Lady Antrim at

---

[30] Letter, dated 25th September 1914 to mother.
[31] Letter, dated 30th September 1914 to mother.
[32] Letter, dated 15th September 1914 to mother.
[33] Letter, dated 4th November 1914 to mother.
[34] Letter, dated 27th September 1914 to mother.
[35] Letter summary, 7th May 1915.
[36] Letter, dated 2nd October 1914 to Polly.

Glenarm Castle she found everyone busy knitting cholera belts. These belts were popular with the soldiers and there were various patterns for knitting them. Broomfield thought that Lady Evelyn Baring's pattern was best. He had been a soldier fighting in the South African war and believed that the belts saved his life.[37] The best were made from wool or silk and they were thought that by keeping the soldiers warm, that this would ensure they didn't catch cholera. It was, of course, a misapprehension, but the belief was firm. Lady Antrim had taken in a family from Belgium, who had been wealthy lace manufacturers in Alost. Their factory, which had employed seven hundred people, had been destroyed when the Germans took over their town and began burning everything.[38] It was obvious that things were changing.

Belgians continued to arrive to Ireland destitute and penniless. Bessie and others began arranging events to raise funds for them. At one such concert which was held in the town hall in Larne, Norah McGarrel Hogg thrilled them all when she danced an Irish jig followed by a Russian dance.[39]

Suspicious Signalling on Agnew's Hill

After mobilization there were no further drastic changes and life returned to a somewhat kind of normal. At the beginning of November Bessie thought it may soon be possible to travel back to America and with this in mind she began sorting out her business affairs for the long absence and tying up other loose ends that she needed to deal with. Larne was now a naval base for the minesweepers. A minefield had been discovered off Londonderry and Portrush, but the minelayer, a German ship flying the Dutch flag, had been caught and the crew interned. At one stage a German mine was found just three miles from Larne and there were 24 battleships in Londonderry harbour.[40] Bessie was justifiably frightened of the mines and hoped that the Atlantic would soon be clear, but decided that instead of travelling from Liverpool to Philadelphia, she would sail on the *Lusitania*.[41] Fortunately, she changed her mind, but unbeknown to her, another Agnew, Thomas and his wife lost their lives on the ill-fated ship. Rumours were circulating that a

---

[37] Letter, dated 23rd October 1914 to Polly.
[38] Letter dated 21st October 1914 to mother.
[39] Letter dated 23rd October 1914 to Polly.
[40] Letter dated 10th November 1914 to mother.
[41] Letter dated 2nd November 1914 to Polly.

Kilwaughter – The Unknown Castle

British cruiser, the, *Audacious* went down in Lough Swilly.[42] Fear was escalating amongst the people. It was said that the Germans thinking they were about to lose everything in Europe, were prepared to risk the rest and land in Ireland.[43]

A week later a curious event happened. Bessie heard that there had been a mysterious signalling from the top of Agnew's Hill. No-one in the area knew what the signalling was about and it was considered strange. A search party was despatched to find the culprit, but to no avail. Bessie was not best pleased. As a foreigner living in Ireland in time of war, she had been particularly careful to remain impartial and did not want to be associated with anyone of dubious connections prowling about her land; but what really rankled her was that, *"Agnew's Hill belongs to me"*. It was clearly part of the lease that she and Galt had originally signed.[44] There had been other signalling too, at Rathlin island and at Malin Head just off Londonderry. The general rumour was that some Nationalists were spying for the Germans, but Crawford the gardener didn't agree with that as he thought it was someone of more importance. The signalling continued, but by mid November 1914, and much to Bessie's relief, it ceased on Agnew's Hill and was now focussed on Islandmagee. Bessie thought it was simply the Ulster Volunteers practising their codes, but it was also rumoured that a German had been hiding out around the Castle and the signalling had been from him. It did not help matters that some of the staff had reported seeing a man, who, *"Looked German"*, at the gate lodge trying to sell jewellery. Rumour was now heaped upon rumour because following the previous signalling from Agnew's Hill, a ship had been blown up after striking a mine somewhere off the coast.[45]

By then stories of spies were circulating thick and fast. A man had been caught dressed as a woman coming out of the lime quarries beside the Castle and raids were expected along the Antrim coast, so farmers had to move all their livestock. A German submarine had surfaced at Ballygally and given petrol from two cars that were thought driven by Irish Nationalists, but which immediately left when the coast guard asked them what they were doing. The

---

[42] It was not a rumour, but a fact. The *Audacious* was being towed to shallower waters by the *Olympic* to save her from German submarines when it overturned and exploded. (Maxtone-Graham (Ed.), 1998, p.163).
[43] Letter dated 3rd November 1914.
[44] Letter dated 10th November 1914 to mother.
[45] Letter dated 17th November 1914 to Edward.

submarine had been seen at Islandmagee where it lay for a week.[46] Large tanks of oil had been found submerged beside the lighthouses at Larne. Submarines had been caught in nets at Larne Harbour and new nets had been strung along the short distance between the Antrim coast and the West of Scotland to stop others getting in.[47] Female spies had even been found on trains between Belfast and Dublin later that summer and to cap it all the ghost of Margaret Jones who died many years previously, had been seen stalking the Castle, making noises and scaring the staff.[48]

Disharmony in the Kitchen

This didn't stop Bessie who had moved on and was busy entertaining the Admiral in charge of the Larne naval base and his wife who were both staying at the Olderfleet Hotel in Larne. Things in Kilwaughter were also beginning to occupy her much more because of some staff in-fighting that had developed. Kilwaughter Castle had remained relatively untouched with the religious problems that had affected people elsewhere in the country, but it was inevitable that eventually it would cause a clash within the staff because Bessie employed people from both religions. Dissension was beginning to filter through and it all seemed to begin with complaints from the staff about the food. One of the new house-maids, Miss Jane O'Kane and Broomfield the butler, were the main culprits behind the quarrelling. Broomfield was a Protestant and Jane a Catholic, and she had referred to Sir Edward Carson as a, *"Traitor to his country"*. This really was asking for trouble from Broomfield and he was furious. When relating the story to Bessie, Broomfield told her that, *"He would be trampled on by a Master or a Mistress, but he would not be trampled on by a Roman Catholic house-maid!"* and that, *"He had had as much dirty water flung in his face as was a disgrace to any Protestant household"*.[49] It turned out that it was not really the food that was the problem, but the fact that they all had to eat together after Jane's insults to the Protestant staff. This unfortunately, was just the start of more problems to come because Rose, another Catholic, though according to Broomfield was quiet, decided that the kitchen door should be left open to disperse the cooking smells. Broomfield complained that this

---

[46] Letter summary, 1st February 1915.
[47] Ibid, 1st March 1915.
[48] Ibid, 6th July 1915.
[49] Letter dated 13th November 1914 to Edward.

meant that all the heat going up the back stairs would be lost and he would be cold and anyway Bessie had said it should remain closed. Rose was having none of it and had replied to him that he could get heat from his pantry fire. She thought Broomfield, *"Hadn't a mind as large as a fly"* and he also reminded her of the Kaiser.[50]

Bessie found the whole thing utterly amusing, but in the end because of another episode and Broomfield's sulks, had to deal with the situation. He was going about subdued and, *"Like a little whipped mouse"* because of an incident that had happened in the kitchen the previous day. It involved Jane O'Kane again. She had asked for a piece of roast mutton that was more thoroughly cooked. Broomfield had taken offence at this simple request and had quarrelled with her. Rose who had cooked the meat, had also taken offence and had left the table in a rage. The following day she brought the meat which was wrapped up in brown paper, to Bessie, to let her decide whether it was cooked properly or not. In the end Bessie told them that she didn't care how much they fought amongst themselves, but the quarrelling should not impact on anything else. Broomfield managed to redeem himself somewhat by teaching some of the maids how to knit double heels on socks and by making lamp mats which he framed.[51] It helped also that Rose was out of action and confined to her room with a sprained ankle which had happened after a fall in part of the house that Bessie had named, *Kennedy Tower*. The staff though, with usual Irish fickleness set all their grievances aside to rally round and make Rose as comfortable as possible – stealing food from the kitchen and keeping her company. Broomfield took her the newspapers and shouted out the local gossip to her through a crack in the door.[52] Even though Rose was a Catholic Broomfield liked her because, *"She was so quiet, you wouldn't know what religion she was"*.[53]

The cease-fire did not last for long however, because two days later, *"O'Kane and Broomfield were near killing each other"* two cut fingers and an old candlestick were produced as evidence. This had happened over an incident when pouring some tea caused the candlestick to be jostled which resulted in some pushing. First Jane gave Bessie her side of the story, then in marched

---

[50] Letter dated 17th November 1914 to Edward.
[51] Ibid, 17th November 1914.
[52] Letter dated 12th December 1914 to mother.
[53] Letter dated 17th November 1914 to Edward.

Broomfield to regale his view of it and this took fifty minutes by which time he had more or less calmed down. His version as usual, ended up ensnared in politics. He hoped he would be, *"Dead and buried deep in his grave before the likes of O'Kane got the upper hand with Home Rule"*. Bessie scolded him and told him that the staff must not resort to physical abuse. The story was not finished yet, because just as Bessie was coming to the end of her conversation with Broomfield, in shuffled Rose on her stick to give her side of the events on the candlestick incident.[54] Bessie had had a trying day, but she was to report that within a short time she saw Broomfield and the house-maid in deep conversation and laughing, the affair forgotten. Bessie even thought that had Rose been younger, then Broomfield would have tried to convert her first to his own religion, before marrying her.

Life Continues with Entertaining

The previous two weeks had been busy as usual at Kilwaughter for Bessie. The dinner party circle had begun again and she had hosted two, attended three more, one luncheon party, five tea parties, one supper and a concert. She reflected that war time in Ireland reminded her of the, *"Life of a metropolis"*. Bessie had always enjoyed her dinner parties at Kilwaughter and took great care that the house was presentable and the menu appropriate. She especially enjoyed guests who were fun and didn't conform to the norm. Three such people who fitted this bill, were the Misses Orr-Owens from Holestone, elderly sisters who had only just moved to the country after the eldest inherited a house from their late uncle. Most of their lives had been spent at their villa on the Riviera or at their house in London and Bessie was sure that they found living a rural life a bit dull. They had various views of the people they mixed with and fell out with them on a regular basis only to become friendly again shortly afterwards. One such man was Lord O'Neill who owned Slemish mountain. The sisters believed that he did not own all of it, but got it into their heads that the eastern part of the mountain was theirs. They took him to court and to the surprise of everyone, won the case. For some time they also took umbrage to Lady Massareene who was too full of life for them to handle – and their dislike was heightened at the Farewell Service for the soldiers from Antrim who were departing for the front. Lady Massareene arrived at the

---

[54] Letter dated 14th December 1914 to mother and family.

service with a kingfisher painted on one cheek and a dragon-fly on the other. The sisters proceeded to state their pity for Lord Massareene in a way that no-one else at the service would have misunderstood.[55]

Bessie thought the sisters great fun and very eccentric and she enjoyed their gossip. They also owned the most exquisite China porcelain and that of course, would have been enough to impress Bessie, but there was a much more serious side to them. They took on the responsibility of looking after the needs of 300 Ulster Volunteers that came from Ballyclare and Doagh. They personally provided all of them with blankets and underwear, suits, mufflers and mittens and anything else that was required.

With Christmas approaching Bessie knew that she would be spending it alone at Kilwaughter as she was still afraid to venture outside Ireland because of the mines and it was now rumoured that these had been laid by Republicans who were in the pay of the Germans.[56] She invited several guests to be with her, but all declined. She did not mind too much sitting alone in the Castle as she enjoyed her own company and Apsley had put in a new fireplace in time for Christmas which had pleased her.[57] It was not to be a time of peace and goodwill in the kitchen however, because Broomfield and Jane were quarrelling again, this time over a dirty fork which Jane had flung across the table on to the floor. Broomfield did not take the bait though which angered Jane even further for the remainder of the day. The next complaint that came was from Rose against Broomfield whom she was thought was a regular, "*Miss Jinnie, thinking always of his stomach and demanding cocoa at 11.00 a.m*". He also wanted cocoa at lunchtime to help him sleep in the evening. Bessie was perplexed and failed to see any connection between cocoa at lunch-time and the evening sleep. She also couldn't understand why they would need food in between meals either. When she mentioned this, a great diatribe was launched at her, as to how close to fainting they all were as it approached 11.00 a.m., so some nourishment at that time was definitely needed. To end the argument and since tea was presently being taxed which made cocoa cheaper, Bessie decreed that they should have cocoa served at every meal and she hoped that that would sort it. At least that's what she thought, but things in the kitchen

---

[55] Letter dated 4th December 1914 to mother.
[56] Letter dated 1st December 1914 to mother.
[57] Letter dated 18th December 1914 to mother.

at Kilwaughter Castle were never that simple. Jane O'Kane didn't like cocoa.[58] Sometime later the servants developed another fad which amused Bessie yet again, because she wrote to her mother to say that they had now taken to using Golden Syrup in their tea instead of sugar.[59]

Bessie gave the staff socks and scarves for Christmas, but was afraid that Crawford and Clarke would, *"Look like convicts"* because of the grey, white and green stripes of their knitwear. Being the Mistress of Kilwaughter she also felt that she should acknowledge others at Christmas – the telegraph boys, post-office workers and the telephone staff amongst others. In total she sent out twenty calendars, numerous books and over 225 Christmas cards. Preparations were in hand for the Christmas dinner and Mrs. Sands had brought them a 21 lb. turkey which was more than enough. Bessie was to eat alone and those staff remaining (not Apsley as he had toothache), would have their meal at 2.00 p.m.[60]

Christmas Alone

Christmas Day was quiet for Bessie at Kilwaughter. She was invited out for tea which she accepted. There had been many presents, cards, letters and calendars delivered – all of which pleased her. Christmas though did not bring a truce to the kitchen and Broomfield was in trouble again, this time over a piece of fish. It all began with a misunderstanding, but thankfully was soon sorted. At the same time some jealousy occurred with an ex-member of staff who had just recently left Bessie's employ. She had allowed him to stay in his house providing he paid rent, but the cook who had a soft spot for him, led him to believe that rent was not necessary. When the Christmas presents to him and his wife were not forthcoming, he was upset and found out that Bessie had decided that he would have nothing before the rent was paid. He duly paid what he owed and received his presents, but not before finding out what the rest of the staff had got just in case his were not as good.

Bessie had enormous patience for the behaviour of her staff who continually kept her amused. She had had to learn a culture that was complicated in the extreme and she had done very well, but she was still

---

[58] Letter dated 21st December 1914 to mother.
[59] Letter dated 22nd January 1917 to mother.
[60] Letter dated 24th December 1914 to mother.

confused when told a story by Lucy McNeill. It turned out that a Larne sailor on board a ship in the middle of a raging battle was found on his knees praying to the Virgin Mary for safety. There was nothing unusal in that apart from the fact that the sailor was a Protestant which added to the complexity of the situation, but Bessie rationalised, that he had tried to conform with everyone else on board, though not very successfully.[61]

Bessie spends another Christmas at Kilwaughter

She continued to remain at Kilwaughter throughout the next year and had to spend another Christmas there because she could not get a passage home. By then many of Bessie's letters were written by someone else, she suffered from arthritis in her hands and sometimes found it difficult to write, especially as her letters were usually very long. In the end she used a typewriter.

The following year of 1916, saw the famous Easter Rising take place in Dublin. Some of the Nationalists had taken over the post office and were demanding full Irish independence. After a week of intense fighting which saw many killed and wounded, it was all over and the executions of those responsible for the siege soon followed. Bessie then dismissed her cook whom she had not long employed, as she thought she was pro-German. The continuing war and the civil unrest dampened life for Bessie somewhat at Kilwaughter. The sewing club that she had been running every Thursday at the Castle for local people to make clothes for the soldiers, had been suspended since all were now involved in helping out in the fields.[62] The sewing club was important to her and she considered it a pleasant event. There were around 12-25 people, but the group had to include at least two, *"Ladies",* as she felt that they would keep the rest of the local people quiet and continually working. Her staff, troublesome at times though they were, on those occasions, kindly forfeited their own supply of butter, sugar and tea, so that the group could enjoy some cakes.

Bessie also later started a herb society at Kilwaughter which was very successful. There were about eighty members who turned up to hear various lectures about herbs and what could be done with them. The herbs were especially used for medicinal purposes in the war – Henbane for absorbing

---

[61] Letter dated 26th December 1914 to mother.
[62] Manko, 1994, p.115.

malaria and Belladonna which reduced fever and also acted as a diuretic. Her gardener planted both of these and he received some of the profits. The herb society became very industrious and even involved the servants who were very enthusiastic about it and held their own meetings and even enlisted the local children to pick the herbs. This business was important and the markets in Belfast were keen to receive them. They paid a good price which was from £9-£13 per hundred weight.[63] Bessie decided that she could use the laundry room for herb drying and thus speed up the process, so she converted it to suit this purpose. The servants were so keen on working with the herbs that Bessie rewarded them by having a Ball at the Castle and allowing them to bring one male friend and one other couple. She also bought them a phonograph player which thrilled the staff.

Yet More Trouble in the Kitchen

Life in the kitchen soon took on a different kind of normality and it all began with the arrival of the new housekeeper Miss Gookin, whom Bessie described as a, *"Black Protestant".* [64] Miss Gookin, like the rest of servants, came with some prejudices. She disliked dirt, alcohol, papists and men, but not gentlemen - and not necessarily in that order. When she began working at the Castle she set about putting her mark on the place as she felt that the Castle housework had been neglected because of Rose's incapacity and it needed to be brought up to her exacting, hygienic standards. Ethel the kitchen maid was included as part of the sweeping clean approach – she looked untidy and Miss Gookin threatened to have her dismissed if she did not improve upon her slovenly ways. The first sanction she brought to bear on Ethel was to refuse her waiting at table. She also made sure that each evening Ethel would have a bath, that had to last a full twenty minutes. Ethel was not the same religion as Miss Gookin and it was thought that this was the reason why she was so hard on the poor maid. On the other hand she liked Rose Rafferty who was a Catholic and who, as we know, had been Bessie's favourite housemaid for twenty-three years. Such was Miss Gookin's respect for Rose that when she

---

[63] Manko, 1994, p.127.
[64] An expression used to describe Ulster Protestants who had the dark hair of the Scots. (Manko, 1994), p.116.

went to visit her in her room, she always took great care to remove her *precious* Ulster Unionist pin as she did not want to offend her.[65]

Miss Gookin made other changes as well. On discovering that the pillowcases of the maids left much to be desired, she instigated regular hair washing and made sure that they were particular about their personal hygiene. She brought in caps of white dotted Swiss lace to cover their hair, but these had to have a black ribbon around them to hide the bad sewing. Miss Gookin herself always wore white for her duties, but would change into black satin for her trips to Larne and when she climbed aboard the *spring van* to sit beside Willie Brennan for the journey, she was thought to have resembled, *"A billowing black sail in full flow"*. Nonetheless she found favour with Bessie who approved of all the changes and although the servants didn't like it, they secretly admired her.

Regardless of their different religions and all their various disagreements the servants maintained a close familial bond with each other and enjoyed working in the Castle. When Bessie's dear housemaid Rose departed Kilwaughter Castle for good on 1st June 1916, there were many tears shed, especially from Bessie. Rose was going to live with her nephew in Belfast as she had become very infirm and was now an elderly lady who hadn't been able to get out of her room for two years. She had gathered a lot of keepsakes over the years from a place that had, in effect, been her whole life. Bessie helped sort all these out, together with Miss Gookin who delighted in cleaning out all the *felth* (filth).[66] Following Rose's departure Miss Gookin was promoted to housekeeper – her rise had been meteoric. Bessie then travelled to England for two weeks with Hannah her personal maid and it was there that she learned how badly the 36th Antrim Division had suffered. In particular, twenty-six men from the Kilwaughter area had either been killed or wounded in France and she knew many of them. Of her tenants Mr. Hewitt had lost three sons and Mr. Wedgwood two. It was so bad, that it put a stop for the first time in 226 years to the 12th July festivities.[67] Bessie felt a pastoral care for many of these people and visited them in their homes which can't have been easy for her and it was at this point that she realised that her place was at Kilwaughter and she put all thoughts of returning to America out of her head. She was an

---

[65] Manko, 1994, p.116.
[66] Ibid, p.118.
[67] Ibid, p.120.

American citizen and would have been prevented from leaving anyway. On the positive side however, she did not pay British taxes.[68]

During the time Bessie had been in London one of her gardener's had left. This meant that Crawford her head gardener (and now her butler as well), had to do extra work. Bessie offered to send out some of the maids to help him, but he was adamant that he didn't want it. He told her that he would, "*Rather work all night as have a woman about the garden. Their feet destroyed the plants and their skirts destroyed the bushes and the amount of work they do won't pay for all the talk there is about it*". It also turned out that Crawford and Miss Gookin had quarrelled. She had complained that Crawford was too thin and that he dyed his hair.[69] More stories were now filtering through about Miss Gookin's treatment of staff and Bessie began to pay attention. Miss Gookin had hired two new maids whilst she had been in England, but what was more serious was that she had begun to abuse the staff physically. Bessie now felt that she had no option, but to dismiss Miss Gookin and wrote to her solicitor Mr. McNinch in Larne, to see if there would be any repercussions if the housekeeper was removed. He advised her that on the abuse issue alone, there were enough grounds for dismissal and so Bessie gave Miss Gookin her notice and a month's wages. Confident as Bessie was ordinarily, this time she was not brave enough to hand Miss Gookin the letter herself, but sent Apsley to do it for her. There now began a war of wills between Bessie and her housekeeper. Before presenting the dismissal letter to Miss Gookin, Apsley had formed a bodyguard in the courtyard with the other men, just in case things got out of hand and when he handed her the letter everyone was amused. Things didn't quite go according to plan because Miss Gookin had an iron resolve and refused to leave. Finally the police had to be called in to sort it out which they did, but not before Bessie also dismissed the two new maids who turned out to be Miss Gookin's own nieces. The housekeeper's plan had been to get rid of all the Catholic staff at Kilwaughter and replace them with her relatives or friends. She also wanted to remain in the Castle whilst Bessie was in America and had begun pilfering the best tinned fruit and vegetables, so that she and her family could live in comfort.[70]

---

[68] Letter summary, 23rd December 1915.
[69] Manko, 1994, p.121.
[70] Ibid, p.124.

After the housekeeper left more horrendous stories began to emerge about the way she had treated the staff. Many of them had left and Bessie now began a recruitment drive to see if she could win some of them back again. In the end though it did not happen, but she managed to get her cook to return. At the same time she decided that four people – Apsley, Hannah and her sister Norah and Chambers who was now the gardener, were enough staff to keep Kilwaughter ticking over.[71] With Bessie alone, she did not use all the rooms and as a result the amount of work that the servants needed to do declined. The smaller number of people in the house also meant that Bessie had time to get to know them better which she wanted to do.

Kennedy Marries

In the autumn Bessie heard from Kennedy that he was to marry, not to Dorothy, the girl Bessie had approved of earlier, but to Gladys Eleanor Fullick, who was a milliner at a shop in Belfast. Gladys's father had died leaving the family in stricken circumstances, so she had had to work.[72] The ceremony was to take place in London, but Bessie was not invited. Bessie had always been fond of Galt's son even though she described him as having, *"Not much back-bone"*. A somewhat unkind comment to make for a man who had fought in the war. She also described him as being discontent and always looking sad.[73] She must have felt somewhat wounded that she would not attend his wedding, but she was more angry than hurt, since a milliner was not her choice of wife for her stepson. She hoped that Gladys might have come from a family who had seen better days. Nonetheless, she decided to invite them to spend part of their honeymoon at Kilwaughter, but they declined. Just ten months later the couple had a baby girl whom they named Joan Katherine after the baby's grandmothers. Kennedy's mother had been called Cornelia which he'd obviously forgotten, but by the time Bessie advised him of that, the child's name had been changed to Valerie.[74]

In the summer of 1919 Kennedy and his family moved to Victoria, Canada, where he ran an agency for oil burners for cookers and ranges.[75] In November

---

[71] Manko, 1994, p.125.
[72] Letter summary, 12th October 1914.
[73] Letter dated 18th October 1914 to mother.
[74] Manko, 1994, p.126.
[75] Letter summary, 1st October 1922.

that year another child was born, this time a son whom they called John Galt, a poignant reminder to Bessie that nothing in life was unchanging for her. The couple had yet another child, who was born just one month before Kennedy died at the early age of 40 years. He had suffered from mustard gas poisoning when on active service duty for the Irish forces in World War 1 which had left him with weakened lungs. His descendants still live in Canada.

The long years of what was supposed to have been a short war were dragging on and there was still no sign of Bessie getting back to see her family in America. March and April of 1917 had brought large drifts of snow up to five feet high and she had lost 21 sheep in the storms. Three ships had been wrecked between Larne and Glenarm and nine men had drowned from one of them. Lord and Lady Antrim had taken in the remaining 20 sailors, to their home at Glenarm Castle where the men remained until they were well enough.[76] In May that year Bessie was given the responsibility for the cheese making in the area.[77]

The Final Year of the War

In 1918 around five hundred American soldiers came to Larne. They were from various states and some of them had never even seen the sea before which caused them severe problems as they had been torpedoed off the coast. Bessie had hoped to entertain many of her countrymen at the Castle and had asked her servants to make quarters ready, but as it happened they were not allowed to leave Larne so her hospitality was not needed. This was a great disappointment to her and the staff. Lucy McNeill had been called upon to deal with the soldiers who had been injured and Bessie also visited and took them little luxuries. She was proud of the soldiers who were considered by the local residents to be, *"So big and fine looking"* and liked it even more when they didn't cause any problems in the area.[78] They left in March with their reputations intact.

On 9th March 1918, an interesting visitor appeared at the Castle. He was a young Australian soldier who was staying with a local farmer. The soldier's name was Agnew and he told a story that his great great grandfather had been

---

[76] Ibid, 15th April 1917.
[77] Letter summary, 31st May 1917.
[78] Letter dated 10th February 1918 to mother.

a stone mason and had built the towers of the Castle that stood adjacent to the front gates. Bessie's servants entertained him regally and he visited the house several times before departing.[79]

Kilwaughter becomes a Convalescent Hospital

In June that year Bessie met Kennedy's new wife and baby in England. She liked them both, but not so the wife's sister whom she thought plain and common. A week later she had a meeting with Lady White who was involved with the hospitals for soldiers. Lady White was looking for volunteers who would turn their homes into convalescent hospitals for the wounded soldiers to have respite care. Bessie put forward Kilwaughter Castle as an appropriate place, but hoped that officers would be sent and not privates, since they were less trouble. As it turned out in the end, she agreed to take ten officers and ten privates who were to be kept separated in the Castle as was the custom of the British army. Bessie had no problem complying with this and placed the best bedrooms at the disposal of the officers together with the library and dining room. The rest would have to make do with the basement, servants quarters (which had thirteen bedrooms), the attic and the bedrooms in the tower.[80]

At the end of September Bessie was sent six officers from Australia who were due to stay until the middle of October. The staff went into overdrive – sorting out the bedrooms that the officers would be using and preparing extra food. Unfortunately two weeks before the soldiers arrived, Bessie's cook decided to leave which caused a real problem, however, Mrs. Massey-Beresford from Belturbet, County Cavan, saved the day by letting Bessie borrow her cook. Bessie of course, entertained her guests magnificently as usual. She took them around the countryside visiting some of her friends at Shane's Castle and *Drumnasole*. She organised a rented car to take the injured officers out and made sure their days were filled with sight-seeing, though left Sundays free for them to enjoy the grounds of Kilwaughter. Meanwhile inside the house, the three remaining servants, Hannah, Little and Sutton, had much to do. They worked tremendously hard, cleaning the officers' rooms, changing the beds, cleaning out the fires and replenishing their toiletries. They made

---

[79] Letter dated 10th March 1918 to mother.
[80] Manko, 1994, p.166.

picnic lunches, did the shopping, chopped wood for the fires and fetched coal for the kitchen. Bessie acknowledged how hard they were working, Hannah and Little worked fourteen hours per day for many weeks without a break.[81] It was all quite different from the Castle's heyday when at least fourteen staff were needed to run the house, now a mere handful would do.

When it came to entertaining the young private soldiers, Bessie moved over and let the servants get on with it, meeting them only at the beginning and end of their stay. They ate with the servants and socialised with them and Hannah kept Bessie up-to-date with all the gossip next day. Sometimes the billeting of soldiers went wrong and was not straight forward. This would happen when Bessie was sent soldiers who were not only injured, but had suffered psychological problems, something we know today as post-traumatic stress. One such soldier, McLean from Scotland, was so ill that he needed round the clock medical help. Sadly after an attempt to jump out of the window and coupled with the injuries he had suffered, he died. The staff who had tried to help him so much were very upset.[82]

War Finally Ends

The war ended in November 1918 and Bessie was made aware of it by the clanging of bells and blowing of whistles. She and Hannah hoisted up two flags on top of the tower to celebrate and it was a joyous occasion. There were parties to attend with extra food and champagne, but even though the war was over in Europe, there were still problems to sort out at home and Home Rule reared its head again. The Irish politicians soon began making local visits and Sir Edward Carson made another appearance in Larne to support Bessie's friend Bertie McCalmont who was hoping to become an MP. He was running against a Sinn Fein candidate, Joseph Maguire who was in jail and Bessie thought this quite preposterous that he should be allowed to run at all. What really angered her though was that the nephew of her old housekeeper Rose Rafferty, was supporting him.

---

[81] Ibid, 1994, pps.137,138.
[82] Ibid, 1994, p.140.

Chapter 10

Things begin to Change

Bessie remained a further year at Kilwaughter after the war ended. She was still busy taking in wounded soldiers until May of 1919. It had been five years since she had seen her family and friends, but she was still in no hurry to return to them, perhaps instinctively knowing that her time left at Kilwaughter was drawing to an end. In the aftermath of the war, life was not that comfortable in the Castle and there were shortages of many things. Few staff remained, Bessie had no cook and the staff didn't want a new one, fearing another Miss Gookin; there was little entertaining and she had to eat in the dining room wrapped in warm furs as there was no fire lit in the house. The furnace wasn't working, but even so coal was scarce and very expensive, as indeed were standard commodities such as dairy products.[1]

On 2nd December 1919, in time for Christmas, Bessie finally set sail for America aboard Cunard's *Carmania*. She had had great difficulty in securing a ticket and was outraged that she had to pay $200 for it and even at that price she still had to share a cabin with two strangers. Her three servants who were accompanying her travelled separately on another ship at a cheaper price.[2]

The Balzani Family can finally visit Kilwaughter Castle

During all the years of the war it had not been possible for any of the Balzani family to visit their Irish home. The Guest Book records that after Ugo's visit in August 1903, no-one came until early 1919. Just two months after the end of the war, Guendalina and her daughter Giorgia visited on 23rd January. This

---

[1] Ibid, 1994, p.143.
[2] Ibid, 1994, p.144.

was the first time that Giorgia had seen the Castle which no doubt, she would have inherited had she lived. She was ill during part of her stay at Kilwaughter and was looked after by one of Bessie's officers.[3] There is no record of her ever returning again. The following month her father, Guido Valensin also arrived – again that would appear to have been his only visit to Kilwaughter Castle.[4] Guendalina Valensin decided then to sell Ballygally Castle which she and her sister Nora had inherited and they sold it to a friend.[5]

In 1921 Bessie's lease expired and it was also the year that Irish Partition began which brought in two separate states, Ulster which was to remain within the control of the British Government and the rest of Ireland which was referred to as the Irish Free State. The partition resulted in civil war and mass destruction and Bessie would have known this. She remained in Wilmington from December 1919 until 1922. Why she decided not to return before then is unclear, but with the end of the war, the long absence from her family, the lease only two years left to run and with Guendalina and Nora still the Castle's owners, so many things had changed for her. She and Galt had wanted to live the lives of the landed gentry in a stately home and in the short time they had been together at Kilwaughter Castle, they had certainly achieved that. It seemed that Bessie had had enough of her life in Ireland and it was time to move on.

Although the lease had expired the previous year, Guendalina and Nora had allowed her one extra year to help clear out the Castle and remove her personal effects, but during that time they had arranged for a new tenant to lease some of the land. The two sisters lives were now totally spent in Italy and with the death of their parents and in particular their mother, it would have been understandable if they had wanted to sever any inclination they felt for spending some of their time in Ireland. It must have been difficult to know what to do with the Irish Castle so far away, that would now very soon, stand empty once more. It was also a huge responsibility for them, but they were determined to hold on to it and the associated Irish identity of both themselves and their mother. They remained the Castle's owners for some time to come until another world war finally brought about the beginning of the Castle's downfall.

---

[3] Letter summary, 23rd February 1919.
[4] Kilwaughter Castle Guest Book.
[5] Letter summary, 16th February 1919.

Bessie leaves for America to visit her Family

Bessie sailed for Ireland in April 1922 aboard the *Seythia* and she was not prepared for what she saw. The civil war had done much more than she could have foreseen. She only remained two days before setting off again, this time for London to visit some of her friends who had been forced from their beautiful homes in Ulster. Shane's Castle, Galgorm Castle and Glenmona had all been burnt.[6] This had upset her enormously because she had visited so many of them in happier times. All had been victims of the bloody civil war.

Bessie did not return to Kilwaughter Castle for three months, spending her time socialising with her various friends around Europe, in Holland, Germany and Denmark. She also presented her niece Nancy at Court on 16th June 1922 where they saw King George V and other members of the royal family. She arrived back at Kilwaughter on 11th August 1922 to arrange for the auction of much of the Castle's contents. Her view was that all her friends were leaving so why shouldn't she? Hannah her maid who had been with her throughout the latter years began the mammoth task of packing thirty years of belongings and personal memories. They sent some of the favourite things back to America and although Bessie was leaving her Irish home, she was not leaving Ireland because Apsley took care of some of her furniture and other belongings in his new house that he had just purchased from Mr. Bailey. The house was large and the deal had included a farmhouse, four tenants' homes and Kilwaughter Village which comprised thirteen houses and the flax mill.

Lord and Lady Massareene offered Bessie the use of three rooms at Antrim Castle which was very much to her liking. She took possession almost at once, decorating them and giving a small room to Hannah. Some of her furniture arrived there together with her six hundred books that she thought probably wouldn't sell at the forthcoming auction. The carpet she brought, had been used in Rose's room and it too, helped her feel more at home.[7]

Edward her brother, arrived for the auction which was to be held during the first week of October. Bessie had chosen Clark & Son, Auctioneers and Valuers of The Mart, 21 Rosemary Street, Belfast, to carry out the auction.[8] [9]

---

[6] Ibid, 22nd May 1922.
[7] Manko, 1994, pps.164-165.
[8] PRONI, T/3549/1.
[9] Larne Historical Centre.

There was so much to be sold and with Kilwaughter Castle being one of Ulster's prime homes, a catalogue was produced to highlight the event and entitled, *Catalogue of the Valuable Collection of Kilwaughter Castle*. Viewing dates were arranged for Friday and Saturday, 29th and 30th September 1922 and five days were set aside for it from 3rd October beginning at 11.00 a.m.[10] Admission was by catalogue, priced at 2s. 6d. Apart from the Castle contents, various other household effects including the carpenter's shop, basement, scullery and courtyard contents were also to be sold. Numerous articles were marked for the *US* which indicated that Bessie was sending these to *Rockwood*. As well as that some things had already been sold beforehand. For the two days of the viewing Bessie and her brother stayed in Belturbet with friends.

As usual at the auction there was a bit of game playing. Apsley and Drummond, his very wealthy cousin, kept the prices high and thus the bidding. On the first day a total of £739 16s 10d. was taken and the following days were equally successful as they made - £509 2s. 9d., £726 17s. 7d., £501 9s. 9d. and the last day, £224 14s. 3d. Altogether the auction brought in just over £2,700[11] which was a good return considering that the war had ended just a short time before.

Bessie took a strangely detached view of the whole proceedings. She had lovingly put together a collection of items for her home over many years, but when it came to seeing these possessions disappear at the auction, she didn't seem to mind at all. She wasn't even concerned that the weather had been bad for part of the time and as a result rain and mud had been carried into the house, almost destroying the wonderful inlaid floors of the old oak hall and the music room, but that too didn't seem to worry her.[12] Guendalina and Nora wanted to reclaim the Castle which was rightly theirs and anything that remained belonged to them and they told her that. Whether this was part of the original lease or not, we cannot be sure, but Bessie was not happy about it and as a result the two Balzani sisters got only, *"Two high post beds, one curtain pole, two stone vases and a cracked dressing glass"*. [13] The fact that the sisters had already found a new tenant may also have upset her, since she wasn't even given the opportunity to renew the lease – an obvious sign that the Balzanis

---

[10] Manko, 1994, p.160.
[11] PRONI, T3549/1.
[12] Manko, 1994, pps.167-168.
[13] Ibid, 1994, p.169.

wanted her out. In Bessie's opinion, they defaulted in their contract.[14] None of this however, stopped her attending the opening of the Ulster Parliament on 12th October 1922.

On 4th November 1922 Bessie left Ireland for America. She returned once more, for the last time, in 1926, but by then Kilwaughter Castle no longer held any interest for her. She died at *Rockwood* following a lengthy illness in 1934. *Rockwood* continued to be the Bringhurst's family home until Bessie's sister Mary died in 1965 aged 100 years. Mary's niece Nancy Sellers Hargraves inherited the house and on her death the property became the responsibility of the local council. They decided to create a museum around its history and artefacts. The house contains Irish artefacts from Kilwaughter Castle.

Kilwaughter Castle's Protector Relinquishes her Responsibility Permanently

Bessie was a remarkable woman, much ahead of her time with her ideas and views, especially in Ireland, then a country where women's opinions were deemed unimportant. She was probably unaware of this female repression and was simply being herself in organising those around her, but it must have been something of an eye-opener in this male-dominated society, to learn that a woman could be successful in business, very much like Margaret Jones before her and long before Bessie moved into Kilwaughter Castle. Those men Bessie worked with must have found her fascinating, though would never have dared admit it. No doubt when Galt died they expected her to return to America, but Bessie was a formidable woman, brimming with self-confidence and well able to run the Kilwaughter estate and her other businesses. Her photographs showed a neatly dressed woman of slight appearance, that belied a steely personality underneath. She could be very controlling and domineering and even manipulative and because of her high-class tendencies, was always seeking out those who were of a more privileged social standing than her.

Bessie certainly forged some very politically powerful friendships, but undoubtedly she had charisma, otherwise her many friends would not have been attracted to her for so long and perhaps her culture intrigued them too – that openness she displayed so much.

---

[14] Ibid, p.9.

She took charge of any situation and could be relied upon to do her best. Her altruism came through during the First World War when she organised many ventures to help the soldiers. She learnt to have patience with the Irish people, as was shown in her relationship with her staff and the workmen at the Castle in the early days. Her many acts of kindness and philanthropy meant that she enjoyed a good reputation. She was an intelligent woman, much experienced in travel and other cultures and probably because of this and her strong personality, her parents deferred to her on many occasions. She enjoyed a good relationship with her father and no doubt inherited many of his characteristics which helped her survive Irish life, since he too, was a successful business man, but her mother was a different matter. It remained a great disappointment to Bessie, that she never made the long journey to Ireland to see her beloved Kilwaughter. Her mother feigned sea-sickness, but the truth was probably that she could not have endured Bessie's bossiness for such a great length of time, in a place from where she could not readily escape.

Bessie and Galt had moved into Kilwaughter after it had stood uninhabited for forty years and together they had brought it to life again after William Agnew had moved to France. Even after Galt's death, she had not stopped loving the Castle and in Bessie, Kilwaughter found a true friend and owed much to her. Its stone walls had echoed with the reverberating noise of her infamous dinner parties and luncheons, to say nothing of the servants' ricocheting squabbles. Now the old building stood alone and empty again and sadly no-one could know at the time, but Elizabeth Bringhurst Smith was to be its last inhabitant. She had not been the Castle's first matriarch, since that honour belonged to Margaret Jones nearly a century before, but with Bessie now gone it had lost a very dear friend who had been its protector for thirty years. As the contents disappeared and the staff too, it took on an air of bleakness about it once more, from which it was never to recover.

Bessie's final account from her solicitor John Bristow, ended all her responsibility for the Castle. It was dated November 1935 and gave a credit to her of £274. 9s. 3d. after taking into account rents from January to November 1921, accountancy and solicitor's fees.[15]

---

[15] PRONI, D1905/10/193.

The Guest Book

The Guest Book that Bessie had opened on 11th May 1892 with her own name, closed with its final entry in September 1922 – a fitting tribute to her brother Edward to whom she was so close and who arrived to help Bessie prepare for the auction. The numerous pages in the book confirmed the great number of guests who enjoyed her hospitality within the safety of the Castle's thick stone walls. Solitary names and addresses, each with its own history. The names of her closest neighbours were there of course – the Antrims of Glenarm Castle, the Macaulays of *Red Hall*, the Magheramornes, the McNeills of Larne, the O'Neills of Shane's Castle, the Turnlys of *Drumnasole* and many more. There were names of exotic places like Madras, Bengal, Bahamas, Egypt, interspersed with such local names as Ballycastle, Ballymena and Belfast. Then Europe was firmly represented and many places from England as well. The Balzani family, the owners of the Castle, added their signatures too, as did their niece Andrienna who, with an obvious sense of humour, signed, *The World* as her place of abode.

At the end of the book, as a reflection of the war years, the pages were taken up with the names of many military staff – the army, navy and RAF - all well represented in the months March to June of 1919 coinciding with the end of the first world war. One striking entry was written on 8th August 1898 when Alice and Angus Kennedy from Culzean Castle in Ayrshire paid a visit. It was striking because more than two and a half centuries before, Sir Patrick Agnew, the first occupant of Kilwaughter in 1622, married Margaret the daughter of Sir Thomas Kennedy of Culzean Castle. That a relationship between Bessie, Kilwaughter Castle's representative and the Culzean Castle descendants was still valid, may have been brought about by an invitation from Bessie, though it is doubtful that she knew so much of the old history of the Agnews. Perhaps the saddest thing though, was the lack of the Agnew name in the Guest Book. It was recorded that Bessie entertained a member of the Agnew family on only three occasions – Quintin Agnew of Lochnaw Castle who came on 27th August 1904 and again on 18th September 1907, this time accompanied by his wife Evelyn and Lt. Col. William Agnew Moore from Londonderry, who visited in January 1919.

Chapter 11

What next for the Castle and Estate?

The Castle and estate now back with its rightful owners, Guendalina Valensin and Nora, opened up new problems, one being what to do with the Castle? Whilst the sisters wanted to keep the estate intact, their homes in Italy were many miles from Ireland. Guendalina also had her husband and daughter who simply could not be uprooted to move to Ulster. The solution was to find someone who could look after the Castle and farm the surrounding land. By then there were just 240 acres, remaining, a substantial reduction from the 13,000 acres once owned by their great uncle William Agnew.

On 14th November 1922, just a few weeks after Bessie had departed, a local farmer signed a lease for a term of twelve years, to farm the demesne lands. The lease was a temporary measure and the contract stated that, *"The operation of the Irish Land Act is expressly excluded"*.[1] In 1926 John Bristow, Solicitor, took over the estate's legal affairs however, one year previously on 28th May 1925, the Northern Ireland Land Act had come into force. This meant that the Land Purchase Commission were legally obliged to request details of all tenanted land including the names of the tenants, descriptions of the holdings, rent payable by the tenants and the tenure under which they held, for the specific purpose that each tenant could purchase, at an agreed price, his holding. Guendalina and Nora's agent passed the necessary details to the Land Purchase Commission, but excluded the demesne lands as these were not considered to come within the Act. The Land Purchase Commission however, required these lands to be included though it was still argued by the agent. John Bristow in a letter to the Italian Ambassador in London, who it would

---

[1] PRONI, D971/9/1

seem was representing the Balzanis, believed that it would be difficult for Guendalina and Nora to exclude the demesne lands unless a claim could be brought to obtain the end of the tenancy agreement with their tenant. It was thought possible that this could be done since he had committed some breaches within the contract. Mr. Bristow then sought further legal advice as he believed that if the lands were brought under the Act, then the value of the Castle as a residence, would be depleted. Unfortunately, the only way to have the demesne lands excluded was to try and evict the tenant which they attempted to do, but he brought conflicting evidence and won his case. It had been a lengthy process and at the time the solicitor thought the case was unique. The result was that the lands were now brought in under the Act, but with certain rights as to the timber and trees, mines, minerals and quarries, bogs and various rights for shooting and sporting activities which formed part of the lease. The lease also did not permit the tenant to damage the lawns around the Castle or the use of the main driveway except on business. It was obvious from the terms of this lease that Guendalina and Nora wanted to keep the Castle for now and its adjoining land for continued use as a residence.

World War Two looms which causes problems for the Balzani Family

The years which followed were difficult for the Balzani sisters as it was not easy for them, as absentee landlords, to find someone to look after their interests, but they still managed to keep hold of the Castle and what remained of its estate. Regrettably the tenant they had found to rent the Castle withdrew his offer. By then the Castle's finances were in an unhealthy place. Its not known what the sisters ultimate objectives were, but we can only assume that they wished to continue to keep their Irish home in the long term. World events were to change that and Europe became enveloped in a catastrophe which, unknown to the Balzanis, would propel Kilwaughter Castle even faster towards its downfall.

At the outbreak of the 2nd World War in September 1939, Mussolini was committed to Hitler's side through the *Pact of Steel*. This meant that Guendalina and Nora were not only prevented from visiting their property by the U-boats circling Irish shores (a similar situation that Bessie also had faced during the last war when she tried to get back to America), but they were also now effectively citizens of an enemy nation. One of the results of this was that the British Government seized all alien property and at some stage during this process, they sequestrated Kilwaughter Castle from its owners.

Kilwaughter Castle seized as Enemy Property

At the end of October 1940, a sale of the remaining furnishings in the Castle was advertised, by order of the Custodian of Enemy Property for Northern Ireland, the proceeds of which would have gone to the Government. Many of the items that weren't sold disappeared and amongst those sadly, were the very old portraits of the Agnews that have never been found. The fact that the building was noted as *enemy property* seemed to come as a shock for local people who knew the history of the place because they also knew that the property was far from being e*nemy*. The Countess Balzani was Irish by birth as were her parents before her and indeed, she was popularly known as, "*The last of the Agnews of Kilwaughter*". [2] Her two daughters Guendalina and Nora could also claim Irish nationality because of her and added to that, Nora was born in England, but unfortunately at the time when war broke out, none of the sisters were living in the property. When taking account of these facts, it is difficult to understand how the authorities could justifiably claim that Kilwaughter Castle should come under the Enemy Property Act, but because of Italy's alien state, it was claimed. The Castle lay empty yet again after this for several more years and its vacant rooms began a long period of deterioration with damp and mould, which helped destroy the rest of the beautiful inlaid floors that had previously begun with Bessie's auction.

Troops Arrive at Kilwaughter Castle

One year after war broke out several military units were stationed at Kilwaughter Castle.

First to arrive was the 6th Battalion of the Royal Berkshire Regiment in June 1940. They remained for four months. They were then followed by the 148th Independent Reconnaissance Company/Squadron in January 1941 and they stayed (apart from a brief period spent at Antrim Castle) until April 1942.

As the war continued Northern Ireland was considered the first country of choice in the United Kingdom, to deploy American troops and amongst the

---

[2] Belfast Telegraph, 24th October 1940.

places made available to billet these people, was the Castle and its grounds. In January 1944, the 644th Tank Destroyer Battalion left New York aboard the *Aquitania,* bound for the United Kingdom.[3] They arrived in the United Kingdom mainland on 22nd January and there the Battalion split. Three Companies (A, B, C), continued their journey by rail, arriving at Kilwaughter Castle on 23rd January 1944. The Larne area had been used to hosting American troops from the last war, but this was a new generation of men. Nonetheless they showed them the same hospitality as before and the troops got on well with local people.

The following excerpts are taken from correspondence sent by some of the members of these Companies.

From Samuel Higginbotham, dated 28th Sept. 2001, 81 years old.

"Only the officers were billeted in the castle, we non-commissioned officers and enlisted men lived in Quonset huts (commonly known as Nissen huts) in the grounds. The kitchen was in the basement or lowest part of the castle. I don't have any idea about the artefacts there. I remember the roof on the castle was sheet lead, must have weighed tons. I worked on our TD's (tank destroyers) a big part of the time we were there. Although they were new, as the Battalion welder I had many modifications to do to them. Most of the guys worked on vehicles etc. I contracted pneumonia while there and spent a month in the hospital. We also had a man killed when the TD he was riding in ran off the road and overturned in a bog. We got passes into Larne several times a week, a truck took us in and brought us back at 10.00 p.m. My buddy and I missed it one night and walked back, we made it back in time for breakfast. I remember the Kings Arms hotel in Larne and some of the pubs. Also the theater (sic) where I went to lots of movies. I met an older lady who had a nice home in Larne who took in sailors, soldiers, RAF fliers, marines, any service men and gave them bed and breakfast at no charge (but anyone could always leave money under the sugar bowl). She was a wonderful woman and I've always been sorry I never properly thanked her, she did a lot for me. She always had a place for me".

---

[3] The Battalion totalled 1,260 men.

Jacqueline Agnew

A further letter from Samuel Higginbotham, dated 1st October 2001.

"As I remember there did not appear to be many out buildings on the grounds, seems we did most of our work outside. The natives and the Battalion had good relations, at least I never heard of any negative incidents. As far as I remember there were no covert operations involved. I spoke to our Major about it and he said 'No'. As I recall the arch at the Castle was still intact while we were there".[4]

From Henry A. Garton, Jr., dated October, 2001, 85 years old.

"The 644th Tank Destroyer Battalion left New York on January 1, 1944 aboard the HMS Aquitania. On January 22, 1944 A,B, and C Companies of the 644th moved by rail to Kilwaughter Castle near Larne, Northern Ireland. Further training was gun service practice, anti-tank range near Bushmills, indirect firing at Sperrin Mountains, artillery range near Draperstown, some firing was done on Collin Top Range about 16 miles from Kilwaughter Castle. Training for combat. Here are a few interesting items. First – There was a caretaker who took care of the grounds, he was often on his hands and knees taking out crab grass, very proud of the grounds. No Kilwaughter Castle staff were there and everything seemed to be removed to make room for us. As for the townsfolk they were very friendly and we got along fine. Major John Girvan (Mayor of Larne) was very good to me and some of my Company. He invited us to breakfast every Sunday morning for eggs, bacon and sausage. There was one sergeant, a Catholic and the Mayor said he couldn't come to breakfast anymore for it would hurt him as Mayor. After that the Battalion said they had the army religion. One time my driver and I had picked up the Battalion pay roll and had gotten lost on our return. A man stopped us and told us to turn around for we were over the border in the Free State, if caught could be held until the war ends. Of course we turned around quickly. As for the Castle we heard the roof was lead and had been removed as needed for the war effort. Just for interest the 644th went all through the war even to the end when the outfit liberated a concentration camp, making the local

---

[4] It was always understood that the troops at Kilwaughter Castle removed the archway to facilitate entry for their heavy equipment.

townspeople go through the camp. Before this I was wounded on November 25, 1944 in the Hurtgen Forrest, my runner was killed stepping on a Shoe Mine. I was hospitalized for months. At the time I was a Captain of 'A' Company and very proud of the Battalion".

The 644th Tank Destroyer Battalion stayed only four months and left Kilwaughter Castle on 11st May 1944 for Belfast where they boarded the *HMS Lancashire* for Newport docks in Wales. Before they left, they wrote on a notice board in the hall, *"Beware of the White Lady"*. A reference made to the Castle ghost. They then travelled on by rail to Hungerford, England. The Battalion later landed on the Normandy beaches and went on to distinguish themselves in the Battle of the Bulge at Ardennes that winter. Kilwaughter Village Hall contains a plaque commemorating the Battalion's sojourn in the area.[5] After they left a notice was placed in the local newspaper in 1946, auctioning off 50 Nissen huts, 500 and 1,000 gallon tanks, stoves and ranges plus much other equipment that had been used by the soldiers. Some of the local residents purchased selected pieces for use on their farms.[6]

Kilwaughter's Final Demise

The years following saw the Castle lie dormant and deteriorate, but in 1951, six full years after the war, it was reported in the local paper that Kilwaughter Castle was to be sold by the Ulster Government. The sale was conducted by W.H. Esler and Sons, Point Street, Larne and the property was bought by E.H. McConnell, a metal company that proceeded with all haste, to push the once magnificent Castle into its total destruction. Mr. McConnell had worked as Regional Manager of Messrs. George Cohen, Sons and Company, though in 1949 resigned from there and opened up his own business in Dalton Street, Belfast.[7] (According to a local resident, McConnell sold the Castle lead on the roof and down pipes, to the Cohen Company). The Company set about dismantling the lead which covered most of the roof, tower turrets, the drains and downpipes for a very good reason. At the time lead was worth £150 per ton. This was a short time after the war and lead was probably hard to come

---

[5] The Ulster American Heritage Trail Plaques, Northern Ireland.
[6] Kilwaughter Castle Camp, Larne, 15th August, 1946.
[7] The Northern Whig & Belfast Post, 2nd and 10th August, 1949.

by, so it was easy to see why the Castle was a big attraction. Not only that, but J. McConnell who was in charge of the operation volunteered that he would be using some of the leaded windows and other materials in a house that he planned to build for himself. The purchase of the lead was even reported as far away as Texas, in the newspaper *Morning Avalanche* in Lubbock, which reported that, "*The high cost of lead was causing the owners to strip the 18th century Kilwaughter Castle in Northern Ireland*"[8] (A journalist error, as the owners did not strip the Castle).

The years following its destruction and with no roof on it to help give at least some kind of protection, the Castle began succumbing to the elements and started its disintegration process in earnest. It was returned in this pitiful state to its rightful owners, the Balzani family. Why the Castle was not given back before its heart was ripped out and it was deliberately completely destroyed is open for debate. The war had long finished and in fact Britain had already begun trading again with both Germany and Italy, but the Government obviously felt it financially prudent to strip it of anything of value before returning it. A total travesty on a John Nash building and sad that the Council of the day could not have seen the folly of this and taken more care that it was preserved not just the area, but also the nation.

It was unfortunate that the sisters resided in a belligerent country at the time of war. In a Treaty signed between the UK and Italy, dated 10th February 1947, the Italian Government undertook to compensate Italian Nationals whose assets were taken under the Trading with The Enemy Legislation, but on enquiring with the appropriate office, no record of either the name Balzani or Valensin was on the data base, as having happened. In fact it was believed that the records of sequestrated property were probably destroyed and only a sample kept for posterity.[9] No compensation for this destruction can be found in any document within the Balzani archives.

Nora, the remaining sister, had died in 1975. She bequeathed her only remaining property, Kilwaughter and what was left of its estate, to her second cousin Countess Bianca Molteni Balzani. Bianca was born in 1908, one of five children and her father had an elevated position within the Bank of Italy. She had married Count Ulisse Balzani, son of Corrado and Maria Cristina and the

---

[8] Morning Avalanche, Lubbock, Texas, 25th February, 1952, p.7.
[9] Foreign & Commonwealth Office, 2016.

couple had three children. At the time of her inheritance from Nora, Countess Bianca Balzani was already a widow and her family grown and had no need of a home many miles away that was no longer habitable, but had become a real liability. In 1980 she decided to sell the Kilwaughter Castle estate and enlisted the help of solicitors, O'Rorke, McDonald and Tweed, of Larne, to deal with the business of getting rid of it. Years before Nora had given most of the earlier remaining artefacts from the Castle to the son of Ulisse's sister who lived in Rome.[10] Over the years the estate had diminished enormously and others had encroached on its lands. Added to that there were missing title documents, which held up the sale, so the whole procedure was not straightforward and took several years.[11] In the end what remained of it, was purchased by several parties and Kilwaughter Castle's past was wiped away with the stroke of a pen. Its last heiress Countess Bianca Balzani who resided beside Lake Maggiore, died peacefully, just two days after her 100th birthday on 27th April, 2008.

Kilwaughter in Ruins

Today the once proud Irish Castle stands decayed and forlorn. It belies its own history and John Nash would no doubt, be appalled at the dishonour paid to his architecture. The crumbling shell gets worse as the years go by. The stone towers are still there at the main driveway which is completely overgrown. Beside them, is the pretty gate lodge, now used as a private home which will hopefully prolong its life. The road at the back entrance to the Castle and now the only access, is full of pitted holes that frequently fill with rain, but the serious looking little grey stone cottage that once was part of the estate, is still there standing guard, but like the Castle, is now completely derelict.

Inside the Castle's decaying mess, there are signs of a previous life. Although the staircases have tumbled to the basement, the shadows of the many fireplaces in the various rooms can still be seen on the walls, as a reminder of the guests who once enjoyed the warmth, the conviviality and the safety that this great Castle provided in times of civil war, world war and undoubted family crises. The beautiful sandstone windowsills endure, as do

---

[10] Kindly recounted by Alessandra Gatti.
[11] Letter from O'Rorke, McDonald & Tweed, 1980.

parts of the original old wall that was built in the 17th century. Trees and undergrowth have laid claim to much of the building. In the end it is only the shell that remains and Kilwaughter, that unknown Castle, faces a bleak future, but nothing can ever destroy its fascinating history.

Afterword

Many of the relatives of both Kilwaughter and Lochnaw Castles went on to achieve interesting lives. Some became officers in various regiments serving in India and elsewhere, others became political or creative and sadly some became involved with the cruel brutality of enslaved people. The following appendices tell a little of their stories.

Appendix 1

The Extended Jones Family

Edward Jones Agnew remained close to his extended family throughout his life and some of them are mentioned in his Will. Many others led compelling lives and are worth mentioning. His half-uncle, Dr. Conway Jones was born in 1721 and died in Lisburn in 1778. He married Mary Wray Todd, daughter of William Todd from Dublin. She was connected to Sir Cecil Wray and to the Harrisons of Magheralave Castle, Lisburn. Mary died a month after her husband in Dublin.[1] and they had five children – William Todd Jones, Valentine Eyer Jones, Edward Jones, Anne Jones and Frances Jones.

William Todd Jones was born 1755 at Cory's Glen near Hillsborough, outside Lisburn. Having decided to become a lawyer he was duly sent to Trinity College, Dublin where he successfully completed his studies and gained entry to the Irish Bar. Coming to the conclusion however, that law was not, after all, what he wanted to do, he resigned and returned home to live the life of a country gentleman. In 1778 whether tiring of idle pursuits or searching for adventure, William joined the Lisburn Fusiliers, one of two infantry corps. He was said to have been an enthusiastic recruit and was well recognised riding through the streets in his resplendent military uniform. Promotion soon followed, first as Lieutenant and then in early 1782 he was again elevated to the rank of Captain. At the same time he was appointed a delegate for Carrickfergus and sent to the Volunteer Convention in Dungannon.[2] Here William began to get a taste for political life and no doubt his early legal

---

[1] These Hallowed Grounds, 2005, Vol. II, p.149.
[2] Member of the Jones family.

training helped him articulate his arguments. The following year he was elected an MP for Lisburn from 1783-90.³ He served two terms.

Like his cousin Edward, both were supporters of Catholic emancipation. William in particular seemed to have been popular with the Catholics and William Drennan referred to this in a letter to his brother-in-law Sam McTier in 1792, that Jones was, *"Idolised"* by the Catholics.⁴ In fact in 1793 the Catholic Committee seemed to reinforce this by allocating various funds to their supporters (presumably they were in their service), amongst whom was William Todd Jones whose remuneration from them rose by £500 to £1,000, with the promise of another £500 in due course.⁵ (They seemed to renege on this promise later on for which Jones took them to task).⁶ In Jones's case this gesture of money may have been ill-advised since according to Martha McTier, he was spending his mornings, *"In dram-drinking and his evenings in wenching"*.⁷

In 1797, just one year before the start of the rebellion, Jones was detained in an English prison for the non-payment of a debt of £2,000. When Martha McTier heard this, she commented to her brother that the Catholic Committee who had earlier agreed to pay Jones substantial funds for his support, should now come forward and pay what they owed him.⁸

William's somewhat debauched life seemed to revolve around brinkmanship and culminated in a duel with Sir Richard Musgrave, an Irish political writer, whose views he felt on the rebellion in 1798, were contentious. Jones challenged Musgrave to a duel and the response to Jones was that his weapon (in this case a sword) would be as ineffective as his pen! Musgrave at first tried to apologise but fearing that he would look a coward accepted the challenge. It seemed that Jones came off best since Musgrave was left wounded, though not seriously.⁹

---

³ Agnew, Luddy, 1998, Vol .I, p.89.
⁴ Ibid, p.409.
⁵ Ibid, p.519.
⁶ Ibid 1999, Vol. II, p.252.
⁷ Ibid 1998, Vol. I, p.520.
⁸ Agnew, Luddy, 1999, Vol.II, p.355.
⁹ Ibid, Vol.III, p.47.

William Todd Jones never married, but fathered an illegitimate son who died at 20 years of age in 1813. Five years later William died as a result of a carriage accident, in Rostrevor, Co. Down.[10] [11]

His brother Edward[12] on the other hand, seemed to have lived a much quieter existence. He was a native of Rostrevor.[13] In 1783 when he was 21 years of age, he felt forced to emigrate to America as by then his more exuberant brother William through his loyal patriotism in Ireland, had caused the loss of much of the family inheritance.[14] [15] Edward initially traded as a merchant and then a lawyer and this obviously raised his profile because just seven years after he arrived in America, he was appointed Solicitor General in the state of North Carolina.[16] [17] He married Mary Elizabeth Mallett in 1790 and the couple had eleven children and if these were not enough, they adopted nine more. He died in 1841.

Their eldest daughter Frances Pollock Jones (1798-1863) married Professor William Hooper (1792-1876) in December 1814 and they had seven children. Hooper began his career by entering the teaching profession, but as a deeply religious man he combined this with the teaching of his faith. He was ordained into the ministry in 1822. He retired from his various commitments one year before his death. His wife had already died and he spent his final year with his daughter Mary Elizabeth and her husband, John de Berniére Hooper. William Hooper was the grandson of one of the signers (William Hooper), of the Declaration of Independence in 1776.[18]

Conway's daughter Frances (the above Frances's aunt), married into the Pollock family of Newry. Her husband Joseph was a barrister and member of the Volunteer Movement, so would inevitably have moved within the same social circles as the Jones'. He was also an avid writer of political pamphlets.[19] The couple had at least three children, Edward, Mary Ann and Frances.

---

[10] Ibid, p.717.
[11] Neill, 1995, Vol.9, pps 14, 18.
[12] Not to be confused with Edward Jones Agnew.
[13] PRONI, T2625/1.
[14] Agnew, Luddy, 1998, Vol. I, p.72.
[15] Member of the Jones family.
[16] Agnew, Luddy, 1999, Vol. II, p.638.
[17] Eccles Family Papers.
[18] Powell, 1988, Vol. III.
[19] Agnew, Luddy, 1999, Vol .III, p.720.

During 1785 and 1786 family life was somewhat difficult for them because Joseph was called to London to repay a debt which was due and the year after, one of their children developed smallpox though survived this.[20] He was a somewhat fickle character because just a short time after his wife's death in August 1789, he was seen to be cheerful and happy that he was once more a single man. In 1796, he was still progressing in his career and was appointed a county judge on an annual salary of £400.[21] He died in 1824.

With regard to their three children, Edward married and had four sons, one of whom James became a well-known physician in London, another son was a lawyer and another Archdeacon. Less is known about the fourth son's career. We do know however, that he travelled to America with his wife and two children, but later returned to live in England. His sister Mary Ann married William Clarke and they had several children including two daughters. Edward's other sister Frances became Mrs. Dowglass (she is mentioned in Edward Jones Agnew's Will) and the couple had two children – Frances and Thomas. Mrs. Dowglass lived part of her life in Rome because her daughter Frances, suffered from tuberculosis and found the climate there to be more agreeable to her health. Mrs. Dowglass died in Rome and her daughter returned to live with her brother. Her nephew (Thomas's son) inherited his father's estate in Ireland.[22]

Conway's other daughter Anne introduced another Huguenot to her family. She married John Anthony de Berniére (1744-1812) around 1778 and it is said by the family that they met in Rostrevor. Being a Colonel in the army he was stationed at various garrisons – Chester in England, Ireland and Canada. During his time spent posted overseas his wife and family resided in England.

The de Berniére family [23] in Ireland, originally descended from Jean Antoine de Berniére[24] who was born near Caen, in Normandy, France and was one of four children. In 1685 he fled his native country for Holland and joined one of Wiliam III's regiments. He eventually arrived in Ireland with Louis Crommelin who was instrumental in shaping the Irish linen industry.

---

[20] Agnew, Luddy, 1998, Vol. I, p.245.
[21] Ibid, 1999, Vol. II, p.208.
[22] PRONI, T2625/7.
[23] PRONI, T2628/7.
[24] PRONI, T2625/8.

Jean Antoine settled in the main linen area of Lisburn and married Mary Magdalen Crommelin, the only daughter of the famous Louis and his wife Anne who was herself a Crommelin and his own cousin. The couple had at least two children and possibly one more. Their son Louis Crommelin de Berniére (born ca.1712), married Elinor Donlevy in 1739, sister-in-law of the Lord Bishop of Down, the Right Rev. George Marley. Louis, a Captain in the British Army, served in Lord Forbe's regiment. Sadly on his way home from Africa in 1762, due to ill-health, he died and was buried at sea. His wife predeceased him, having died on 29th August 1759. The couple's eight children were now orphans and the family unit was split. The children were sent to various relatives to be cared for. Their eldest son, John Anthony who married Conway's daughter Ann, was sent to his mother's sister Elizabeth Donlevy (wife of the aforementioned George Marley). (His aunt Elizabeth became the great grandmother of the 7th Duchess of Rutland).

John Anthony and his wife Anne went on to have at least 12 children and in 1799 after John had resigned his commission in the army, they followed Anne's brother Edward's example and took the whole family to live in America.[25] John Anthony held the distinguished title of being the progenitor of the de Berniére family there. They settled, like Edward in North Carolina. In 1812 John Anthony died and his wife Ann lived on with her daughters in Charleston, South Carolina until 1821 when she too, passed away. Both were buried in St. Phillip's Churchyard, Charleston.

---

[25] PRONI, T2625/1.

Appendix 2

Sir James Willson (sic) Agnew (1815-1901)

Lt. Col. Alexander of Whitehills was born in 1609 and died in 1695. He was the son of Sir Patrick, the 8th Hereditary Sheriff of Galloway. Alexander who often accompanied his brother Andrew, Sir Patrick's heir, to Ireland, had several children. One of these, John, was the ancestor of Sir James Willson Agnew who was Premier of Tasmania for a brief period from 1886-87. James, was born in Ballyclare, County Antrim on 2nd October 1815, one of two sons, to James William Agnew, a doctor and Yeoman Cavalry officer and his wife Ellen Stewart. His grandfather had also been a doctor and army officer and so following on in the family tradition, James decided to study medicine, first in London where he obtained his surgeon's qualifications in 1838 and then in Paris and Glasgow. On completion of his training he emigrated to Australia, settling first in Sydney before moving to Melbourne. During his time there he was offered an appointment as private secretary to Sir John Franklin who was the Lieutenant-Governor of Van Diemen's Land, present day Tasmania. James accepted this prestigious position, but unfortunately for him by the time he arrived in Hobart, the post had been filled. Nevertheless, he made up his mind to stay and began practising medicine.

In 1841 he was assistant surgeon to the agricultural establishment and as his reputation became known, he was offered the post of assistant surgeon to the Saltwater River probation station on the Tasman Peninsula. (A later position was taken up by James, namely, to accompany the ship, *Lady Franklin* which was full of convicts, to Norfolk Island).

By 1845 James was granted the right of private practice and had also been appointed Colonial Surgeon in Hobart. One year later on 27th April 1846 he married Louisa Mary Fraser, the daughter of Major Fraser of the 78th

Regiment. The couple had six children, but unfortunately only two of them survived to adulthood, a daughter Evelyn Robina who married an Englishman Robert Buxton Heinekey, son of Robert Heinekey, of Streatham, Surrey, and a son Charles Stewart who married Lucy Emmeline Reid.[1] Sadly James lost this remaining son too, as he drowned in his bath in the Coogee, some years later, leaving a widow and six children.

Following the cessation of convict transportation in 1853, James' position as Colonial Surgeon ended, but by now he had become actively involved in Tasmanian life and had been elected to the Council of the Royal Society in 1851. He was Honorary Secretary from 1861-81 and also became the first Chairman of the Management Board of the Tasmanian Museum and Art Gallery and Chairman of the trustees of the Hobart Public Library, a position he kept until the year of his death.

In March 1868 his wife Lousia died when the youngest child Evelyn Robina was just two years old. Ten years later in November 1878 James married again. His second wife was Blanche (née Legge), the widow of the Rev. Samuel Parsons, but there were no further children from this marriage.

James had retired from the medical profession by 1877 as his vast array of interests lay elsewhere, not least in politics for in the same year he was elected to the Legislative Council, but only four years later, he resigned his position and left Tasmania to spend some time in England.

When he returned again to Tasmania in 1884, his love for politics had remained undimmed during his time abroad, because he was soon re-elected to the Legislative Council and just two years later his popularity was such that he was elected Premier. His premiership lasted just one year and was unremarkable in that it left no record of any legislative accomplishment. On his defeat he gave up public life having served ten years on the Council, but he did not give up politics completely for he became a member of the Council of Higher Education. His interests ranged wide including ethnology and in 1888 he produced a pamphlet on the, *"Last of the Tasmanians"*. In 1890 he was on the council of the University of Tasmania, but his highest achievement was yet to come five years later, when Queen Victoria honoured him with a knighthood for his services to the community.

---

[1] When Evelyn's husband died she changed the family name to Buxton (Agnew, M.V., p.438).

Jacqueline Agnew

On the eve of his 84th birthday, Sir James was again honoured, this time with a tribute and photograph of himself and the executive officers of the Royal Society of Tasmania. He was held in very high esteem and the address which was given, was effusive in its glowing terms of his character, of his intellect and of his many acts of kindness.

The year 1901 saw Sir James' health deteriorating. Added to that the shock of his son drowning in the bath had only exacerbated his frail condition. He died at his home on 8th November 1901, aged 86 years and was buried in the Cornelian Bay Cemetery in Hobart town.

From his early life that had begun in the small Irish village of Ballyclare, Sir James had achieved much in his professional life to be proud of which was just as well as his family life was marked by tragedy. He was known as, *"Good Doctor Agnew"* and was a popular and sociable man. He was a great fan of horse racing and indeed, became the President of the Tasmanian Racing Club. As a keen angler in his spare time, he donated £800, to pay for a consignment of salmon ova to be brought from his native Ireland to stock the rivers and lakes of Tasmania. His expertise in the health field was greatly acknowledged too and he was said to be, *"One of the best informed men in the colony in scientific development"*. With his knighthood and presentation on his 84th birthday, Sir James must have been left in no doubt that he had made a remarkable and long-lasting contribution to his adopted land.[2] [3]

---

[2] Papers from the Tasmanian Parliamentary Library, 2002.
[3] National Biography, 2004, pps.464-465.

Appendix 3

The Agnew Slave Plantation

Another son of Lt. Col. Alexander Agnew of Whitehills, James, was born in 1645 at Balloo in Bangor, County Down. He married Eleanor Jamieson and in 1671 their son James was born. Sadly his father died just ten years later in 1681. His grandfather Alexander, is thought to have taken young James back to Scotland to rear, because we find that some years later when he had become a father to yet another James, both emigrated from Scotland in 1717, to Gettysburg, Pennsylvania. At the time the youngest James was just six years old. This James had two marriages, firstly to Margaret whose maiden name was thought to have been Ochiltree and secondly to Rebecca Scott whom he married in 1737. He died in 1770, the same year as his own father's death and was buried in Lower Marsh Creek Presbyterian Graveyard, Gettysburg.[1] His Will showed that by the time of his death he had accumulated much wealth and a substantial plantation. His estate was divided between his wife Rebecca and ten children.[2] One of those, Colonel James Agnew, became a revolutionary soldier in the Continental Army and was wounded in a battle in New Jersey. At the time he would have been facing his namesake, Brigadier General James Agnew, a Lochnaw Agnew and probably a distant relative, who fought on the side of the British,[3] though it's highly unlikely that they would have known this had they confronted one another.

Colonel James' brother Samuel, moved to Abbeville in South Carolina where the family was instrumental in establishing Presbyterianism and helped found the Presbyterian Seminary and College in the Due West area of that

---

[1] Agnew, M.V. ,1926, p.450.
[2] Information kindly recounted by Jimmie Robbins, a descendant.
[3] Agnew, M.V., 1926, p.420.

state. They are said to have enjoyed a good life and prospered there. A grandson Enoch (born in 1809), later moved with his brother Joseph (born in 1831) to Mississippi in 1852, in what was then called Tippah County where they acquired substantial land.[4] Dr. Enoch Agnew and his wife Letitia Todd Simpson (1809-1879), whom he married in 1832, had a son Samuel Andrew, who was born in 1833. Samuel was a Presbyterian Minister for 40 years. His father Enoch owned the Agnew Plantation, which neighboured the Brice Plantation and the slaves from both mixed frequently as is recorded by Samuel who wrote an extensive diary of the plantation's day-to-day life. The diary included the names of some of the slaves and gave us an insight into what life was like for them. Whilst life on the plantation was cruel and tough, there were, some moments of lightness, such as the time when two of the slaves married and the event was said to be merry. [5]

Dr. Enoch Agnew died in 1871 and the grand plantation family home where Samuel Andrew lived no longer exists.

---

[4] Information kindly recounted by Jimmie Robbins, a descendant.
[5] Samuel Andrew Agnew's Diary, September 27, 1863-June 30, 1864, University of North Carolina.

Appendix 4

Thomas Agnew (1794-1871)

In 2007 Agnew's Art Gallery[1] in London, celebrated 190 years as art dealers. Its founder was Thomas Agnew who claimed descent from Sir Patrick Agnew of Sheuchan, the first Baronet of Lochnaw, Leswalt. Thomas became apprenticed to Vittore Zanetti in Manchester, Zanetti was an Italian craftsman, carver and gilder. In 1816, Thomas bought into Zanetti's company and the firm became Zanetti & Agnew dealing in high quality print publishing.

In 1828 Zanetti retired to his estate in Lake Maggiore, but by then his son Joseph had joined the company together with Charles Allen Du Val[2] who was a painter and from his paintings engravings were made and sold as prints. This enhanced the growing business and Thomas's reputation soon spread. Eventually Thomas moved to meet the market demand of contemporary art and the business developed further, so much so that after his two sons were taken into the partnership, they decided to open a branch in London and concentrate the business from there, so the Manchester branch closed in 1923.

Thomas and his wife Jane Garnet Lockett had 13 children and when he died in 1871 two of his children, William (later 1st Baronet of Great Stanhope Street, London) and Thomas were instrumental in continuing the growth of Agnew's as it became known. Their premises in Old Bond Street soon began trading in Old Master pictures and they gained an international reputation. Sir William, a Liberal in his thinking, was a friend of Gladstone's and became a Member of Parliament for South East Lancashire in 1880.

---

[1] For more information on the history of Agnew's Art Gallery, see Oxford Dictionary of National Biography, 2004, pps. 362,461.
[2] Charles Du Val painted a portrait of Daniel O'Connell, the Irish politician and activist. For more information on Duval, see www.charlesduval.org

After many years of successful trading, it was decided to close the art gallery and in 2013, Agnew's was purchased privately.[3]

---

[3] https://worsleycivictrust.org/Tales_of_St_Marks_Graveyard_files/The%20%20AGNEWS.pdf

Appendix 5

Thomas Frederick Andrew Agnew (1834-1924)

Thomas, born in 1834, was the penultimate son of Sir Andrew Agnew's ten children. Sir Andrew was the 7th Baronet of Lochnaw, Leswalt and married Madeline Carnegie, the daughter of Sir David Carnegie. Sir Andrew's father married Martha de Courcy, but sadly he died six months before his son was born. Sir Andrew succeeded his grandfather to the baronetcy and was a Scottish politician and a great believer of Sabbatarianism. He corresponded with Prime Minister W.E. Gladstone concerning Sunday observance and in a letter to Sir Andrew, Gladstone stated his own support for the, "*Strict observance of the Lord's Day*". [1]

Sir Andrew's son, Thomas, began his career in commerce in Liverpool, but also developed a philanthropic conscience. After spending time in India during the Indian Mutiny, he joined the Madras Volunteer Cavalry, but it was on a trip to New York in 1881, that an idea began to form in his head after a visit to the New York Society for the Prevention of Cruelty of Children. He knew that in Liverpool many children lived in appalling conditions. Thomas was so impressed with what he saw in New York, that he decided, with the help of some others, to create a similar establishment in Liverpool. In 1883 nothing like this existed in the UK and so from Thomas's idea began the precursor for the present-day NSPCC.

The following year another similar establishment was formed in London and this eventually amalgamated with the Liverpool society in 1954, but it is thanks to the inspiration of Thomas that many children will have been lifted out of abuse and poverty.

---

[1] The National Archives of Scotland, GD154-921-00004, 21st February 1849.

Appendix 6

Kilwaughter Castle Ghost Stories

As everyone knows a real castle that's worth anything must have its own ghost and Kilwaughter Castle is no exception. In fact the Castle has two ghostly stories. The first one is told about *The White Lady,* who was a former tenant of Kilwaughter House which originally stood behind the Castle. In 1780 she was thought to be a distraught and love-sick Miss Agnew who had been badly let down by her unfaithful lover. She apparently died in sad circumstances in 1745 and on a very dark night, it is said that her spirit can still be seen on top of the Castle's tower looking out over the estate.

The second story again takes place in the 18th century when one of the workers of the Castle stayed late to help with the calving. After midnight a heifer calf was safely delivered and the worker began making his way home along the back avenue of the Castle. It was a clear night in March and there was a full moon so visibility was good. Suddenly he spotted some movement in a field which was known as the *Shepherd's Park*. Next to this field was another, called the *Long Hill* in which corn had just been sown that day, which meant that the ground was very even and tidy. The worker's attention was drawn to something happening over the hedge and as he glanced across, he was in time to see three horsemen galloping down *Shepherd's Park* with their riding capes billowing out behind them. They sped on into *Long Hill* where the corn had been sown and the worker was annoyed because he realised that the field would be ruined and next day the work would have to be done all over again. The horsemen jumped the fence over the back avenue and went on through the orchard towards the lake before disappearing into the forest.

As the worker continued his journey home, he was angry because he knew that he would have to rectify the damage caused by the riders. Next day before milking the cows, he decided to have a look at the damaged field to see what needed to be done to fix it. When he reached the corn field however, he was amazed and couldn't believe what he saw because there was no damage whatsoever to the field and not even any sign of hoof marks. He reported the event to the staff of the Castle, but there was never any explanation given as to the cause of this very unusual occurrence.[1]

Postscript

An interesting entry discovered on the internet, states that the name *Agnew* is one used not just by those who were born into it, but bizarrely by the BBC as a pseudonym. The name *David Agnew* was apparently commonly used in the 1970's for television drama programmes for contractual purposes, i.e. when episodes had been re-written or when writers had asked for their names to be removed from the final listings. It is still used periodically by students of film studies. Probably the most famous programme in which it was used twice was *Doctor Who*.[2]

---

[1] Larne Gazette, 2000.
[2] Wikipedia, the free encyclopedia.

References

Books

Agnew, Sir Andrew, (1893). The Hereditary Sheriffs of Galloway.
Adam & Charles Black, Edinburgh.
Agnew, Sir Andrew, (1864). A History of the Hereditary Sheriffs of Galloway.
Adam & Charles Black, Edinburgh.
Agnew, M.V., (1926). The Book of the Agnews.
Philadelphia.
Agnew, Sir James, National Biography, (2004), Vol.1, pp.464-5.
Oxford University Press.
Agnew, J., (Ed.), (1995). Funeral Register of the First Presbyterian Church of Belfast, 1712-36.
Ulster Historical Foundation, Belfast.
Agnew, J., (1996). Belfast Merchant Families in the Seventeenth Century.
Four Courts Press, Dublin.
Agnew, J., (Ed.), Luddy, M., (Gen.Ed.). (1998). The Drennan-McTier Letters, Vol.1. 1776-1793.
The Women's History Project in Association with Irish Manuscripts Commission, Ireland.
Agnew, J., (Ed.), Luddy, M., (Gen.Ed.). (1999). The Drennan-McTier Letters, Vol. 2, 1794-1801.
The Women's History Project in Association with Irish Manuscripts Commission, Ireland.
Agnew, J., (Ed.), Luddy, M., (Gen.Ed.). (1999). The Drennan-McTier Letters, Vol. 3. 1802-1819.
The Women's History Project in Association with Irish Manuscripts Commission, Ireland.

Barzilay, D., (1978). The British Army in Ulster, Vol.3.
Century Books, Belfast.
Benn's History of Belfast. (1877). Reminiscences of Three Belfast Families. Second Volume.
Marcus Ward & Company (London).
Blair, M., (2007). Hiring Fairs and Market Places.
Appletree Press Ltd., Belfast.
Blaney, R., (1996). Presbyterians and the Irish Language.
Ulster Historical Foundation and Ultach Trust, Belfast.
Brown, Dr. D. (2023). The Glynns, Glens of Antrim Historical Society Magazine, Vol.50.
Clifford, B., (1989). Belfast in the French Revolution.
Belfast Historical and Educational Association, Belfast.
Collins, B., (1994). Flax to Fabric. The Story of Irish Linen.
An Irish Linen Centre & Lisburn Museum Publication, Lisburn.
Crowley, J., Smyth, W.J., Murphy, M. (Editors). (2012). Atlas of the Great Irish Famine 1845-52.
Cork University Press, Cork.
Dallat, C., (1990). The Road to the Glens.
The Friar's Bush Press, Belfast.
Dickson, C. (1997). Revolt in the North, Antrim and Down in 1798.
Constable and Company Ltd., London.
Elliott, M., (2000). The Catholics of Ulster.
Allan Lane, The Penguin Press, London.
Foy, R.H. (1999). Remembering all the Orrs. The Story of the Orr families of Antrim and their Involvement in the 1798 Rebellion.
Ulster Historical Foundation, Belfast.
Gibson, Rev. W., (1860). The Year of Grace: A History of Ulster Revival 1859.
Andrew Elliott, Edinburgh.
Gillespie, R., (1985). Colonial Ulster. The Settlement of East Ulster 1600-1641.
Cork University Press, Cork.
Gun, W.T.J., (1934). Harrow School Register, 1571-1800.
Londman's Green & Co., London.
Haddick-Flynn, K., (1999). Orangeism. The Making of a Tradition.
Wolfhound Press Ltd., Dublin.
Hames, J.H., (2001). Arthur O'Connor, United Irishman,

The Collins Press, Cork.
Hill, M., Pollock, V. (1994). Women of Ireland, Image and Experience, ca. 1880-1920.
W. & G. Baird Ltd., Belfast.
Hossack, B.H. (1986). Kirkwall in the Orkneys. Reprint of 1900 Edition.
The Kirkwall Press, Kirkwall.
Hume, Dr. D. (2007). People of the Lough Shore. A Memoir of Past Lives and Bygone Times from Ballycarry, Glynn, Islandmagee, Magheramorne and Whitehead, 1790-1950.
Trafford Publishing, Canada.
Johnston-Liik, E.M., (2002). History of the Irish Parliament, 1692-1800, Vol.4, No.1124, p.510.
Ulster Historical Foundation, Belfast.
Kennedy, Brian, (1995). Scots-Irish in the Hills of Tennessee.
Causeway Press, Londonderry/Ambassador Productions, Belfast.
Laxton, E., (1997). The Famine Ships, The Irish Exodus to America 1846-51.
Bloomsbury Publishing, PLC, London.
Lee, J., (1979). The Modernisation of Irish Society, 1848-1918.
Gill & Macmillan Ltd., Dublin.
Luddy, M., (1995). Women in Ireland 1800-1918.
Cork University Press, Cork.
Maxtone-Graham, J., (1998). Titanic Survivor. The Memoirs of Violet Jessop, Stewardess.
Sutton Publishing Ltd., Gloucestershire.
Merrick, A.C.W., Clarke, R.S.J. (ed.), (1991). Old Belfast Families and The New Burying Ground, Vol.4.
The Ulster Historical Foundation, Belfast.
Morgan, H., (1993). Tyrone's Rebellion,
Gill & Macmillan Ltd., Dublin.
McCreary, A., (2000). A Vintage Port, Larne and its People.
Greystone Press, Antrim, Northern Ireland.
McCutcheon, W.A., (1980). The Industrial Archaelogy of Northern Ireland.
Fairleigh Dickinson University Press.
McDonnell, H., (1993). The Journal of the Glens of Antrim Historical Society. Vol.21.
McDonnell, H., (1996). The Wild Geese of the Antrim MacDonnells.
Irish Academic Press, Dublin.

McDonnell, H., (2013). Glenarm Friary and the Bissets, Glens of Antrim Historical Society. Accessed 2024, https://antrimhistory.net/glenarm-friary

McKerlie, P.H., (1994). History of the Lands and their Owners in Galloway. Vol.1.,

G.C. Book Publishers Ltd., Wigtown.

McKillop, F., (1987). Glenarm A Local History.

Ulster Journals, Belfast.

McKillop, F., (2005). History of Larne and East Antrim.

Ulster Journals, Belfast.

McKillop, F., (2006). Townlands, People and Traditions.

McKillop, Glenarm.

O'Brien, J., Guinness, D., (1992). Great Irish Houses and Castles.

George Weidenfeld & Nicholson Ltd., London.

O'Faolain, S. (1992). The Great O'Neill.

The Mercier Press, Dublin.

O'Laverty, Rev. J. (1884). Diocese of Down and Connor.

James Duffy & Sons, Dublin.

(Reprinted 1981, Davidson Books, Spa, Ballynahinch).

Oxford Dictionary of National Biography (2004), pp. 461, 462. Agnew's Art Gallery.

Oxford University Press.

Oxford Dictionary of National Biography (2004), Vol.24, pp. 471-474.

Oxford University Press.

Powell, W.S.(Ed.). Dictionary of North Carolina Biography, Vol.3.

University of North Carolina Press.

Rankin, K. (2002). The Linen Houses of the Lagan Valley. The story of their families.

Ulster Historical Foundation, Belfast.

Rogers, N. (2009). Ireland, Slavery and Anti-Slavery 1612-1865.

Palgrave MacMillan, Hampshire.

Rutherford, G. (ed. Clarke R.S.J.). (2004). Old Families of Larne & District.

Gravestone Inscriptions, County Antrim, Vol.4. Ulster Historical Foundation, Belfast.

Stewart, A.T.Q., (1977). The Narrow Ground, Aspects of Ulster, 1609-1969.

Faber & Faber Ltd., London.

Stewart, A.T.Q., (1995). The Summer Soldiers, The 1798 Rebellion in Antrim and Down.
The Blackstaff Press, Belfast.
These Hallowed Ground, (2005), Vol.2 p.149.
Lisburn Branch of the North of Ireland Family History Society.
Truxes, T.M., (Ed.), (2001). Letterbook of Greg & Cunningham 1756-57. Merchants of New York and Belfast. Oxford University Press, Oxford.
Wilsdon, B., (1997). The Sites of the 1798 Rising in Antrim and Down.
The Blackstaff Press, Belfast.

Primary Sources

Agnew, W., Wills dated 27th July 1886, 23rd October 1888, 29th July 1889.
Rockwood Museum.
Agnew Genealogical Table (from the late Mrs. Nancy Agnew Ferns, Nova Scotia).
Balzani, Maria Augusta. Grave Paper, Ref. 1975/48-3695, dated 23rd October 1981.
Census, (1851).
Gladstone, Rt. Hon. W.E., copy of letter dated 21st February, 1849, to Sir Andrew Agnew.
The National Archives of Scotland, Edinburgh, GD154-921.
Kilwaughter Castle Guest Book. 11th May 1892-22nd September 1922.
The Historical Society of Delaware.
Lambert, J.H. Will dated 8th October 1886.
Rockwood Museum, Delaware.
Letters of Elizabeth Bringhurst Galt Smith during her time at Kilwaughter Castle.
The Historical Society of Delaware. Also Summaries of Letters from Elizabeth Bringhurst Smith to family and friends, from 1886-1922.
Rockwood Museum, Delaware.
Letters from members of 644th American Tank Destroyer Battalion, dated September/October 2001.
Letter from O"Rorke, McDonald & Tweed, Solicitors, 29 The Roddens, Larne, dated 9th September 1980 concerning sale of Kilwaughter Castle.
Marriage Certificate between T.C. Simon and M. Agnew, dated 16th May 1844, No.102.

MIC/1805. Obituary of Valentine Jones, dated 22nd March 1805, Belfast News Letter. Linen Hall Library, Belfast.

OB/1/84/A. Letters from Count Ugo Balzani to Oscar Browning, 1895-1913. King's College Library, Cambridge.

Porter, Rev. Classon, (undated). The Agnews of Ireland. (Courtesy of Mr. Frank Ferguson).

Porter, Rev. Classon, (undated). Conversation with Margaret Jones. Nineteenth century notes on the Agnew Family.

Porter, Rev. Classon, (undated). Nineteenth century notes of the Agnew Family.

PRONI DA106/57-10. "Irish Landed Gentry – when Cromwell came to Ireland".

PRONI D300/1/5/244. Will of William Agnew, dated 17th April 1851.

PRONI D300/1/5/862. Information of Rev. Classon Porter's Estate.

PRONI D300/1/5/2. Will of Patrick Agnew, dated lst July 1724.

PRONI D971/9/1. Italian Marriage Settlement between Donna Guendolina Balzani and Senor Guido David Valensin, dated 9th June 1905.

PRONI D971/9/1. Indenture between H.J. McNeale, Regent Street, London and Maria Augusta Balzani and John Galt Smith, dated 2nd November 1891. Lease of Kilwaughter Castle.

PRONI D971/9/1. Letter from John Bristow to His Excellency The Italian Ambassador, London, dated 16th April 1932.

PRONI D1326/2/6. Indenture between William Agnew and Maria Augusta Simon, dated 15th April 1878.

PRONI D1326/2/6. Statement from Henry Thomas McNeale to William Neill and William Augustus, Ferrar Solicitors, dated 8th April 1892.

PRONI D1326/2/19. Search for Judgement for James Agnew Farrell from 1789-1823. Certificates of Satisfaction.

PRONI D1754/32. Ulster Folk Museum.

PRONI D1905/10/193. Final Account of Mrs. Galt Smith of Kilwaughter Castle, Larne. County Antrim.

PRONI D1954/4/273. Renewal of Life, Lord Dungannon/James Agnew Farrell.

PRONI D2095/6. Letter from Mary Gilbraith to Edward Jones Agnew, dated 30th May 1832.

PRONI D2095/14. Letter from Margaret Jones to William and Maria Agnew, dated 25th October 1832.

PRONI D2095/18. Anonymous Address, "The Oakboys, the Hearts of Steel, the Volunteers of the United Irishmen of Larne and Neighbourhood".

PRONI D2453/9. Letter from Rachel Galbraith to Miss Jones, dated 6th August, 1834.

PRONI D2453/63. The Agnew Family Document, Kilwaughter 1200-1951. Untitled letter, dated, 17th June, 1815 and 19th June, 1815.

PRONI LPC 1040. Will of Edward Jones Agnew.

PRONI T206/1. Perogative Wills, etc., of persons of surname Agnew.

PRONI T281/1/8. Will of Valentine Jones of Kilmacmurnerty, Portadown, dated 1st September 1825.

PRONI T502/68. Affidavit for Inland Revenue made in John Lambert's name.

PRONI T559/36. Stewart Genealogy.

PRONI T808/46. Will of William Agnew, dated 27th January 1775.

PRONI T808. Tennison Groves Genealogical Notes.

PRONI T956/54. Marriage Settlement between Roger Moore and Catherine (Kitty) Jones, dated 1808.

PRONI T1009/390. Will of Margaret Jones, dated 19th October 1847.

PRONI T1282/1. Part of The Stewart of Killymoon Papers.

PRONI T2625/1. Two letters from John Anthony de Bernière to Edward Jones, North Carolina.

PRONI T2625/1. Notes on two letters from John Anthony de Bernière to Edward Jones, North Carolina.

PRONI T2625/7. Anonymous address but written by sibling of Dr. Jones.

PRONI T2625/7. Introduction to the de Bernière family written by Mary de Bernière Barnwell.

PRONI T2625/8. Will of Jean Antoine de Bernière, dated 11th February 1725.

PRONI T3549/1. Catalogue of the Valuable Collection of Kilwaughter Castle, dated 1922.

PRONI LPC/1040. Will of Edward Jones Agnew, dated 9th June 1825.

The Journal of the Barbados Museum and Historical Society, Vols., XV, XVI, XVII, XXV, XIV. Minutes of the Barbados Assembly. National Library Service, Bridgetown 2, Barbados, West Indies.

The National Archives of Scotland, GD154-517, dated 30th November 1654. Depositions by Captain John Agnew and James Shaw of Ballygally concerning the least granted by the Earl of Antrim to Sir Patrick Agnew.

The National Archives of Scotland, GD154-687-2-1-00011, dated 5th October 1818. Letter from James Agnew Farrell to Sir Andrew Agnew, Lochnaw Castle.
The National Archives of Scotland, GD154-532, dated 1693-1708. Rent rolls and accounts of payment of rents of Kilwaughter by Patrick Agnew.
The National Archives of Scotland, GD154-921-00004, dated 21st February 1849. Letter from Rt. Hon. W.E. Gladstone to Sir A. Andrew on the Sunday Observance Question.
The New York Times. 3rd June 1886.
William Welch Collection. The Alan Mason Chesney Medical Archives, Folder 137/5. Address by Countess Nora Balzani on, *"Training for Social Work in Italy"* (undated).
The Johns Hopkins Medical Institution, Baltimore, USA.

Secondary Sources

Agnew Association of the UK, Newsletter, February 1984, No.5.
Agnew Association of USA, Newsletter, January 1985, No.3.
(Courtesy of Sir Crispin Agnew).
Agnew Association of USA, Newsletter, May/June 1985, No.4.
Agnew Association of the UK, Newsletter, October 1992, No.11.
Agnew Association of the UK, Newsletter, October 1993, No.12.
Agnew Genealogical Table (undated).
Agnew of Kilwaughter, family descent (Courtesy of Sir Crispin Agnew).
Agnew – The Newsletter of the Agnew Family, (Oct. 2004), Vol.1, No.8.
Belfast Commercial Chronicle, dated 8th April 1805. Legacy from Valentine Jones to Belfast Charitable Society.
Belfast Commercial Chronical, dated 15th June, 1805. Sale of the lease of a farm in Malone.
Best, E.J. (1997). The Huguenots of Lisburn.
Lisburn Historical Society.
Blair, S.A., undated. Kilraughts, A Kirk and Its People.
Brett, C.E.B., Buildings of County Antrim.
A joint publication of the Ulster Architectural Heritage Society and the Ulster Historical Foundation.
Belfast, 1996.
Burke's Peerage, (2003), 107th Edition, Vol.1.

Belfast News Letter, (22nd March 1805). Obituary of Valentine Jones. MIC/1805.

Linen Hall Library, Belfast.

Belfast New Letter, (19th June 1829). Northern Yacht Club. Issue 9603.

Belfast News Letter, 31st January 1861. Donation for coal and blankets.

Belfast News Letter, (22nd January 1863). The Rev. Francis Dobbs. Issue 15493.

Belfast New Letter, (13th May 1876). Agency of Kilwaughter Castle. Issue 18969.

Belfast News Letter, (22nd October 1886). Reduction of Rents. Issue 22254.

Belfast News Letter, (30th March 1891). Ulster Intelligence. Issue 23629.

Belfast News Letter, (30th March 1891). The Linen Hall. Issue 23629.

Belfast News Letter, (lst May 1891). County Antrim. To be let by Private Contract. Issue 23657.

Belfast News Letter, (12th September 1891). Advertisements and Notices (Auction of household effects). Issue 23772.

Belfast News Letter, (13th October 1891). Advertisements of Notices (Auction of Kilwaughter Castle Farms). Issue 23798.

Belfast News Letter, (27th July 1893). The Church of Ireland. Issue 24357.

Belfast News Letter, 4th August 1893.

Belfast News Letter, (24th August 1894). Larne Horse Show Society. Issue 24684.

Belfast News Letter, (13th February 1896). Life in America. Issue 25143.

Belfast News Letter, (6th August 1897). The Royal Visit to Ireland. Issue 25599.

Belfast News Letter, (11th August 1898). Accident at Larne. Issue 25902.

Belfast News Letter, (26th April 1899). Death of Mr. John Galt Smith JP. Issue 26123.

Belfast News Letter, (7th March 1940). Article by Colin Johnston Robb on Valentine Jones.

Belfast Telegraph, dated 24th October 1940.

Ceylon A People's History 1793-1844, from the newspaper, Asia Economy 1804-1843, Part 2.

Centre for Migration Studies, Ulster-American Folk Park, Omagh.

Coleraine Chronicle, 24th June 1846. Appointment to the Commission of the Peace for the County of Antrim.

Congregational Memoirs of the Old Presbyterian Congregation of Larne and Kilwaughter, 1864.

Day, A., McWilliams, P. (Eds.)., (1991). Ordnance Survey Memoirs of Ireland, Vol. 10, Parishes of County Antrim III, 1833, 1835, 1839-40. Larne and Island Magee.

Deed by Randle McDonnell Earl of Antrim to Patrick Agnew of Kilwaughter. 14th November 1713. Recorded 20th April 1716. Dublin Registry of Deeds, Bk 15, p.249, No. 7399.

Dictionary of Irish Architects, 1720-1940. 2024.

Dublin Evening Post, 8th October 1850. Reduction of Rents.

Foreign & Commonwealth Office, relating to Enemy Property, emails dated 27th September 2016.

Freeman's Journal and Daily Commercial Advertiser, (7th May 1839). Births, Deaths, Marriages and Obituaries. Dublin.

Friends of Rockwood, Newsletter, Vol.3, No.2, Spring 1989.

History Guide, Carnfunnock County Park.

A Larne Borough Council Publication.

Holmes, R.F.G., (1992). Irish Presbyterianism.

Presbyterian Historical Society of Ireland.

Hughes, A.J., (1998-2000). Études Celtique, Vol.34.

The Institute of Irish Studies, The Queen's University of Belfast, in association with The Royal Irish Academy, Dublin.

Jope, Professor E.M. Kilwaughter Castle, Near Larne, Co. Antrim. Undated report from the Department of Archaeology, Queen's University, Belfast

Land Owners in Ireland Register 1876, Antrim County entry.

Linen Hall Library, Belfast.

Larne Gazette, dated 13th December 2000.

Larne Historical Centre, Larne.

Larne Times, dated 14th June 1951.

Larne Times, dated 25th October 1951.

Larne Times, dated 29th November 1951.

Letter from the Congregation of Larne and Kilwaughter, dated March, 1916, to Nora Balzani.

McKillop, F. (2005). Scots-Irish Links. History of Larne and East Antrim.

Neill, T. (1995). Lisburn's Charter of 1662, Vol.9, pps.14, 18.

Northern Whig, 28th April 1899. Obituary of John Galt Smith.

North-Eastern Education and Library Board. Indenture, dated 2nd May 1896 between Count Ugo Balzani and others.
O'Hart, J., 2nd Ed., (1887). J. Duff & Sons, Dublin.
O'Regan, R., (2010). Mercer Press, Cork.
Ramsey, S. (undated). Two Papers on the Early History of Belfast. Read before the Rosemary Street Presbyterian Church, Young Men's Guild.
Register of Parks, Gardens and Demesnes of Special Historic Interest, NI. Department for Communities.
Romantic Rockwood, Rural Gothic Villa in Delaware. Booklet from Rockwood Museum, 1982.
Spreti, M.V., (1928-36), Vol.1. Enciclopedia Storico-Nobiliare Italiana. Milano.
Tasmanian Parliamentary Papers:-
- Australian Dictionary of Biography, Vol.3, pps.18-19.
- Bennett, S., Bennett, B. (1980). Biographical Register of the Tasmanian Parliament, 1851-
1960. Australian National University Press, Canberra.
- Green, F.C. (1956). A Century of Responsible Government, 1856-1956. Hobart: Government Printers, pps.166-167.
- Newman, T. (1988). Tasmanian Premiers 1856-1988. A Biographical Handbook, p.39.
- Royal Society of Tasmania 1899-present. Biographical file – James Agnew.
The Agnews, Genealogical Information Relating to the Family (undated).
The Bigtown Gazette, 1842. Canada.
The Corran, Setember 1977, No. 4.
Larne and District Folklore Society.
The Corran, Summer 1980.
Larne and District Folklore Society.
The Corran, Spring 1986, No.38.
Larne and District Folkore Society.
The Glynns, Journal of the Glens of Antrim Historical Society. (2004), Vol.32, Cushendall, Co. Antrim.
The New York Times (3rd June, 1886). Marriage of Elizabeth Bringhurst Shipley and John Galt Smith.
The New York Times (1st July 1892). Costly for the Importers.

The Times, (16th May 1857). Death Announcement of Maria Simon, in Ballysax. Page 1.

The Times, (26th April 1878). Marriage Announcement of Maria Augusta Simon and Count Ugo Balzani, in London. Page 1.

The Times, (13th January 1891). Death Announcement of William Agnew. Page 1.

The Times, (12th July 1895). Obituary of Countess Balzani. Page 10.

The Times, (24th December 1896). Marriage Announcement of Andreina Alessandra Balzani and William Malcolm Hailey in Bombay. Page 1.

The Times, (3rd March, 1919). The By-Elections, Oxford University Polling Dates. Page 8.

The Times, (31st January 1939). Obituary of Lady Andreina Hailey. Page 17.

The Times, (3rd February 1939). Funeral Announcement of Lady Andreina Hailey. Page 15.

The Writings of George Washington from the Original Manuscript Sources, 1745-1799. John C. Fitzpatrick, Editor.

Library of Congress, Washington.

Ulster Journal of Archaelogy, (1901), 2nd series, Vol. VII.

Ulster Journal of Archaelogy, (1901), 2nd series, Vol. VII. (Rev. Classon Porter).

Ulster Journal Archaelogy, (1901), No. 2, Vol. VII. Ballygally Castle, Rev. Classon Porter.

Ulster Journal Archaelogy, 3rd series, Vol. 19, 1956.

Theses

King, A., (2023). Dear William: Female Novelists and the Scots Language; Diary Novels and Dialect: the Ó Gnímh Bards and Agnew Sheriffs.

Manko, K.L., (1994). Letters from Abroad, Elizabeth Bringhurst Smith's Letters from Kilwaughter Castle, Ireland, 1886-1922.

Web References

Agnew Family Genealogy Forum. https://www.genealogy.com/forum/surnames/topics/agnew/1128/ Accessed 11th August 2024.

Agnew, Samuel Andrew. Diary, 1823-1902, (27th September 1863- 30th June 1864).

University of North Carolina, Chapel Hill Libraries.
https://docsouth.unc.edu/imls/agnew/agnew.html
Accessed 11th August 2024.
Barbados Plantation History.
www.CreoleLinks.com@2010
Accessed 31st January 2023.
Biographies of Crown Forces Generals
https://www.revwar75.com/crown/oldstuff/bio.htm
Accessed 16th July 2005.
British Orderly Books – Headquarters and Brigades Database
https://revwar75.com/crown/brigade2.htm
Accessed 16th July 2005.
Depositions 1641, Trinity College Dublin.
http://1641.tcd.ie/.
Accessed 22nd July, 2024.
Description of the Smith Knapp Wedding, Irish Emigration Database, 25th December, 2015.
http://www.dippam.ac.uk/ied/records/21899.transcript
Accessed 14th September, 2016.
Eccles Family Papers, Manuscripts Dept., Library of the University of North Carolina. https://finding-aids.lib.unc.edu/03504/
Faulkner's Dublin Journal. July 1765.
Dublin, Ireland.
https://www.irishnewsarchive.com/the-dublin-journal-faulkner-newspaper-archives
Kilwaughter Castle Camp, Larne. Larne Times, 15th August, 1946.
https://www.findmypast.co.uk
Accessed 10th August, 2016.
Obituary, St. Sepulchre's Cemetery, Oxford.
https://www.stsepulchres.org.uk/burials/simon_thomas.html
Accessed 17th October 2021.
Larne - History of Carnfunnock.
https://www.midandeastantrim.gov.uk/downloads/CCP_History_Guide.pdf
Larne Gazette Newspaper, 13th September 2000.
https://media.info/newspapers/titles/larne-gazette
Larne Gazette Newspaper, 29th November 2000.

https://media.info/newspapers/titles/larne-gazette
Morning Avalanche, Lubbock, Texas, 25th February 1952.
https://www.findmypast.co.uk
Accessed 10th August 2016.
McDonnell, H., (2013). Glenarm Friary and the Bissets, Glens of Antrim Historical Society.
https://antrimhistory.net/glenarm-friary
Accessed 4th February 2024.
New Burying Ground at Kilwaughter, 15th July 1876.
https://www.findmypast.co.uk
Accessed 13th August, 2016.
Official USA Embassy, Florence.
https://it.usembassy.gov/embassy-consulates/florence/
Accessed 6th October 2023.
Place Names N.I.
www.placenamesni.org
Accessed 11th August 2024
The Belfast Newsletter Index.
https://ucs.louisiana.edu>bni
Accessed 11th August 2024.
The Centre for the Study of Legacies of British Slavery, William Smith
https://www.ucl.ac.uk/1bs/person/view/2146654619
Accessed 17th January 2022.
The Centre for the Study of Legacies of British Slavery, Charles McGarel.
https://www.ucl.ac.uk/1bs/person/view/6914
Accessed 27th July 2024.
The Complete Newgate Calendar, Vol. 3.
https://archive.org/details/in.ernet.dli.2015.37104
Accessed 20th November 2010.
Official USA Embassy, Florence.
http://www.usembassy.it/florence/cons/files/palazzo.htm
PRONI, Summary of The Stewart of Killymoon Papers.
http://proni.nics.gov.uk/records/private/stewart.htm
Accessed 2nd February 2002.
Rolston, B., (2003). "A Lying Old Scoundrel". Waddell Cunningham and Belfast's Role in the Slave Trade.
Trade, Vol.II, No.1 (Spring Edition).

https://www.historyireland.com/a-lying-old-scoundrel/
Scots-Irish Links.
https://www.ancestry.com
Accessed 22nd September, 2010.
The Canadian Biographical Dictionary and Patriot Gallery of Eminent and Self-Made Men, (1880).
Ontario Volume.
https://www.canadiana.ca/view/oocihm.08545/5
The Ulster American Heritage Trail Plaques, Northern Ireland.
http://www.larne.com/tourism/heritage/plaques.asp
Accessed 13th July, 2000.
Villa Balzani.
https://www.bolognawelcome.com/en/places/towers-historic-buildings/villa-balzani-2

Index

148th Independent Reconnaissance Company/Squadron, 186
1641 Rebellion, 8
36th Antrim Division, 171
5th Earl of Antrim, 23
644th American Tank Destroyer Battalion, ii
644th Tank Destroyer Battalion, v, 187, 188, 189
Abercorn, of, Duchess, 157
Achison, Mr., 52, 53
Adair, Lady, 133, 160
Adair, William, 68
Agnew, i, iii, v, vii, ix, xi, xii, 1, 2, 3, 4, 5, 6, 7, 8, 9, 10, 11, 12, 13, 15, 16, 17, 18, 19, 20, 21, 23, 24, 25, 26, 27, 34, 36, 39, 40, 41, 42, 43, 44, 46, 47, 48, 51, 52, 55, 56, 57, 58, 59, 60, 61, 63, 66, 67, 68, 69, 70, 71, 74, 75, 79, 80, 81, 83, 84, 85, 87, 102, 107, 108, 111, 122, 123, 125, 145, 147, 150, 157, 158, 162, 163, 174, 183, 186, 194, 195, 196, 198, 199, 200, 201, 202, 203, 204, 206, 207
Agnew Bards, i, xi, 1, 58
Agnew Plantation, 202

Agnew, Agnes, 7
Agnew, Alexander, Lt., Col., 201
Agnew, Andrew, Captain, 150
Agnew, Andrew, Frederick, Thomas, 205
Agnew, Andrew, Samuel, 202
Agnew, Andrew, Sir, i, 3, 11, 13, 16, 60, 123, 205
Agnew, Andrew, Sir, 10th Sheriff of Galloway, 11, 12
Agnew, Andrew, Sir, 10th Sheriff of Kilwaughter, i, 12, 13, 123
Agnew, Andrew, Sir, 7th Sheriff of Galloway, 3
Agnew, Andrew, Sir, 8th Baronet, i, 3, 11, 13, 60, 123, 205
Agnew, Andrew, Sir, 9th Sheriff of Galloway, i, 3, 6, 10, 11, 13, 60, 123, 205
Agnew, Andrew, Sir, Lochnaw, of, Baronet, 7th, i, 3, 11, 13, 60, 123, 205
Agnew, Andrew, Sir, son of Agnew, James, Sir, 16
Agnew, Callwell, Jane, 119, 122
Agnew, Charles, 80

225

Agnew, Charles, Captain, 7, 9, 20, 58, 61, 62, 80, 81, 102, 138, 199, 203
Agnew, Charles, grandson of Agnew, James 1st of Larne, 62
Agnew, Charles, grandson of Agnew, James, 1st of Larne, 62
Agnew, Dr., 51
Agnew, Eleanor, 16
Agnew, Elizabeth, 7
Agnew, Ellen, 26, 27, 63, 123, 198
Agnew, Enoch, Dr., 202
Agnew, Evelyn, 183
Agnew, Francis, 7, 10, 19
Agnew, George, Captain, 16
Agnew, Grace, 20
Agnew, Helen, 9, 12, 13, 148
Agnew, Henry, 20
Agnew, Hugh, 20
Agnew, James, 6
Agnew, James, 1st of Larne, 19, 26, 43, 50, 55, 56, 57, 58, 59, 60, 61, 62, 70, 80, 114, 157
Agnew, James, Brigadier General, 18
Agnew, James, Col., 201
Agnew, James, General, Brigadier, 18, 201
Agnew, James, grandson of Agnew, James 1st of Larne, 62
Agnew, James, Major, 18
Agnew, James, Sir, 12, 13, 14, 15, 16, 18, 61, 81, 198, 200
Agnew, James, son of Agnew, Alexander, Lt., Col., 19, 26, 43, 50, 55, 56, 57, 58, 59, 60, 61, 62, 70, 80, 114, 157

Agnew, James, son of Agnew, James, Major, 19
Agnew, Jane, 7
Agnew, Jean, ii, v, 20, 30, 41
Agnew, John, 16
Agnew, John, Captain, i, iii, v, vii, xi, 4, 6, 7, 8, 9, 10, 12, 19, 21, 29, 37, 39, 40, 41, 42, 44, 46, 51, 52, 55, 59, 63, 64, 72, 81, 83, 84, 85, 101, 107, 111, 119, 127, 132, 140, 147, 174, 182, 184, 190, 191, 195, 196, 197, 198
Agnew, John, Hearts of Steel, 46
Agnew, Jones, Edward, vii, 4, 16, 20, 21, 26, 27, 34, 43, 44, 45, 46, 47, 48, 49, 50, 51, 54, 55, 56, 58, 59, 63, 64, 65, 66, 67, 68, 69, 70, 71, 72, 73, 74, 77, 80, 81, 103, 108, 111, 113, 114, 117, 131, 136, 137, 138, 139, 142, 143, 144, 145, 147, 148, 151, 152, 156, 157, 159, 163, 164, 165, 179, 183, 193, 194, 195, 196, 197
Agnew, Jones. Edward, 43
Agnew, Margaret, 16, 17, 18, 55
Agnew, Margaret (wife of James Farrell), 55
Agnew, Margaret, daughter of Agnew, Patrick, 3rd of Kilwaughter, 20
Agnew, Margaret, daughter of Wilson, James, 19, 21, 55, 183
Agnew, Maria, ii, 40, 68, 69, 72, 80, 83, 84, 85, 86, 87, 99, 121, 125, 150, 190
Agnew, Marie, 7
Agnew, Mary, Lady, 15, 16, 17
Agnew, Patrick of Sheuchan, 6

Agnew, Patrick, 1st of Kilwaughter, 12
Agnew, Patrick, 2nd of Kilwaughter, 13, 19, 20, 21, 23
Agnew, Patrick, 3rd of Kilwaughter, 18
Agnew, Patrick, 3rd of Kilwaughter, 8, 13, 14, 19, 20, 21
Agnew, Patrick, Agnew, Patrick, 3rd of Kilwaughter, 19
Agnew, Patrick, of Ballykeel, 7
Agnew, Patrick, Sir, 4
Agnew, Patrick, Sir, 8th Sheriff of Galloway, vii, 2, 3, 4, 6, 7, 10, 11, 102, 133, 183, 198, 203
Agnew, Patrick, Sir, 9th Sheriff of Galloway, vii, 2, 7, 10, 11, 133, 183, 203
Agnew, Patrick, son of Agnew, John, Captain, 12
Agnew, Patrick, son of Agnew, Patrick, 1st of Kilwaughter, 12
Agnew, Patrick, son of Captain John Agnew, 10
Agnew, Quintin, 183
Agnew, Robert, 18, 116
Agnew, Robert, Captain, 18
Agnew, Rosina, 7
Agnew, Sir Andrew, 2, 6, 60
Agnew, Stair, Sir, 16
Agnew, Susanna, 16
Agnew, Thomas, 6, 162
Agnew, Thomas, Captain of Creoch, 6, 16, 203
Agnew, Valentine, 43
Agnew, William, vii, 6, 10, 13, 16, 17, 19, 20, 21, 23, 24, 25, 26, 27, 29, 30, 33, 34, 39, 41, 42, 43, 47, 53, 55, 62, 63, 67, 68, 69, 70, 72, 74, 75, 76, 77, 79, 80, 81, 82, 83, 84, 85, 86, 87, 102, 103, 107, 108, 110, 111, 118, 125, 149, 155, 160, 182, 183, 193, 194,195, 196, 203
Agnew, William, James, 198
Agnew, William, Major General, 20
Agnew, William, son of Agnew, James, 1st of Larne, 62
Agnew, William, son of Agnew, Jones, Edward, 68, 69, 70, 72, 74, 79, 80, 81, 82, 83, 84, 86, 108, 110, 118, 182, 184
Agnew, William, son of Agnew, Patrick, 3rd of Kilwaughter, 2, 19, 20, 21, 23, 24, 26, 27, 51, 55, 60, 63, 67, 83, 101, 122
Agnew, William, son of Agnew, Patrick, 3rd son of Kilwaughter, 25
Agnew, William, The Hynd, 19
Agnew, Willson, James, Sir, 198
Agnewe, Andrew, 2
Agnews of Kilwaughter, i, ii, iii, v, ix, xi, xii, xiii, 1, 2, 3, 4, 5, 6, 7, 8, 9, 10, 11, 12, 13, 14, 15, 19, 20, 21, 23, 24, 25, 26, 27, 36, 43, 44, 45, 48, 49, 52, 54, 55, 58, 59, 60, 61, 62, 63, 64, 65, 66, 67, 68, 69, 70, 71, 74, 77, 79, 80, 81, 82, 83, 85, 86, 87, 99, 101, 102, 104, 105, 106, 107, 108, 109, 110, 112, 114, 115, 116, 117, 118, 119, 120, 121, 122, 123, 125, 126, 127, 128, 129, 130, 132, 133, 135, 136, 137, 138, 140, 142, 143, 145, 146, 147, 148, 149, 151,

152, 153, 154, 156, 157, 158, 159, 160, 161, 164, 166, 167, 168, 169, 171, 172, 173, 175, 177, 178, 179, 180, 181, 182, 183, 185, 186, 187, 188, 189, 190, 191, 192, 206
Agnews of Kilwaughter Castle, 25
Agnews of Lochnaw, i, xi, 2, 9, 11, 13, 15, 19, 60, 145, 183, 192
Alexandra, Queen, 144
Ambassador, Italian, 184
Anglo-Norman, 1
Antrim Castle, 179, 186
Antrim Iron Ore Company, 150
Antrim, Lady, 158, 161
Antrim, Lady and Lord, 174
Antrim, Lord, 27, 53
Appendices, 192
Apsley, 153, 159, 160, 167, 168, 172, 173, 179, 180
Aquitania, 146, 187, 188
Auction, xiii, 104, 110, 111, 112, 135, 179, 180, 183, 186
Australia, v, 30, 41, 174, 175, 198
Baillie, J., 7
Ballygally Castle, 7, 9, 10, 21, 51, 52, 53, 58, 69, 72, 86, 163, 178
Ballymoney, 23
Ballysax Rectory, 85
Ballysax, St. Paul's graveyard, 85
Baltimore, v, 68, 69, 73
Balzani, ii, iii, v, xi, xii, xiii, 83, 99, 100, 101, 108, 120, 121, 122, 124, 125, 126, 127, 140, 177, 180, 183, 185, 190, 191
Balzani, Andrea, Count, 100
Balzani, Annibale, Count, 121

Balzani, Augusta, Countess, iii, vii, 84, 120
Balzani, Francesca, ii, v
Balzani, Guendalina, vii, 101, 121, 125, 126, 127, 129, 177, 178, 180, 184, 185, 186
Balzani, Molteni, Bianca, Countess, vii, 190
Balzani, Nora, iii, vii, 86, 101, 125, 127, 129, 178, 180, 184, 185, 186, 190
Balzani, Simon, August, Countess, iii, vii, 84, 120
Balzani, Simon, August, Simon, 85, 86, 99, 101, 111, 120, 121, 122, 123, 124, 129, 130, 140
Balzani, Simon, Augusta, Countess, iii, vii, 84, 85, 86, 99, 100, 101, 108, 110, 117, 120, 121, 122, 123, 124, 129, 130, 140, 145, 186, 190
Balzani, Stefanoni, Maria, 121
Balzani, Ugo, Count, vii, 99, 100, 120, 122, 123, 124, 125, 126, 127, 128, 129, 177
Balzani, Ulisse, Count, 190
Balzani, Valensin, Guendalina, vii, 101, 121, 125, 126, 127, 129, 177, 178, 180, 184, 185, 186
Balzani, Villa, 99, 100
Bamber, Brown, Richard, 76
Bamber, George, 76
Barbados, v, xii, 32, 33, 34, 36, 37, 39, 41
Barbados, Assembly, 17, 32, 33, 40
Barbados, House of Assembly, 32

Barbados, St. Michael's Lodge, 32
Baring, Evelyn, Lady, 159, 162
Barklie, Archibald, 70
Barklie, Helen, 148
Baron of de Bethmann, 84
Baronet of Nova Scotia, 4
Barracks, The, 68
Battle of Kinsale, 3
Belfast, v, xi, 14, 15, 16, 21, 26, 27, 28, 29, 30, 31, 32, 36, 37, 39, 40, 41, 42, 43, 45, 46, 50, 57, 59, 68, 69, 71, 80, 83, 86, 101, 105, 106, 111, 112, 114, 118, 122, 124, 130, 134, 136, 139, 141, 148, 151, 164, 170, 171, 173, 179, 183, 186, 189
Belfast, Miller and Nelson, 64
Belgium, 161
Berniére, de, Anthony, John, 196
Berniére, de, Antoine, Jean, 196
Berniére, de, Crommelin, Louis, 197
Besant, Mrs., 135
Bird, Miss, 115
Bissetts, 1
Blair, Elizabeth, 20
Blair, James, Major, 20
Blair, Sam, 46
Blennerhassett, Conway, 18
Blennerhassett, Harman, 18
Boissy-St-Leger, 83
Bologna, ii, 99, 127
Boneparte, Lucien, Prince, 121
Borghese, Maria, Anna, Princess, 127
Borghese, Scipione, Prince, 127
Boyd, 52, 131, 132, 133
Boyd, Sarah, 41

Brandywine Cemetery, 140
Breen, Philip, 44
Brennan, Mrs., 132
Brennan, Willie, 171
Brice Plantation, 202
Bridgetown, 32
Bringhurst Family, 104
Bringhurst, Edith, 117, 131, 133, 136, 140
Bringhurst, Edward, vii, 4, 16, 20, 21, 26, 27, 34, 43, 44, 45, 46, 47, 48, 49, 50, 51, 54, 55, 56, 58, 59, 63, 64, 65, 66, 67, 68, 69, 70, 71, 72, 73, 74, 77, 80, 103, 108, 111, 113, 114, 115, 117, 118, 131, 136, 137, 138, 139, 140, 142, 143, 145, 147, 148, 151, 152, 156, 157, 159, 163, 164, 165, 179, 183, 193, 194, 195, 196, 197
Bringhurst, Mary, 103, 117
Brisbane, Isabella, 7
Bristow, James, 42, 80, 147, 152, 185
Bristow, John, 147, 152, 182, 184
Broomfield, 153, 155, 158, 159, 162, 164, 165, 167, 168
Browning, Oscar, 100, 128, 129
Bryan, Marianne, 102
Bunting, Edward, 16
Burgess and Guilds-Brother of Ayr, 19
Byrne, Morgan, Henry, 101
Cairndhu, 116
Canada, v, 59, 61, 72, 144, 173, 196
Canevaro, Carlo, Count, 125
Canevaro, Guiseppe, Count, 125
Canevaro, Palazzo, 127
Carmania, 177

Carnegie, David, Sir, 205
Carnegie, Madeline, 205
Carson, Lord, 151, 158, 159, 164, 176
Casement, McGildowney, Edmund, 80, 83
Casement, Montgomery, John, 72, 83
Castle, Kilwaughter, of Ghosts, 189
Cathcart, John, 7
Ceylon, 59, 60
Chaine, James, 62, 116, 161
Chaine, William, 149
Château, xii, 83, 84
Chichester, Colonel, 157
Chichester, Lady, 133
Christmas, Osborne, William, 125
Churchill, Winston, 161
Cimitero Acattolico, 124
Clark & Son, 179
Clark, Mrs., 116
Clark, Stewart, Mr., 111, 115, 116, 139, 179
Clarke, 168
Clarke, William, 196
Cleveland, Grover, 150
Clyde Valley, 150
Cohen Company, 189
Colonna, Prospero, Prince, 128
Constable, Archibald, 125
Conway, Lord, 30
Cooke, Alan, 12
Cork, 47, 85, 101, 124
County Antrim, 3, 4, 7, 40, 45, 47, 50, 51, 62, 72, 78, 79, 85, 141, 198
Court Case, 114

Craddocj, Mr., 156
Crawford, 26, 156, 163, 168, 172
Crawford, James, 20
Crawford, William, 26, 43
Crommelin, Louis, 30, 196
Crommelin, Magdalen, Mary, 197
Cromwell, 9
Crowe, McCulloch, Tullis, Andrew, 72
Culzean Castle, 102, 183
Cunningham, Waddell, 27, 31, 32, 37
Cunninghame, James, Major-General, 32
Curran, 62, 83, 149
Custodian of Enemy Property, xiii, 186
Custodian of Enemy Property for Northern Ireland, xiii, 186
Dalling, Maggie, 150
Debille, Miss, Governess, 69
Declaration of Independence, 27, 195
Delaware, v, xii, 101, 103, 118, 119, 140, 178
Delaware, Rockwood, 84, 103, 104, 105, 106, 132, 135, 138, 139, 140, 145, 180, 181
Depositions, 8, 10
Dobbs, Francis, Captain, 59
Donegore, 51, 58
Donlevy, Elinor, 197
Douglas, William, 6
Downshire, Marquess of, 25
Drennan, William, 26, 39, 41, 47, 75, 76, 194
Drennan, William, Dr., 26, 37, 39, 41, 47, 75, 76, 194

Drennan/McTier, 74
Drennan-McTier Letters, ii
Drumalis, 62, 115, 116, 151
Drumnasole, 59, 154, 157, 158, 175, 183
Dublin, v, 18, 26, 43, 48, 49, 67, 82, 86, 111, 119, 136, 139, 144, 148, 153, 161, 164, 169, 193
Dufferin, Lady, 157, 161
Duke and Duchess of York, 139
Duke of Leinster, 119
Dunbar, Elizabeth, 16
Dunbar, James, Sir of Mochrum, 16
Dunluce Castle, 5, 10
E.H. McConnell, 189
Earl of Antrim, 7, 10, 14, 20, 23, 72, 78
Earl of Donegall, 38
Earl of Galloway, 6, 11
Earl of Shaftesbury, 114
Easter Rising, 169
Edward VII, King, 144
Edward, VII, King, 144
Edwards, Sarah, xi, 41, 154
Emily, 154
Enemy Property Act, 186
Era, Jones, Valentine, ii
Ethel, 170
Farrell, Agnew, 55, 56, 57, 61
Farrell, Agnew, James, 19, 47, 50, 51, 55, 56, 57, 58, 59, 60, 61, 62, 70, 114, 146, 157
Farrell, Agnew, James, son of Farrell, Agnew, James, 19, 51, 55, 56, 57, 58, 59, 60, 61, 62, 70, 114, 157
Farrell, Catherine, 59
Farrell, James, 19, 55, 61

Farrell, James, The Hynd, 19, 55
First World War, xii, 70, 146, 150, 151, 174, 182
Fitz Warins, 1
Florence, 99, 106, 110, 115, 117, 125, 126, 127, 129, 137, 141, 142, 143
Fort, 1, 4, 5, 15
France, 16, 31, 33, 45, 49, 50, 57, 83, 84, 87, 106, 109, 125, 128, 148, 150, 152, 171, 182, 196
Franklin, John, Sir, 198
Fraser, Mary, Louisa, 198
Fraud, xii, 35
Fricker, 113, 131
Fullick, Eleanor, Gladys, 173
Galbraith Family, 67
Galbraith, (Nellie), Eleanor, 67, 68, 69
Galbraith, Eleanor (Nellie), 21
Galbraith, Rachel, 73
Galgorm Castle, 157, 179
Galloway, Sheriffs of, i
Galt, Ann, 41
Gardener, Mr., 154
Garron Tower, 131
Garton, A., Henry, 188
Gate Lodge, xiii, 64, 132, 163, 191
George, Lloyd, David, 161
George, V, King, 179
Getty, Mr., 9
Gingles Family, 21
Gingles, John, 63
Girvan, John, Major, 188
Glenarm, 1, 2, 3, 23, 52, 53, 54, 66, 78, 158, 162, 174, 183
Glenmona House, 179
Gookin, Miss, 170, 171, 172, 177

231

Gordon, Elizabeth, 6
Gordon, Mr., 36
Gordon, William, 6
Graeme, Elizabeth, 34, 36
Graeme, Mr., 36
Great Irish Famine, xii
Green, Mrs., 135
Greer, Mrs., 131
Gregg, Thomas, 31
Guest Book, 115, 119, 155, 177, 178, 183
Gun-running 1914, 157
Gun-Running, 1914, 148
Gwynn, Stephen, Rev., 69
Hailey, Andreina, Lady, 120, 121
Hailey, Lady, xii
Hailey, Lord, 121
Hailey, Malcolm, William, Sir, 121
Hall, Village, Kilwaughter, 189
Halliday, Alexander, Dr., 37
Hamburg, 149
Hannah, 104, 171, 173, 175, 176, 179
Hargraves, Sellers, Bringhurst, Nancy, v, 150, 179, 181
Harries, Edward, 20
Harrison, Robert, 31, 40
Harrow, 43
Hattie, Cousin, 140
Haywood, Margaret, 19
Hearts of Oak, 46
Hearts of Steel, 46
Heinekey, Buxton, Robert, 199
Herb Society, 169
Higginbotham, Samuel, 187, 188
Higginson Family, 157
High Sheriff of the County of Antrim, 39

Hogg, McGarel, Gerald, Hon., 113
Hogg, McGarel, James, Sir, 61
Hogg, McGarrel, Norah, 162
Hooper, Berniére, de, John, 195
Hooper, William (grandson), 27, 195
Hooper, William (Signer), 27, 195
Hooper, William, Professor, 195
Hottinguer Bankers, 84
Houston, Martha, 19, 20, 26, 34, 37, 39, 41, 47, 69, 147, 194, 205
Howlish Hall, 18, 19
Huguenot, 84, 196
Huguenots, 30
Hunter, John, 52
Hurricane, 33
Hynd, 19, 62
Illegitimate, xii, 5, 72, 80, 87, 195
India, 20, 41, 121, 192, 205
International History Congress, 127, 128
Ireland, i, ii, v, xi, xiii, 1, 3, 4, 6, 7, 9, 12, 16, 18, 19, 22, 23, 29, 31, 34, 36, 37, 38, 41, 43, 44, 45, 46, 47, 49, 50, 55, 57, 58, 59, 63, 67, 68, 69, 73, 74, 75, 76, 78, 80, 81, 82, 83, 84, 85, 87, 101, 102, 105, 106, 109, 112, 118, 122, 123, 131, 133, 135, 137, 138, 139, 143, 144, 146, 148, 149, 151, 152, 153, 156, 158, 159, 161, 162, 163, 166, 167, 178, 179, 181, 182, 184, 186, 188, 189, 190, 195, 196, 198, 200
Irish Civil War, xii, xiii
Irish Parliament, 7, 44, 45, 48, 49, 63, 71, 111

Irving, John, 59
Italy, i, ii, v, xiii, 25, 99, 101, 106, 122, 124, 127, 128, 178, 184, 186, 190
James VI, King, 4
Jamieson, Eleanor, 201
Jock the Fool, 25, 63
John the Footman, 132
Jones Plantation, 32
Jones, Alice, 30
Jones, Anne, 193
Jones, Conway, Dr., 193
Jones, Edward, vii, 4, 21, 26, 27, 34, 43, 50, 54, 55, 58, 59, 63, 66, 68, 69, 71, 80, 108, 111, 114, 117, 147, 157, 193, 195, 196
Jones, Edward, son of Dr. Conway Jones, vii, 4, 21, 26, 27, 34, 43, 50, 54, 55, 58, 59, 63, 66, 68, 69, 71, 80, 108, 111, 114, 117, 147, 157, 193, 195, 196
Jones, Elizabeth, 29
Jones, Ellen, 26, 27, 63, 123, 198
Jones, Eyer, Valentine, 193
Jones, Frances, 193
Jones, Jane, 31, 41, 108
Jones, Kitty, 40, 67
Jones, Louis, 30, 41, 138, 196
Jones, Margaret, vii, 26, 40, 43, 44, 45, 63, 67, 68, 70, 72, 73, 74, 75, 76, 77, 78, 79, 80, 81, 82, 85, 143, 164, 181, 182
Jones, Maria, 40
Jones, Mary, 30, 59
Jones, Mary Anne, 31, 40
Jones, Pollock, Frances, 27, 195
Jones, Thomas, 29

Jones, Todd, William, 193, 194, 195
Jones, Valentine, 30
Jones, Valentine (Barbados 1), 31, 32, 33, 34, 36, 39, 40, 44, 46
Jones, Valentine (Barbados 1), Court of Common Pleas, Judge, 32
Jones, Valentine (Barbados 2), 34, 40
Jones, Valentine (Barbados 3), ii, iii, xii, 26, 29, 30, 31, 34, 35, 36, 37, 38, 39, 40, 42, 43
Jones, Valentine (Father), 30
Jones, Valentine (of Portadown), 29
Jones, Valentine (Officer), 30
Jones, Valentine (the Elder), ii, iii, xii, 26, 27, 29, 30, 31, 32, 34, 35, 36, 37, 38, 39, 40, 42, 43, 45, 81
Jones, Valentine (the Elder}, 27, 29, 30, 31, 32, 36, 37, 38, 39, 42, 45
Jones, Valentine, son of Jones,Valentine (the Elder), 31
Jope, E.M., Professor, 4, 5, 64
Kennedy Family of Cassilis of Scotland, 102
Kennedy, Angus, and Alice, 183
Kennedy, Gilbert, 6
Kennedy, Gilbert, Rev., 102
Kennedy, John, Lord, 6
Kennedy, Margaret, 102
Kennedy, Marion, 6
Kennedy, Thomas, Hon. Sir, 6
Kennedy, Thomas, Sir, 102, 183
Kerr, W., 67
Killymoon, 12, 13, 26, 43, 63, 64, 74

Killymoon Castle, 12, 13, 26, 43, 63, 64, 74
Kilwaughter, i, ii, iii, v, xi, xii, xiii, 1, 2, 3, 4, 5, 7, 8, 9, 10, 11, 12, 13, 14, 15, 19, 20, 21, 24, 25, 26, 27, 43, 44, 45, 48, 49, 52, 54, 60, 62, 63, 64, 65, 66, 67, 70, 71, 74, 77, 79, 80, 81, 82, 83, 85, 86, 87, 99, 101, 104, 105, 106, 107, 108, 109, 110, 112, 114, 115, 116, 117, 118, 119, 120, 121, 122, 123, 125, 126, 127, 128, 129, 130, 132, 133, 135, 136, 137, 138, 140, 142, 143, 145, 146, 147, 148, 149, 151, 152, 153, 154, 156, 157, 158, 159, 160, 161, 164, 166, 167, 168, 169, 171, 172, 173, 175, 177, 178, 179, 180, 181, 182, 183, 185, 186, 187, 188, 189, 190, 191, 192, 206
Kilwaughter Castle, i, ii, v, xi, xii, xiii, 4, 12, 20, 21, 52, 63, 64, 65, 70, 71, 74, 79, 80, 81, 85, 86, 104, 107, 108, 110, 116, 119, 127, 128, 133, 145, 148, 151, 152, 160, 164, 168, 171, 175, 177, 178, 179, 180, 181, 183, 185, 186, 187, 188, 189, 191, 206
Kilwaughter Castle Convalescent Hospital, 175
Kilwaughter Castle fire, 9, 65, 66, 113, 135, 165, 177
Kilwaughter Castle Ghost Stories, 206
Kilwaughter Castle Towers, 175
Kilwaughter Deer Park, 21
Kilwaughter Estate, ii, xii, 5, 8, 10, 12, 14, 19, 24, 25, 26, 67, 79, 80, 87, 126, 181
Kilwaughter Graveyard, 81
Kilwaughter House, xi, xii, 4, 12, 20, 52, 63, 65, 206
Kilwaughter, Battalion, 160
Kirk, William, 102, 114, 143
Kitchener, Lord, 156, 161
Knapp, Cyrus, 102
Knapp, H., Cornelia, 102, 173
Knox, John, General, 47
Knox. John, 4
Kyle, Martha, 69
Lacy, de, Hugh, 1
Laing, Mr., 147
Lake, Artificial, 64, 113, 115, 117, 134, 137, 138, 147, 152, 206
Lake, General, 50
Lambert, Hay, John, 81, 83, 84
Land Purchase Commission, xiii, 184
Larne, i, v, xi, 2, 5, 8, 9, 19, 20, 24, 25, 26, 43, 45, 46, 51, 53, 55, 56, 57, 58, 60, 61, 62, 64, 68, 69, 70, 77, 101, 110, 116, 121, 122, 123, 129, 135, 136, 139, 147, 149, 150, 151, 152, 154, 155, 156, 157, 159, 160, 162, 164, 169, 171, 172, 174, 176, 179, 183, 187, 188, 189, 191, 207
Larne and Kilwaughter Church, 25
Larne Refugee Camp, 8
Law, Satterthwaite and Jones, 32
Lily, 153
Listyagnew, 2
Little, 7, 175
Lochnaw Castle, i, xi, 2, 6, 9, 10, 11, 12, 14, 15, 16, 60, 145, 183, 192, 201, 203, 205

Lochnaw, Constabulary of, 6
Lockett, Garnet, Jane, 203
Londonderry, Lady, 157
Lucien, Prince, xii, 121
Luddy, Maria, ii
Lusitania, 162
Macaulay, John, Mrs. and Mr., 119
Macauley, John, Mr. and Mrs., 122
Macauley, John, Mrs. and Mr., 119
MacDonnell, Randal, Sir, xi, 1, 2, 4, 8, 10
MacDonnell, Sorley, Boy, 3, 5
Magennises, 8
Magheramorne Estate, 9, 19, 51, 55, 56, 57, 58, 59, 60, 61, 62, 70, 112, 113, 114, 116, 150, 157
Magheramorne, Lady, 112, 114
Magheramorne, Lord, 113, 114, 116, 133, 136, 183
Magnier Family, 84
Magnier, Armance, Catherine, Marie, Mlle, 84
Magnier, François, Pierre, 84
Majorie, 153, 154
Mallett, Elizabeth, Mary, 195
Mamiani, Terenzio, Count, 99
Mandeville, de, 1
Manko, Katino, ii
Marchioness of Londonderry, 78, 131
Margherita, Queen, 123
Marjorie, 153, 154
Marley, George, Rev., Right, 197
Marquis of Donegall, 56, 83
Massareene, Lady, 166, 179
Massareene, Lord, 167

Massey-Beresford, Mrs., 175
McCalmont, Bertie, 136, 146, 148, 151, 157, 159, 176
McCalmont, Lady, 133
McCalmont, Mrs., 148, 159
McCay, Cassie, xi, 48, 110
McClarty, Fred, 63
McConnell, J., 190
McCormick, 132
McCracken, Joy, Henry, 57
McCullough, John, 9
McCullough, Rachel, 155
McDonnell, Hector, 2
McDonnell, Randle, Earl of Antrim, 14
McDowall, Alexander, 7
McDowall, Hew, 7
McDowall, Uchtrad, 7
McGarel, Charles, 61
McGildowney, Mrs., 158
McGill, David, 6
McGill, Elizabeth, 6
McHenry, James, 58
McLean, 176
McNeale, Thomas, Henry, 87, 120
McNeill, Colonel, 160
McNeill, Lucy, 149, 157, 169, 174, 199
McNeill, Malcolm, 83, 87, 101
McNinch, Mr., 172
McTear, Frances, 118
McTier, Martha, 26, 34, 37, 41, 47, 194
McTier, Sam, 194
Meadowbank, 105, 106, 107, 108, 118, 119, 143
Mearns, Robert, 55
Mistress, 67, 73

Montgomerie, Alexander, 8th Earl of Eglington, 15
Montgomery, Hugh, Sir, 7
Moore Family, 70
Moore, Agnew, William, Lt.-Col., 70
Moore, John and Marbella, 40
Moore, Katherine, 40
Morand, George, 84
Mountjoy, 150, 157
Mountjoy, Lord, 3
Muller, Max, 100
Mullins, Thomas,Ventry, Lord, 18
Murdoch, Corrado, 99
Musgrave, Richard, Sir, 194
Mussolini, 185
Naples, 121, 126, 128
Napoleon I, xii, 121
Nash, John, i, xi, 12, 44, 63, 64, 190, 191
NATO, 126
Nelson, Betty, Jennie, 69
New Burying Ground, 86
New York, 18, 101, 102, 106, 112, 115, 132, 134, 140, 141, 143, 144, 150, 157, 159, 187, 188, 205
New York Society for the Prevention of Cruelty of Children, 205
Nisbet, Anne, 16
Nisbet, James, 17
Nisbet, William, 17
Norah, 173
North Carolina, 27, 195, 197, 202
Northern Star, 50
Nova Scotia, v, 4, 150
Nugent, General, Major, 57

Ó Gnímh, i, xi, 1, 2, 4, 58, 60, 66, 129
O'Connor, Arthur, 47
O'Hale, Brian, 23
O'Kane, Jane, 164, 165, 167
O'Neill, Hugh, 1, 3, 20, 53
O'Neill, John, 46
O'Neill, Lord, 57, 157, 166
O'Neill, Moira, 157
Oakboys, 24
Of the 40 Lots, 9
Ogilvie, Blair, James, 21
Ogilvie, William, 20
Ogilvie, William, Rev., 20
Olderfleet Hotel, 164
Orebaugh, W., Walter, 127
Orebaugh, W., Walter, Consul, 126
Ormond, 1
Orr-Owens, Misses, 166
Palazzo Canevaro, 125, 127
Paris, v, xii, 18, 83, 84, 87, 99, 106, 107, 113, 120, 127, 135, 198
Parliament, 7, 9, 22, 37, 38, 45, 70, 181, 203
Peers, Margaret, 29
Peers, Mary, 29
Peers, Thomas, Rev., 29
Penry, G.S., 150
Peo, 45
Père Lachaise Cemetery, 84
Peru, 125
Phoenix, Mr., 117
Plantation, 3, 7, 22, 29, 32, 201
Plantation House, 4, 5, 63
Plantation of Ulster, 3, 4, 5, 8, 12, 17, 61, 63, 201, 202

Plantation of Wales, 3, 4, 5, 8, 12, 17, 61, 63, 201, 202
Poirez, Lewis, 30
Poiriez, Lewis, 30
Porter, Classon, Rev., 7, 9, 19, 20, 23, 25, 44, 55, 58, 59, 63, 67, 68, 69, 70, 74, 80, 81, 83
Premier of Tasmania, 198
Presbyterians, 3, 22, 25, 49, 102
PRONI, ii, 8, 9, 12, 13, 19, 20, 24, 26, 29, 40, 46, 50, 51, 55, 56, 57, 58, 59, 62, 65, 69, 70, 72, 73, 80, 83, 84, 86, 87, 108, 125, 126, 179, 180, 182, 184, 195, 196, 197
Purnell, Catherine, 61
Rafferty, Rose, 107, 124, 131, 147, 153, 154, 155, 159, 164, 165, 166, 167, 170, 171, 176, 179
Rebellion, 52, 55, 58, 63
Redhall, 67, 119, 122
Reid, Emmeline, Lucy, 199
Rennie, John, 55
Revolution, 18, 45, 49
Ridolfi, Luisa, 125
Rochet, Louis, 30, 31, 41, 138, 196
Rochette, Poirie, Moses, Jean, 31
Rockwood, 84, 103, 104, 105, 106, 132, 135, 138, 139, 140, 145, 180, 181
Rome, iii, 3, 99, 100, 101, 121, 123, 124, 125, 126, 127, 128, 129, 191, 196
Rome, San Pietro, 3
Ross, James, 27, 63, 80
Ross, William, 27
Royal Africa Company, 31
Royal Berkshire Regiment, 186

Rutland, Duchess, 7th, 197
Sams, 131, 141, 147
Sands, Mrs., 154, 158, 159, 168
Saurin, James, Rev., 75
Saurin, William, 75
Savage Family, 1, 2
Sayers, Mr., 36
Scotland, v, 2, 3, 5, 10, 11, 12, 14, 17, 58, 60, 102, 105, 123, 135, 146, 152, 153, 159, 164, 176, 201, 205
Scots-Irish Links, 8, 13, 19
Scott, Rebecca, 201
Scottish Presbyterians, 9, 14
Second World War, ii
Settignano Cemetery, 126
Sewing Club, 169
Seythia, 179
Shaftesbury, Lord, 151
Shaw, 7, 21, 52, 53, 54, 69
Shaw, Eleanor, 7, 16, 21, 67, 201
Shaw, Henry, 51, 54, 69
Shaw, James, 10
Shaw, James, Captain, 7
Shaw, John, 9
Shaw, Margaret, 19, 21, 183
Shaw, William, 55, 69
Shepherd, William, 155
Sheuchan, of, Agnew, Thomas, 6, 16, 203
Shipley, Joseph, 103
Shipley, William, 103
Siddons, Sarah, Mrs., xi
Simon, Augusta, Maria, 83, 85, 86, 87, 99
Simon, Collyns, Thomas, 69, 80, 84, 85, 86
Simon, Frederick, William, 85
Simon, Peter, 84

Simpson, Todd, Letitia, 202
Sinclair, Mr., 25, 60
Skeffington, Chichester, 4th Earl of Massereene, 50
Slave Trade, 32
Smiley, H.H., Mr., 115, 116, 139
Smiley, Lady, 159, 161
Smiley, Mrs. and Mr., 115, 121
Smith (1), Galt, John, iii, vii, 37, 39, 41, 42, 46, 101, 107, 140
Smith (2), Galt, John, ii, iii, vii, 30, 31, 37, 39, 41, 42, 46, 80, 101, 102, 105, 106, 107, 108, 109, 111, 112, 113, 114, 115, 116, 117, 118, 119, 120, 122, 123, 124, 125, 130, 132, 133, 134, 135, 136, 137, 138, 139, 140, 141, 142, 145, 147, 155, 163, 173, 174, 178, 181, 182
Smith, Bringhurst, Edward, ii, ix, xii, 41, 102, 103, 104, 105, 106, 107, 108, 109, 110, 111, 112, 113, 114, 115, 116, 117, 118, 119, 120, 122, 123, 124, 130, 131, 132, 133, 134, 135, 136, 137, 138, 139, 140, 141, 142, 143, 144, 145, 146, 147, 148, 150, 151, 152, 153, 154, 155, 156, 157, 158, 159, 160, 161, 162, 163, 164, 165, 166, 167, 168, 169, 170, 171, 172, 173, 174, 175, 176, 177, 178, 179, 180, 181, 182, 183, 184, 185, 186
Smith, Bringhurst, Elizabeth, ii, vii, ix, xii, 41, 101, 102, 103, 104, 105, 106, 107, 108, 109, 110, 111, 112, 113, 114, 115, 116, 117, 118, 119, 120, 122, 123, 124, 130, 131, 132, 133, 134, 135, 136, 137, 138, 139, 140, 141, 142, 143, 144, 145, 146, 147, 148, 150, 151, 152, 153, 154, 155, 156, 157, 158, 159, 160, 161, 162, 163, 164, 165, 166, 167, 168, 169, 170, 171, 172, 173, 174, 175, 176, 177, 178, 179, 180, 181, 182, 183, 184, 185, 186
Smith, Bringhurst, Kennedy, George, ii, ix, xii, 41, 102, 103, 104, 105, 106, 107, 108, 109, 110, 111, 112, 113, 114, 115, 116, 117, 118, 119, 120, 122, 123, 124, 130, 131, 132, 133, 134, 135, 136, 137, 138, 139, 140, 141, 142, 143, 144, 145, 146, 147, 148, 150, 151, 152, 153, 154, 155, 156, 157, 158, 159, 160, 161, 162, 163, 164, 165, 166, 167, 168, 169, 170, 171, 172, 173, 174, 175, 176, 177, 178, 179, 180, 181, 182, 183, 184, 185, 186
Smith, Galt, Elizabeth, ii, ix, xii, 41, 102, 103, 104, 105, 106, 107, 108, 109, 110, 111, 112, 113, 114, 115, 116, 117, 118, 119, 120, 122, 123, 124, 130, 131, 132, 133, 134, 135, 136, 137, 138, 139, 140, 141, 142, 143, 144, 145, 146, 147, 148, 150, 151, 152, 153, 154, 155, 156, 157, 158, 159, 160, 161, 162, 163, 164, 165, 166, 167, 168, 169, 170, 171, 172, 173, 174, 175, 176, 177, 178, 179, 180, 181, 182, 183, 184, 185, 186
Smith, Galt, Florence, 85, 99, 100, 102, 106, 110, 115, 117,

125, 126, 127, 129, 137, 141, 142, 143, 160, 173
Smith, Galt, Jane, 42
Smith, Galt, John, ii, iii, vii, 30, 31, 37, 39, 41, 42, 46, 80, 101, 102, 105, 106, 107, 108, 109, 111, 112, 113, 114, 115, 116, 117, 118, 119, 120, 122, 123, 124, 125, 130, 132, 133, 134, 135, 136, 137, 138, 139, 140, 141, 142, 145, 147, 155, 163, 173, 174, 178, 181, 182
Smith, Galt, John (1), 39, 41, 42, 46
Smith, Galt, Katherine, Joan, 173
Smith, Galt, Kennedy, George, 6, 102, 106, 110, 115, 117, 137, 138, 140, 142, 143, 159, 160, 165, 173, 175, 183
Smith, Galt, Mrs., 156
Smith, Galt, Valerie, 173
Smith, John (Jack), 41
Smith, Jones, Edward, 80
Smith, Kennedy, Florence, 106
Smith, Kennedy, George, 102, 105, 134
Smith, Kennedy, George, son of Kennedy, Gilbert, Rev., 102
Smith, Samuel, 15, 41, 102
Smith, William, 41, 42
Somerled, 2, 51
South Carolina, 32, 197, 201
SS Glendun, 150
St. Anne's Cathedral, 16
St. Anne's Parish Church, 16
St. Cedma's Parish Church, 119
St. Giles Anglican Church, 101
St. Magnus Cathedral, 17
St. Mary Abbot's Church, London, 99

St. Sepulchre's Cemetery, 85, 86
Stewart, 3, 11, 12, 13, 38, 47, 51, 52, 54, 58, 63, 68, 116, 198, 199
Stewart, James, 12, 13, 26, 43
Stewart, Margart, 26
Stewart, William, 26, 63
Sutherland, John, 64
Sutton, 175
Swift, Jonathan, 56
Tasmania, v, 198, 199, 200
Tempest-Vane, Herbert, Lord, 131
Tenant Rights, 82
Tennant, Emerson, James, Sir, 81
Terheun, Catherine, 102
The Flight of the Earls, 3
The Great Famine, 78
Thompson, Robert, 65
Todd, William, 193, 194, 195
Todd, Wray, Mary, 193
Tone, Wolfe, Theobald, 45, 50
Trading with The Enemy Legislation, 190
Treaty of Mellifont, 3
Tredozio, 126
Trevozzo, 126
Troops, 186
Turnly, Armenella, Letitia, 59
Turnly, Francis, 59, 157
Ulster, ii, v, 2, 3, 8, 14, 21, 22, 37, 44, 49, 56, 59, 74, 82, 105, 118, 146, 148, 154, 157, 163, 167, 170, 171, 178, 179, 180, 181, 184, 189
Ulster Custom, 82
Umberto I, King, v, 2, 4, 16, 18, 33, 36, 38, 42, 50, 55, 57, 100,

118, 123, 128, 135, 144, 145, 179
United Irishmen, xii, 1, 19, 37, 45, 47, 50, 51, 54, 55, 56, 57, 58
UVF, 146, 151, 157, 158, 159
Val, Du, Allen, Charles, 203
Valensin, 178, 190
Valensin, David, Guido, 125, 126, 178
Valensin, Giorgia, 126, 127, 177
Valensin, Giorgio, 125
Valensin, Luisa, Maria, 125
Vanderbilts, 115, 133
Villeroy, 83
Vinadio, di, Balbo, Ferdinando, 125
W.H. Esler and Sons, 189
Waddell, Ross, Jane, 27
Wales, of, Prince, 130, 144
Ward, Ralph, Rev., 68, 72, 80
Wards of Bangor Castle, 134
Ware, William, 16

Waring, John, 29
Webb, James, Anna, 103
West Indies, 27, 31, 32, 34, 35
Westminster Abbey, 121
Wheeler, Mrs, 114, 117, 131
Wheeler, Mrs., 114, 117, 131
White, Lady, 145, 175
Wilkinson, Elizabeth, 18
Wilkinson, George, 144
Will, xii, 7, 11, 12, 19, 20, 26, 28, 29, 30, 39, 43, 55, 63, 68, 72, 73, 80, 83, 84, 105, 142, 193, 196, 201
William Henry, Price, 33
Williamson, Robert, 76
Wilmont, Dunmurry, 42
Wilson, James, 19, 55
World War 2, xi, xiii
World War Two, 185
Zanetti & Agnew, 203
Zanetti, Vittore, 203
Zoagli, of, Duke, 125

www.ingramcontent.com/pod-product-compliance
Lightning Source LLC
Chambersburg PA
CBHW061229070526
44584CB00030B/4048